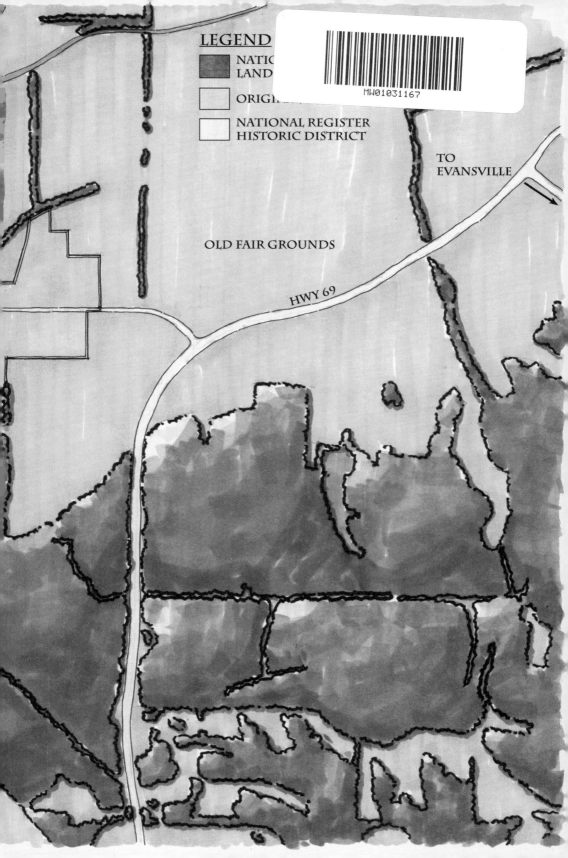

LEGEND

NATIO
LAND

ORIGI

NATIONAL REGISTER
HISTORIC DISTRICT

TO
EVANSVILLE

OLD FAIR GROUNDS

HWY 69

New Harmony

INDIANA

"We are a river of time, and it keeps on flowing."

JANE BLAFFER OWEN

APRIL 18, 1915–JUNE 21, 2010

New Harmony
INDIANA

Like a River Not a Lake · A Memoir

JANE BLAFFER OWEN

AFTERWORDS BY

Anne Dale Owen and Jane Dale Owen

EDITED BY

Nancy Mangum McCaslin

INDIANA UNIVERSITY PRESS   *Bloomington & Indianapolis*

This book is a publication of

Indiana University Press
Office of Scholarly Publishing
Herman B Wells Library 350
1320 East 10th Street
Bloomington, Indiana 47405 USA

iupress.indiana.edu

| *Telephone* | 800-842-6796 |
| *Fax* | 812-855-7931 |

Manufactured in China

Cataloging information is available from the Library of Congress.

ISBN 978-0-253-01624-9 (cloth)
ISBN 978-0-253-01663-8 (e-book)

2 3 4 5 20 19 18 17 16 15

FRONTIS: *Jane Blaffer, Portrait 3, 1936.* Vera Prasilova Scott took many photographs
of the Blaffer family. Her originals are now archived in the Vera Prasilova
Scott portraiture collection, MS 497, Woodson Research Center,
Fondren Library, Rice University, Houston, TX, © Rice University.
Courtesy of Rice University. Blaffer-Owen family photograph.
PAGE III: *Fish above the Lab* © 1988 John Hubbard. Courtesy of John Hubbard.
ENDPAPERS: *Area Map* and *Town Map* © 2013 Kenneth A. Schuette.

Dedicated to
THE TOWNSPEOPLE OF NEW HARMONY—
PAST, PRESENT, AND
FUTURE.

I will never leave this house of light, I will never
leave this blessed town
for here I have found my love and here I will stay
for the rest of my life.
If this world turns into a sea of trouble
I will brave the waves and steer my mind's ship
to the safe shore of love.

If you are a seeker looking for profit, go on
and may God be with you,
but I am not willing to exchange my truth,
I have found the heart and will never leave
this house of light.

—Jalaludin Mohamad Rumi,
Thirteenth-century Sufi mystic,
from Rumi Hidden Music.

Reprinted by permission of HarperCollins Publishers Ltd.
© Azima Melita Kolin and Maryam Mafi, translators, (2001).

Contents

Foreword

John Philip Newell

❖ JANE BLAFFER OWEN ranks among the most beautiful and wise women the modern world has known. I met her over ten years ago. She was already in her mid-eighties. And I fell in love with her immediately, as have countless other men and women of every age and stage. Yes, she was beautiful physically as well as intellectually and emotionally. But it was the way she embodied vision that drew most of us to her. And we who love her have come from many, many disciplines, ranging from art and culture to science and religion.

Carl Jung, the founder of analytical psychology, said that the Spirit is a *coniunctio oppositorum,* a conjoining of what has been considered opposite: heaven and earth, spirit and matter, the feminine and the masculine, East and West, the night and the day, the unconscious and the conscious, the head and the heart, spirituality and sexuality, our individual stories and the one story, the story of the Universe. Jane Owen lived among us as a messenger of Spirit. She was forever weaving together what has been torn apart.

Close to the heart of her vision is the Roofless Church of New Harmony. It has four defining walls but truly no roof. It is to me one of the most prophetic sites of prayer in the Western world. Over fifty years ago, well in advance of the earth-awareness of today, Jane Owen saw that our sacred sites must not be cut off from the temple of the earth. Our places of prayer must not represent separateness from the other species and the other people of the world. The Roofless Church stands as an abiding testimony to this vision. The primary context of religion, and indeed of life itself, must be the great and living cathedral of earth, sea, and sky. If we are to be whole, we must come back into relationship with Creation.

Jane Blaffer Owen with John Philip Newell.

Photograph by Alison Erazmus, 2010.

On May 1, 2010, we rededicated the Roofless Church on the fiftieth anniversary of its consecration. It was as if Jane Owen, who died the next month at the age of ninety-five, was determined to celebrate its jubilee, such was the significance of the church to her vision.[1] The next day, in studying photographs of the celebration, I pointed out to her that she had been gazing around quite a bit during the procession, to which she replied, "I was just counting the number of people." Jane Owen was forever passionate about continuing the vision.

At the heart of the Roofless Church is her most cherished work of art *Descent of the Holy Spirit* (*Notre Dame de Liesse*) by Jacques Lipchitz.[2] The sculpture is of the Spirit, in the shape of a dove, descending on an abstract divine feminine form that is opening to give birth. At one level Lipchitz is pointing to the story of Jesus, who was conceived by the Spirit in the womb of Mary. But at another level Lipchitz is pointing to the story of the Universe. Everything that has being has been conceived by the Spirit in the womb of the Universe. In other words, everything is sacred. This is the vision that guided Jane Owen to commit herself to reweaving the strands of life—between nations, between cultures, between religions, between any of the so-called opposites that have tragically separated us in our lives and world.

She knew the sacredness and the beauty of life. But never did she forget the brokenness and pain of life. At the other end of the Roofless Church is another sculpture, *Pietà* by Stephen De Staebler. It is a primitive, naked, feminine form. In her sides and feet are the nail marks of crucifixion. And her breast is split open to reveal the head of her crucified son emerging from within her. When our child suffers or when one we love is in agony, we experience their suffering not from afar but as coming from deep within us. Jane Owen knew such suffering in her family and life. She also knew, as De Staebler's sculpture so powerfully communicates, that if there is to be real healing in our world, we must know the brokenness of other nations, other species, other families as part of our own brokenness. Jane's countenance was beautiful. Yet it was a countenance that showed also deep sorrow with the brokenness of the world.

One of the last things she said to me was that New Harmony saved her. Was I mishearing her? Many have said, and many will continue to say, that Jane Blaffer Owen saved New Harmony. Certainly this is part of the story. But Jane Owen was disclosing to me another truth, a more hidden part of the story. New Harmony saved her because she found in this town and in its people the object of her love. That is why she called it her "second marriage." She knew that it was only because she faithfully gave herself in love to New Harmony that she truly found herself. Such is the way of love. It is in giving our heart to the well-being of the other that we most truly become well ourselves.

Jane Owen would often say that the great ones in our lives who have died are like "allies" on the other side of death. "And maybe," she would say, "just maybe, they can do more for us on the other side than they did on this side." I agree. And I believe that Jane Owen is one of these great ones. We will never again see her picking peonies to give to New Harmony residents and visitors alike. We will never again hear her laughter at table as she works her magic of bringing different people and disciplines together. We will never again receive one of her many handwritten notes suggesting the next way of serving the dream of a new harmony in our world. But we need never lose communion with her heart and her vision. For she is a great ally. And her work with us is not finished.

The Reverend Dr. John Philip Newell, Edinburgh, Scotland, is internationally acclaimed for his work in the field of Celtic spirituality as a minister and peacemaker, and the author of more than fifteen books, including A New Harmony: The Spirit, the Earth, and the Human Soul.

Foreword

J. Pittman McGehee

❖ FOR THE BEST OF THREE DECADES, I was Jane Blaffer Owen's priest. I helped usher her into the next realm as homilist at her burial office in Houston.[1] I knew Jane well. This memoir should be read with an image of her standing in the nave of a roofless church, beneath a floppy hat, her eyes fluttering, and her smile as wide as the Wabash River. It should be read with the animation she brought to her life and to the lives of the many she touched.

I spent many an evening with Jane, both at her home in Houston and in New Harmony. I especially relish the memories of our times together in New Harmony. She invited me there to lecture, lead a retreat, or bless a new building. Inevitably we would settle into her den with refreshment and talk. She loved a story, and she told them well. Jane spoke of priests and poets, artists and archbishops, all people she had known. She shared her own spiritual journey and deep appreciation for the mystery, telling how she had experienced the transcendent in her ordinary life. She also spoke of her losses, disappointments, and moments of quiet desperation. Jane never tried to hide her humanity. At her funeral, I spoke about the word *eccentric,* meaning "out of the center." Jane's eccentricity was not strange or unattractive but authentic. Her authenticity brought appeal not only from powerful agents of change but also from humble partners in her efforts.

This is primarily a story of the evolution of her New Harmony mission. But more so, it is a story of how a woman served her purpose well and how the world benefited. New Harmony was her organizing principle. As this principle evolves, we will be introduced to artists, architects, theologians, ecclesiastical leaders, writers, and poets, all of whom added their presence to the soul of New Harmony. You will read about the history of that sacred space and be enlightened by poetry, literature, and myth. Jane weaves the tapestry of a life lived in service to a calling to bring beauty and meaning to a world needing both.

Although the memoir focuses primarily on New Harmony, Jane's influence there was not exerted at the expense of her hometown. The University of Houston, the Museum of Fine Arts, Houston, the C. G. Jung Educational Center, Episcopal High School, and Christ Church Cathedral, among many others, benefited from her exuberant benevolence. I mention these to highlight the many seeds sown as Jane sought to satiate her curiosity for the novel and her longing for the divine. She lived the larger life. She did not bury her talents in the ground but spent them in service of meaning and purpose.

This reflective memoir shows the brightness of her touch and the depth of her search for the sacred in nature, creativity, literature, symbols, art, and even in suffering. Her life, though abundant, was not without illness, the darkness of loss, and the vicissitudes of the human predicament.

Jane Blaffer Owen was given much, and much was demanded from her.

She responded with a courageous and creative life. At the balance of her days, she had the fulfillment of all that she had given away. Jane often quoted Luke 12:48: "From everyone who has been given much, much will be demanded, and from the one who has been entrusted with much, much more will be asked."

The Very Reverend J. Pittman McGehee, DD, is a Jungian analyst and director of Broadacres Center for spirituality and psychology; former dean of Christ Church Cathedral, Houston, Texas.

Preface

Jane Blaffer Owen

May 1, 2010
Fiftieth Golden Anniversary Rededication
of the Roofless Church

The first half of life is biography,
where we allow our story to be written for us by others . . . .
The second half of life must be autobiography,
authored by the Self.

J. Pittman McGehee and Damon J. Thomas,
*The Invisible Church: Finding Spirituality
Where You Are*

❖ IN CONTRAST TO THE WAY in which most of us in the modern world live our lives, early Celtic artisans represented the commingling of their yesterdays and tomorrows in the strands that form their everlasting and interlacing designs drawn in manuscripts and carved on monuments. I experience a similar commingling of time in New Harmony.

Extraordinary men and women brought their visions, scientific minds, talents, and, as with Robert Owen and William Maclure, their personal fortunes to New Harmony in 1826. Their likenesses adorn spaces in the national art galleries of England, Scotland, and Wales, the M. and M. Karolik Collection of Boston's Museum of Fine Arts, and Washington's Smithsonian Institution. In New Harmony, their portraits hang in the Working Men's Institute and inside the historical houses that my husband, Kenneth Dale Owen, restored. Numerous biographies document their achievements and limitations.

Readers of history, however, shall not learn from these books, portraits, or bronze effigies the extent to which the undying dead of New Harmony have directed the course of my life and impacted the lives of fellow residents, some of them close friends and allies for over half a century. Today's visitors, whatever their reasons for coming to New Harmony, enter a community of energetic and caring citizens who, consciously or not, inhabit the past, present, and future.

The powerful river that partly encircles this town of less than nine hundred people offers another metaphor for the conjoined seasons of our lives and for my personal approach to New Harmony's rich and varied legacies. Whether the current of its journey south is languid or swift, whether its surface darkens with filtered mud or mirrors a sky flushed with rose and lavender, the Wabash flows onward, totally alive—like the town of New Harmony itself—reminding us it is an unpredictable river, not a placid, circumscribed lake. However threatening on some days or safe and picturesque on others, this river challenged me, forcefully and fatefully, from my first arrival in New Harmony in 1941. (See the area map on the front endpaper.)

While the Wabash has provided a title for my tale of New Harmony, it does not explain why I have chosen to bind these pages with five bands of different colors, placed vertically, not horizontally. These colors and their alignment represent a philosophy bred into me by my parents and nourished by the people who, after them, have influenced and enlightened me. I owe a few words of gratitude to the remarkable man who inspired the black, red, white, yellow, and brown bands of color. But first, the genesis of our friendship.

Sometime in the early 1960s, I was invited to join an organization founded by men I admire: the theologian Paul Tillich, the psychologist Rollo May, the mythologist Joseph Campbell, the Harvard biblical scholar Amos N. Wilder, and many others, each of whom was a seminal figure in his field of study.[1] The organization was formally named the Society for the Arts, Religion, and Contemporary Culture, but members and fellows always spoke of it by the initials A.R.C., as though to call attention to what the founders of the society took to be an indivisible trinity of three abiding realities—art, religion, and culture.

At an ARC annual conference, I had the good fortune to meet Frederick Franck. Born in Holland of agnostic parents, he stepped upon the world stage when he joined the medical staff of Albert Schweitzer's famous Lambaréné clinic as an oral surgeon. Franck brought pencils, paintbrushes, and an unerring eye with him to Africa. He chronicled the so-

Frederick Franck's *Saint Francis and the Birds* beside Swan Lake with
Stephen De Staebler's *Chapel of the Little Portion* in the distance.

*Photograph by Janet Lorence, 2013. Saint Francis and the Birds © 2004 Frederick
Franck. Courtesy the Estate of Frederick Franck and Pacem in Terris.*

journs and experiences of a long, creative life in his books and freestanding
artworks around the world. Frederick designed *Saint Francis and the Birds,*
a Corten steel sculpture, to place beside small Swan Lake behind the New
Harmony Inn in 2004 (see numbers 1, 2, and 3 on the town map on the
back endpaper). Guests and residents should smile to learn that our version contains one dove more than Franck's similar statue in Assisi, birth-
place of the patron of animals. St. Francis was an anointed prince of peace,
not merely an image suitable for decorating birdbaths and feeders.

Franck is best remembered for Pacem in Terris, a place for people of
different faiths who share a common devotion to art, music, and drama.[2]
I have attended plays, "transreligious" services, and concerts in this triangular enclosure, built on the stone foundation of an old mill. When Frederick
and his indomitable wife Claske found and bought the remains of the mill

in Warwick, New York, its interior space was a repository for neighborhood garbage. Water no longer turned the wheel that had once ground grain into flour. The once-beautiful face of the mill was disfigured, like the face of the leper whom St. Francis kissed at the beginning of his ministry a thousand years ago. A burning passion for healing turned the heart-wheels of selfless volunteers as they carted truckloads of kitchen and backyard detritus from the stone perimeter and created a stage and terraced seats within new walls. For forty years, the Francks brought music and drama to the stage of this chapel-theater. Frederick died on June 5, 2006, but his son, Lukas, Claske, and colleagues continue the work of Pacem in Terris.[3]

I relate this brief history of Pacem in Terris because it embodies my belief that preservation, be it of buildings or values, is better served by sustained commitment from local people than by philanthropists alone, however welcome they have been and always will be.

The chapters that follow honor other passionate preservers: Robert Owen, whose New Lanark Mills were a shining exception during the bleak reality of the Industrial Revolution; George MacLeod, who resurrected Iona; and, lastly, the men and women who have labored with me to preserve New Harmony. But before introducing these latter-day "Franciscans," the refrain of this book's song requires that I trace the stripes of color on its cover to their origin.

For too many years, the thriving Port of Houston lacked an adequate welcoming center for seamen on leave from their ships. A few valiant chaplains from Catholic and Protestant churches offered shelter and hospitality from a corrugated tin shack in a dangerous, poorly policed area near the port. Seamen were robbed, mugged, and sometimes killed. I was among a group of Houstonians, including Jack Brannen, MD, Howard Tellepsen Sr., and David Red, who found this sin of omission in a prosperous city scandalous. In 1968, we were joined by Jack Turner, of the Port Authority, who donated seven cyclone-fenced acres near the Ship Channel. The area was transformed into a baseball diamond, a soccer field, basketball and volleyball courts, an Olympic-size swimming pool, tracks for runners, and a pavilion. Generous citizens and foundations contributed funds for a substantial multipurpose building; members of Houston's garden clubs provided landscaping.

The addition of a small chapel that would not emphasize one denomination over another became my responsibility. I sought the ingenuity of

Frederick Franck. His response to my SOS was immediate but cautious. He would meet with the chaplains and the center's board of directors—if they were willing to open their minds to new ideas. My faith in my mentor's powers of persuasion was not misplaced. Though reluctant at first, the governing bodies obeyed his request for the hatch of a beached fishing boat, from which he fashioned an altar.

Frederick asked the wives of the chaplains and me to embroider leaves on the bare limbs of a large tree he had sketched on a rectangle of burlap. His proviso, however, was that we use black, red, white, yellow, and brown thread, not green. Each color was to be a welcoming beacon, inviting sailors from around the world, regardless of their nation or race, to the chapel. This hand-sewn, rough-hewn tapestry hangs above the sea-washed altar. He also duplicated a tubular banner, representing the colors and interdependence of humanity, like one at Pacem in Terris, which I hope shall fly not only over the Houston International Seafarers' Center but, one day, over every human habitation.[4]

In view of my enthusiasm for the humble materials that Franck selected for the chapel, the reader may well wonder why I chose costly art for the altar of the church I envisioned for New Harmony. Some may well ask why I was so bent on providing an altar in the first place. Reasonable or not, wise or profligate, I herewith submit the stimuli that ignited my endeavors in New Harmony sixty-nine years ago.

The Roofless Church with its altar and ceremonial gate in 1962.

Photograph by James K. Mellow. Courtesy of James K. Mellow.

Acknowledgments

❖ I WISH TO EXPRESS my gratitude to family and friends who encouraged me for many years to write about my life. While some of it would provide interesting or entertaining memories as social history over many decades, the most meaningful part of my life, after motherhood, can be found within the small town of my husband's Owen ancestors, New Harmony, Indiana. My father, Robert Lee Blaffer, and after him my brother, John, never ceased to support my belief in New Harmony.

Over the years, I have been asked to give interviews, write introductions, speak in various settings, and provide information for historians, biographers, and scholars. I always envisioned, however, writing about my New Harmony adventures and revealing the full story myself.

I appreciate the efforts of those who were directly involved in transforming the idea of a book into reality.

Two women helped in the beginning. Barbara Conrey worked with me in New Harmony on individual chapters. Roger Rasbach introduced Donna Mosher, a busy editor with Segue Communications, to me at lunch, knowing of my need for assistance. Donna graciously transformed my handwritten pages into a coherent form on the computer.

I asked my good Houston friend Ted Estess, Founding Dean of the Honors College at the University of Houston, to read the rough draft. His wife, Sybil Pittman Estess, my longtime friend and a wonderful poet, read along with him. Ted devoted considerable time in the fall of 2008 to reviewing the draft and knew it would benefit from extensive research before revising. Ted gave me the best advice possible when he recommended Nancy, who had worked with him on his recent book *Be Well: Reflections on Graduating from College.*

My gratitude and appreciation for Nancy Mangum McCaslin, who became my personal editor, is boundless. Nancy understood immediately that a mother measures time and events in relation to her children rather than by a calendar, and her research assistance was always sensitive and more accurate than a bloodhound following a scent. Her editing was intuitive and gentle. Her tireless efforts on my behalf are invaluable, as is our close friendship. She also suggested two knowledgeable readers who would bring their expertise to my memoir.

Connie Weinzapfel, Director of Historic New Harmony, read my manuscript for the accuracy of historical references as well as contemporary details related to New Harmony. A dear friend and collaborator on several other projects, Connie worked most recently with me on the foreword for *New Harmony Then and Now,* with text by Donald E. Pitzer and photographs by Darryl D. Jones, available through Indiana University Press, Quarry Books. Other photographs by Darryl are included in the following pages.

Ben Nicholson, Associate Professor of Architecture, Interior Architecture, and Designed Objects at the School of the Art Institute of Chicago, read my manuscript in his capacity as co-editor of the forthcoming *Forms of Spirituality: Modern Architecture, Landscape, and Preservation in New Harmony.* Laura Foster Nicholson, naturally, read along with him. They are more recent transplants to New Harmony with whom I enjoy a rich friendship; each brought unique talents that enrich our community. Laura is one of the top weavers in the country, with a studio full of glorious works in progress on her looms. Ben can often be found patiently creating labyrinths with whatever nature has to offer him, such as multicolored autumnal leaves. While reading an early draft of *Forms of Spirituality,* I began to consider it as a companion book to mine that would balance two perspectives, the scholarly with the personal.

I also want to thank William R. Crout, Founder and Curator, the Paul Tillich Lectures, the Memorial Church, Harvard University. Bill is a former student, editorial assistant, and friend of Paul Tillich. Always a southern gentleman at heart and my East Coast friend for over a decade, Bill graciously provided helpful information about Tillich. He and Nancy were indefatigable allies of mine concerning chronological details about Paul Tillich for my memoir.

I was pleased to renew communication with Ralph G. Schwarz, and I thank him for aiding my memories about his time in New Harmony.

The maps of New Harmony, which will orient readers to our town and its surrounding area, were graciously designed by my friend Kenneth A. "Kent" Schuette, Clinical Professor, Landscape Architecture, at Purdue University, and illustrated by Roy Boswell, with technical assistance provided by Nicholas Mitchel and Tony Gillund.

I also thank the many individuals and archivists who responded so willingly to Nancy's requests and provided valuable assistance and information, including Preston and Pauline Bolton; Claske Franck, Pacem in Terris; Ted Lechner; Michelangelo Sabatino, PhD, Associate Professor, Gerald D. Hines College of Architecture, University of Houston and co-editor of *Forms of Spirituality*; Cammie McAtee; Laura McGuire; Lorraine A. Stuart, Archives Director, and David Aylsworth, Collections Registrar, Museum of Fine Arts, Houston; Betty L. Fischer, Archivist, University of St. Thomas; Lee Pecht, Head of Special Collections, and Rebecca Russell, Archivist/Special Collections Librarian, Woodson Research Center, Rice University; Stephen Fox, Architectural Historian, Fellow of the Anchorage Foundation of Texas; Vicki List McIntosh, Owen Offices; Judy Alsop, Red Geranium Enterprises Archives; Chris Laughbaum of the Robert Lee Blaffer Foundation, Robert Lee Blaffer Trust Archive and Paul Tillich Archive; Jodi Moore, Property Manager, David Dale Owen Laboratory, Rapp-Maclure-Owen House, and Rawlings House; Linda Warrum, Interpreter, Historic New Harmony; Martha J. Breeze, Posey County Recorder, and Mary J. Rhoades, Chief Deputy; Philip Werry, Werry Funeral Homes, Inc.; Martha Mathews; Sherry Graves, Margaret Scherzinger, and M. Ryan Rokicki, Director, Working Men's Institute; Amanda Bryden, Historic Sites Collections Manager, Indiana State Museum and Historic Sites; Letitia "Tish" Mumford; Bishop and Liz Mumford; Priscilla Jackson, Archivist, and Stephen Reynolds, Director of Information Technology, the Ethel Walker School; Fiona de Young, School Archivist and Assistant Librarian, Moran Upper School Library, the Kinkaid School; Linda Caruso-Haviland, Associate Professor, Founder and Director of the Dance Program, Bryn Mawr College; Serene Jones, President, as well as Leah Rousmaniere, Associate Director of Development for Stewardship and Research, Union Theological Seminary;

Sr. Élise and the Community of the Holy Spirit; Mrs. Shanks, Lexington
Public Library Reference and Information Center; Diane Ney, Manager
of Archives and Records, and Beverly Brown of Washington National
Cathedral; Fr. Rivers Patout, Rev. James and Carol Scott, and Patricia
Poulos, Houston International Seafarers' Center; Barbara Morris; Marisa
Bourgoin, Richard Manoogian Chief of Reference Services, Archives of
American Art, Smithsonian Institution; Geraldine Aramanda, Archivist,
and Mary Kadish, Collections Registrar, the Menil Collection; Duane
Hampton; Ritsert Rinsma; Tom Straw; Jane Martin, Michelle Harris,
Jenny Wright, and Karen Turner, Support Services Administrator, the
Iona Community; Michelle Andersson, Photo Librarian, Historic Scot-
land; James Clifton, Director, Leslie Scattone, Assistant Curator, and
Sarah Pierce, Administrative Assistant, Sarah Campbell Blaffer Founda-
tion; Kathy Sales and Angie Hein, New Harmony Inn; Janet Lorence;
Meredith "Merri" Leffel; Drs. Niels C. Nielson Jr. and Adrian Neil
"Sandy" Havens, Professors Emeriti, Rice University; Dr. Barbara Trues-
dell, Assistant Director, Indiana University Center for the Study of History
and Memory; Elizabeth A. Novara, Curator, and Amanda Moore, His-
toric Preservation Graduate Assistant, Historical Manuscripts Special
Collections, Frederick L. Rath Jr. Papers and the Charles Hosmer Papers,
Hornbake Library, University of Maryland; Jennifer Greene, Reference
and Archives Librarian, David L. Rice Library, University of Southern In-
diana; Vickie Cato, Clerk, Vanderburg County Clerk's Office, Evansville,
Indiana; Justin Davis, Librarian, Indiana State Library; Clair Wezet,
Poseyville Carnegie Public Library; Claudia Schmuckli, Director and
Chief Curator, Blaffer Art Museum, University of Houston; Tina Blue-
field; Darryl D. Jones, Photographer; Cheryl Wilburn, Episcopal Diocese
of Washington; and Sarah Buffington, Curator, Old Economy Village.
For assistance with French translations after June 2010: Andrea Heggen;
Cammie McAtee, PhD; Monique Singley, Executive Assistant to James J.
Coleman Jr.; and Leslie J. Roberts, PhD, Professor Emeritus of French,
University of Southern Indiana. For assistance with permissions and
rights requests: Mutie Tillich Farris, PhD, Estate of Paul Tillich and Es-
tate of Hannah Tillich; Sr. Catherine Grace, CHS, Community of the
Holy Spirit; Lukas Franck, Pacem in Terris; Danae Mattes and Jill Ther-
rien, Studio Archivist, Stephen De Staebler Estate; Hanno D. Mott of the
Lipchitz family, including Lolya R. Lipchitz and Frank L. Mott; Brittany

Piccuirro, Press Archivist, Marlborough Gallery; Margaret Rosati Norton, Estate of James Rosati; Robert Hernandez, Interim Manager of Rights and Reproductions, the Menil Collection; Michael Shulman, Director, Publishing, Broadcast and Film, Magnum Photos; Kevin Swank, Visuals Editor, *Evansville Courier & Press;* Isabelle Le Druillennec, Responsable Unité Collections, Assistant Curator, and Caroline Sormay, Assistante Éditions/Communication, Musée Picasso, Antibes; Hannah Rhadigan, Permissions Assistant, ARS—Artists Rights Society; and Maryam Mafi. In memoriam: Robert "Bob" Schneider and Jeanne Blair.

Gratitude goes to the professionals who made the publication possible. At Indiana University Press: Linda Oblack, Sponsoring Editor; Sarah Jacobi, Assistant Sponsoring Editor; Pam Rude, Senior Artist and Book Designer, and the Indiana University Press team. In addition, IUP's anonymous peer review recommendations proved insightful and helpful, although some were beyond the scope of a literary work: Reader #1 requested the addition of an index, and Reader #2 requested the inclusion of a brief explanation about the memoir-writing process and source material, which was also accomplished through some additional endnotes. At Westchester Publishing Services: Debbie Masi, Production Supervisor, Editorial Services. For copyediting: Sue Warga. For the index: Meridith Murray, MLM Indexing Service. And for proofreading page proofs and the index: Donna Mosher, Segue Communications, returned to the project a decade later.

Historical Note

Connie A. Weinzapfel

❖ JANE BLAFFER OWEN's memoir begins with her 1941 entry into New Harmony, Indiana, a town with a substantial and significant history. A brief overview of its history and development will provide a helpful orientation to her many references to its past.

New Harmony is the site of two of America's important early communal experiments. The first utopians—the Harmonie Society of Iptingen, Germany, from within the area of Württemberg—were led by Georg Johann Rapp (1757–1847) from their first settlement to the Northwest Territory in 1814. (Members of the Harmonie Society have been referred to as Rappites or Harmonists.) "Father Rapp," the title given him by his Pietist flock, and his adopted son Frederick hired engineers from Vincennes, Indiana, to design their new town, Harmonie. Streets were laid out in a perfect grid and were named for their utilitarian purposes—Church, Granary, Steammill, and Brewery, as well as East, West, North, and South streets (see the town map). The Harmonists efficiently constructed their single-family houses in a process we would today call prefabrication, as pieces were cut and numbered off-site at their mill and assembled on each town lot. Gardens for vegetables, herbs, and flowers were incorporated into the plan, and two thousand acres immediately surrounding the town were used for the Harmonists' agricultural endeavors and formed the basis for their substantial commercial success. In keeping with their providential path as God's chosen people, the Harmonie Society placed New Harmony for sale in 1824 in order to relocate to western Pennsylvania. Considering New Harmony's remote location on the frontier, the Harmonists' dwellings and public buildings were quite remarkable. The American Planning Association recognized their exemplary community

design in 1998 when it designated New Harmony as a National Planning
Landmark.

During the years of the Harmonie Society's ventures in America, a parallel utopian movement was taking shape in Europe and Great Britain. In
New Lanark, Scotland, Robert Owen (1771–1858) was instituting systems
for the improvement of the lives of his cotton mill workers. In response to
the degradations to laborers brought on by the Industrial Revolution,
Owen promulgated theories that promoted education as the great equal-
izer for the inequities of social classes. This included planned housing and
schools for all of his New Lanark employees. Owen also created an Institute for the Formation of Character in New Lanark, which, in essence, was
a community education center.

Owen tried unsuccessfully for years to influence the British Parlia-
ment to enact social reforms. Likewise, he was rebuffed by other industri-
alists, who saw in Owen's plans only depletion of profits. When word
came that the Harmonists had placed for sale their town in the wilderness
of Indiana, Owen became interested; he was already acquainted with the
community, for he had corresponded with the Rapps since 1818. In 1825
Robert Owen spent much of his fortune to buy New Harmony.

Soon after purchasing the town of New Harmony, Robert Owen found
a like-minded Scotsman, social reformer, and scientist William Maclure
(1763–1840), who believed that the basis for the improvement of society
was education. Maclure was a founder and president of the Academy of
Natural Sciences in Philadelphia. While there, Robert Owen was reintroduced to the Pestalozzian educator Marie Duclos Fretageot. Under the
patronage of Maclure, Fretageot headed a school and was well acquainted
with the local intellectual community. Through her introduction, Owen
met the group of people who would add substance and longevity to his
utopian dream. Some went straightaway to New Harmony, like Dr.
Gerard Troost—a geologist, mineralogist, zoologist, and chemist, and the
first president of the Academy of Natural Sciences. Others waited for
transport on the keelboat *Philantropist* with Robert Owen and William
Maclure via the Ohio River to New Harmony during the winter of 1825–26.[1]
Not surprisingly, it was dubbed "The Boatload of Knowledge" for the
many world-renowned scientists, educators, and professionals aboard,
including Charles-Alexandre Lesueur, paleontologist, archaeologist, ichthyologist, and zoologist, together with three of his students; Thomas

Say, entomologist, conchologist, and artist; Thomas Stedman Whitwell, an English architect who designed Owen's quadrangular community design, a structure intended to be built just south of New Harmony where the ultimate realization of Owen's millennial dream would take place; Dr. William Price, physician; Robert Dale Owen, eldest son of Robert Owen; the Pestalozzian educators Marie Duclos Fretageot and William S. Phiquepal, with ten students; and Lucy Sistare, artist and educator, among others.[2]

The Owen/Maclure community introduced educational and social reforms to America and was to be a model for other villages to be built around the world. After only two years, the envisioned community of mutual cooperation did not survive as a cohesive unit, due primarily to a lack of "mutual cooperation" among the throngs of disparate people attracted to the ideals of the utopian experiment.

Although William Maclure and Robert Owen both left the community, many of the scientists, educators, and professionals remained. Robert Owen's sons Robert Dale, Richard, David Dale, and William, and one daughter, Jane Dale Owen Fauntleroy, provided continuity and made important contributions during New Harmony's Post Communal Period from 1828 to 1858. New Harmony provided geological and natural science collections for the foundation of the Smithsonian Institution. Indeed, New Harmony became a national center for scientific and educational innovation until the Civil War. During these years, New Harmony was one of the most important training and research centers for the study of the natural sciences in America.

In the early 1900s, one hundred years after the Harmonists founded the town, New Harmony experienced a renewed vigor in the lives of the townspeople and the physical environment of the town, as evidenced in the photographs of William F. Lichtenberger and Homer Fauntleroy.[3] Prosperity from agriculture built many fine Victorian homes among the comparatively modest Harmonist dwellings. Strong leadership and planning enabled the town to erect monumental public buildings, including the 1894 Working Men's Institute and the 1913 Murphy Auditorium. Pride in community and recognition of the town's historical importance enabled New Harmony to overcome losses from the 1908 Monitor Corner fire and the 1913 flood.

In early 1913, the New Harmony Town Council created a Centennial Commission, consisting of its own members, the trustees of the Working

Men's Institute, and ten citizens of the town to be appointed by the president of the Town Council, "five of whom must be women recommended by the Woman's Library Club." In the *Program of the Centennial Celebration at New Harmony, Indiana,* the opening statement to the public declares, "No town or city in the United States boasts a history of greater romantic or sociological interest."

A great celebration marked New Harmony's centennial in 1914, and we began our yearlong bicentennial celebrations with pealing church bells and sparklers at midnight on New Year's Day 2014. The New Harmony Bicentennial Commission is pleased to remember the contributions of Jane Blaffer Owen posthumously as the bicentennial honoree. As Jane Owen remarked in an interview in May 2008, "The dreams of the people who have come before are finally being realized now, 200 years later."[4]

Nature provided the lure for both Native Americans and the Harmonie Society to settle here. It provided subject matter for the scientists and artists of the Owen/Maclure community and created a fertile base for agriculture. The natural beauty of New Harmony continues as an attraction today. I believe that the present inhabitants will honor the endeavors and good intentions of our forebears and continue to care for our past, make the most of the moment, and work together toward the ideal.

Connie A. Weinzapfel, Director, Historic New Harmony—a unified program of the University of Southern Indiana and the Indiana State Museum and Historic Sites, Inc.

From Spoken to Written Words

Nancy Mangum McCaslin

❖ PEOPLE WHO KNEW Jane Blaffer Owen considered her a consummate storyteller. Throughout her long life, she told many of the stories
and anecdotes that follow, but she always hoped to commit them to a
cohesive and meaningful written form. She admitted wondering if enough
time had passed to enable some distance from and insight into the experiences of her life. She was in her late eighties when she started writing,
around 2003.

Jane Owen wrote about one aspect of her life specifically: all that led to
and radiated from her New Harmony experiences, from her arrival in 1941
through the early 1970s. A literal chronology was less important to her as
an organizing principle than sequences created spontaneously through
natural associations and connections. She borrowed a comparison about
her writing style from a well-worn phrase about the difference in one's religious orientation: following the spirit rather than the letter of the law.
Like her oral storytelling, her written narrative flows freely, often jumping from present to past or future; it reminds me of the path of the Cathedral Labyrinth she would walk in New Harmony, which led, albeit circu-
itously, to the center before retracing the path outward again. While on
the current path, the feet attempt to balance between the one just walked
and the one yet to come, manifesting in each step on its smooth granite
surface the fluid interplay of present, past, and future. Such is the nature
of writing from hindsight.

As part of the revising process, which began in early 2009, she and I
consulted a wide array of resources, both her own and archival material,
including correspondence, journals, and her previous publications, such

as forewords and presentation papers. We endeavored to support the narrative while also remaining true to the memory. For Jane Owen, the primary purpose of her writing would be to tell the personal story. She would leave to scholars the task of interpreting her legacy.

Chartres Labyrinth Image.
© Jeff Saward, Labyrinthos Photo Archive.
Courtesy of Jeff Saward/Labyrinthos.

NEW HARMONY
INDIANA

JANE BLAFFER OWEN

My life is for myself and not for spectacle. I much prefer that it be of a lower strain, so it be genuine and equal, than that it should be glittering and unsteady. . . . To be yourself in a world that is constantly trying to make you something else is the greatest accomplishment.

—Ralph Waldo Emerson, "Self-Reliance"

CHAPTER 1

Twin Vows

I grew up in a small, exclusive neighborhood of impressive homes with magnolia-, jasmine-, and rose-filled gardens. The several families who had built these fine homes and gardens owned stock in the same companies, belonged to the same clubs, sent their children to the same schools, and attended the same church (institutions that were segregated in those days). The presumption that long and enduring friendships would blossom among the beneficiaries of this elite segment of society was in my case never justified.

In the decades between two world wars, children—especially young women—seldom disappointed parental expectations, however often they might have wished to bolt imposed boundaries. My long-suppressed rebellious spirit came close to volcanic eruption in Houston during 1936, my first year after college. Well-intentioned and loyal friends of my parents gave endless lunches, dinners, and dances, for I was considered a proper debutante in my Parisian haute couture wardrobe. Not so. I had done nothing to merit the attention of kind hosts. I saw myself as a wild,

alien creature who had been forcefully herded down from her native habi-
tat into a glittering show ring and ordered to go through prescribed paces.
I searched in vain for some loose planks in my imaginary enclosure but
found none.

Nor was there an acceptable exit from societal expectations after my
engagement to Kenneth Dale Owen, the estimable man who would be
my husband for sixty-one years. My future role as an active member of
Houston society and a promoter of good causes cast its long shadow
before me. My family background and education together with Kenneth's
own impeccable credentials would place me in a position of leadership in
the energy and oil capital of the world. Would I take a bold leap over
my enclosure, embarrass the people I loved, break my legs, and smash my
foolish face in the doing? Happily, and I believe by the grace of God, I
didn't have to kick over the traces.

A way out of confining expectations presented itself shortly after my
marriage in July 1941 and opened the way for a second marriage. From my
perspective today, I firmly believe that every first marriage can be preserved if a cerebral and spiritual marriage follows. The rumblings of dis-
content in our hearts can lead either to strained relationships and divorces
or to life-enhancing breakthroughs. It is unwise to expect happiness
solely from another person. Other women have saved their marriages by
taking a law degree, answering a call to the ministry, or cultivating an un-
developed talent. Had anyone predicted that a sleepy, dusty little Indiana
town would be my threshold to a higher consciousness, I would not have
believed it. But something did happen in that unlikely place to redirect
my life.

That something began with a stopover in New Harmony one hot
August day in 1941, three weeks after our wedding at Ste. Anne, my family's
summer place in Ontario. As we were driving from Canada to Texas,
Kenneth wanted me to see the town of his birth before pushing on to
Houston. I had, of course, consented but not with enthusiasm. I had heard
about my husband's illustrious ancestors and had read Frank Podmore's
life of Robert Owen with my father before I met Kenneth. Daddy admired
Owen for his factory and child labor reforms and initiated similar social
benefits and an employee stock ownership plan for the Humble Oil

Blaffer sisters "Titi"
(Cecil), Jane, and Joyce.

*Blaffer-Owen family
photograph.*

Mr. and Mrs. Kenneth
Dale Owen.

*Blaffer-Owen family
photograph.*

Company that he helped found. For me, the legacy of Robert Owen and his fellow passengers on "The Boatload of Knowledge" existed chiefly in history books and biographies.

Our car pulled up before an unusual house known as the David Dale Owen Laboratory, which I soon learned had been built in 1859 (4 on town map on back endpaper). David Dale Owen was a geologist.[1] David's elder brother Robert Dale, who was an early trustee of the Smithsonian, had chosen James Renwick Jr. as the architect for that institution, America's first castle of science and first national museum.

David Dale had worked and taught in three laboratories before building this one: the Harmonist Community House No. 3 and the Harmonist shoe factory (both long gone from town), followed by seventeen years in the Harmonist stone Granary behind the Laboratory (5, 6, and 7 on town map, respectively). Successive generations of non-geologist Owens had converted David's Laboratory into a family residence, and my husband called it home. I felt more like bowing my head than looking up because I was, in essence, bringing a wreath to the graves of noble men and women. But an alive and unforgettable presence was standing in the doorway to greet us: Kenneth's elderly aunt Aline Owen Neal.

Auntie's freshly laundered white cotton dress, full and floor-length, did not conceal or diminish her somewhat triangular shape. A black, curving ear trumpet emerged like a ram's horn from the left side of her well-coiffed hair but was quickly lowered so both arms could embrace her nephew. Auntie didn't grasp what we were saying, but no matter: sweetly smiling, she nodded assent to Kenneth's every word. She had helped raise him. Ever since his first oil well, Kenneth had maintained her as the châtelaine of the Laboratory, a living monument to the Owen family.

I was no sooner inside than, like a stray cat, I wanted out. The twenty-foot-tall living room, designed to be a lecture hall with a gallery on three sides, was not hospitable. Several tables were stacked high with outdated newspapers and greeting cards. Auntie threw nothing away, perhaps because her nature was too gentle, her mind too comfortable in the past. As we hastened through the clutter to the circular dining room with its arched and diamond-hearted windows, I thought of the fairy tale that had captured my childhood imagination, where everyone, even the flies on the windowsills, had slept for a hundred years. In the story, a beautiful princess lay under an enchantment in a round tower. In the Laboratory,

The David Dale Owen Laboratory as it appeared on May 24, 1940,
in the Historic American Buildings Survey.

*Library of Congress, Prints & Photographs Division, HABS IND,
65-NEHAR, 1—2, Photograph by Lester Jones.*

something as beautiful as a princess seemed to lie asleep, hidden from
view, yet nonetheless palpably present. Could we summon enough love
from our own hearts to awaken her and enough patience to recover her
buried treasures?

My husband brought me out of my reveries and unanswered questions.
"It's awfully hot in here, Jane. Let's step outside," he said, and held open
the west door for me to enter an Old World courtyard, a square green
space enclosed by a wall overhung with trumpet vines. A pair of gates had
long ago opened for Owen carriages.

Beyond the north fence rose the sandstone and brick wall of the Granary, a massive structure that the German Harmonists had begun in 1814
and completed in 1822. Intended as a storehouse for food and grain, it

could also serve as a fortress for protection. The Harmonists were avowed pacifists, so never a shot was fired from the tall, narrow slits of the ground floor. These openings were ventilators, not loopholes or *meurtriers,* the name of which was drawn from the French word for "murder."

Turning back toward the Laboratory, I looked up in wonder at the conical witch's-hat roof of the dining room and its weather vane. The directional markers—which would have pointed north, south, east, and west—were missing, but my eye lingered on a long, corkscrew-shaped column that supported a strange wooden fish. Time had battered its stomach and chewed its contours. Sensing my curiosity, Kenneth explained that the Paleozoic fossil fish had been great-uncle David's tribute to the naturalist Charles-Alexandre Lesueur, one of the passengers on "The Boatload of Knowledge." Lesueur had not only studied the anatomy of fish but, an accomplished artist, also drawn and painted them. I later learned that the supporting rod itself is an enlargement of both a blastoid, *Pentremites,* as the base and a bryozoan, *Archimedes,* a corkscrew-shaped fossil dear to the hearts of geologists and an apt colophon for a laboratory dedicated to science.

Kenneth's blue eyes saddened as he ended his explanations. "We'll have to find a good craftsman to replace this tired old fossil. Enough of this gloomy, run-down place," he said. "I'll take you across this mess of lawn to the white-pillared house on the far corner of the property that once belonged to us. The Lab is the only house in town still in my family."

I remembered the same diffident look on Kenneth's handsome face a few years earlier beside an entrance door of my own parents' home. He had no idea I was watching through a window, fascinated by his gesture. Having rung the doorbell, he stepped back and with his right hand rubbed the signet ring on the little finger of his left hand. The ring was engraved with the double eagle that Hadrian's Roman army had brought to New Lanark in the second century AD. Robert Owen had adopted this image for his own crest and, being egalitarian, placed identical eagles on the buttons of the coats of his employees. The intensity of Kenneth's gesture seemed an unmistakable appeal to his ancestors for help in his pursuit of a difficult, pampered girl.

An appeal to ancestors for courage should come naturally from us, not only from a man in love. Many years later, words from Julie Dash's film *Daughters of the Dust* powerfully underscored my belief and spelled out the challenge given and taken by Kenneth. In a graveyard scene, a Gullah African American woman named Nana Peazant addresses her great-grandson Eli: "Those in this grave, like those who're across the sea, they're with us. They're all the same. The ancestors and the womb are one. Call on your ancestors, Eli. Let them guide you. You need their strength. Eli, I need you to make the family strong again, like we used to be."[2]

Through the window at my parents' house, I saw a sensitive man appealing for guidance from earlier Owens and a never-to-be-underestimated mother. At the time, I could not yet appreciate the burden an alcoholic father places on a son's shoulders. Witnessing his appeal achieved what the daily arrival of a dozen pink roses and at Christmas a pair of antique Italian armchairs had failed to accomplish. At last, after two years of indifference to Kenneth's courtship, my self-centered ego moved over to make room for love and understanding. My parents announced our engagement shortly after my fortuitous awakening.

On that hot August day in New Harmony, the house that Kenneth and I were approaching stood on the sandstone foundation of Father George Rapp's 1822 mansion, which was originally a dignified three-story house (8 on town map). (Thomas Say's watercolor of the house is at the American Philosophical Society in Philadelphia.) William Maclure, father of American geology and Robert Owen's financial partner, had owned Rapp's mansion. Maclure's brother Alexander inherited it. After a disastrous fire demolished all but the cellar and the apricot-colored foundation stones, Alexander planned the reconstruction.

Kenneth's briefing resumed. "The 1844 fire destroyed the Rapp house and much of the Maclure library, which was a great loss. Alexander built this really elegant house, thanks to a first-rate carpenter and contractor from England named John Beale.[3] My great-grandfather Richard bought it from the Maclure estate in the 1850s and lived there. His son, Horace, sold it in 1901 to a prosperous grain merchant Captain John Corbin. That was lucky for the house and our family, as my grandfather could not afford

The Rapp-Maclure-Owen House circa 1935, showing exterior detail of
front portico, in the Historic American Buildings Survey.

Library of Congress, Prints & Photographs Division,
HABS IND, 65-NEHAR, 12—2, *Photograph by Alexander Piaget,*
Piaget-van Ravenswaay Photography.

to maintain it. The Corbins are fine people and good custodians," he
concluded.

I feel grateful to Alexander Maclure, who chose not to rebuild in the
Harmonists' style, with short German windows and low walls; instead,
fourteen-foot-high walls frame ten-foot-high windows. He also added the
distinctly southern long white veranda to the east entrance. But even with
these positive changes, the house we were observing that sweltering
August day in 1941 did not reflect Alexander's accomplishment. The shut-
tered windows and the once white-painted brick walls were now layered
with soot from the soft coal the town used at that time.

As we returned across the lawn between the two houses, the faded neg-
ative of the Laboratory developed into a sharper, more credible image. Its

black ironwork—scalloped and thick like Irish lace—embroidered the eaves of the slate roof, the front portico, and the entablature of the windows and doorways. An octagonal lantern crowned the roof of the erstwhile lecture hall. Chimney pots that individually reflected geometric shapes stood guard, alert sentinels.

"All of this for a working, teaching laboratory?" I asked myself. Then a revelation struck me: David Dale Owen, albeit a scholar-scientist, was also an artist and a romantic. Letters in the Owen archives bear witness to his love for his wife, Caroline. But even greater than conjugal love, here in his laboratory stood incontestable testimony of the driving force of his life: geology, his second marriage. He devoted the last years of his life to preparing a bridal bower for his beloved geology that others might share his passion and nurture a still-young and promising profession. David, with no thought of enriching himself or his family, had surveyed fourteen states, pointing the way to wealth for individuals and large companies that benefited from his discoveries.

Lines from a poem by Rumi accurately describe David Dale:

Love is recklessness, not reason.
Reason seeks a profit.
Love comes on strong, consuming herself,
    unabashed.[4]

I began to understand his two passions, that for his profession and that for his wife, Caro, as twin vows. David introduced me to the idea of a second marriage while married to the same person—an insurance policy for the safekeeping of a marriage covenant.

I did not share my fantasies with Kenneth, for his scientific mind would have thrown the light of reason upon my emotional response to his heritage. Having had to face practical and critical issues all his life, Kenneth sensibly outlined steps for the restoration of the Laboratory.[5]

"The damn roof leaks, and every room needs replastering and fresh paint. Auntie's invasive memorabilia need some weeding out. Not that we'll begin right now."

"Oh, of course not now," I replied. "Only don't forget your plans for a new fossil fish!"

There had not been even a suggestion of a breeze during our tour, but suddenly a wind began to spin the fish westward, toward the route we would take across the Wabash to Texas. Of all my impressions of New

Harmony and its imperatives, the parting image of the bruised but inde-structible fish remains vivid, a symbol of the continuing challenge ahead.

This particular fish, high above a circular tower, is an apt emblem for New Harmony's two utopian experiments. The pious Harmonists would have valued it for its importance to the early Christian church, for the five initial letters of each word in the Greek phrase "Jesus Christ, Son of God, Savior" form the acronym ICHTHUS, meaning "fish." The Owenites would have seen in the fish identified by Charles-Alexandre Lesueur an appropriate symbol of their belief in the redemption of the world through scientific discovery and education. Was the wind that spun the fish telling us that, back to back, science and religion could together accomplish the unrealized hopes of Harmonists and Owenites?

The Laboratory in its present condition was unsuitable for overnight lodging, so we stayed the night at the McCurdy Hotel in Evansville, re-turning the next day for our farewells to Auntie. We didn't linger this time because Kenneth had planned our journey to Texas to include a visit to his cousin Natalie Wilson of Wilson, Arkansas. He wished for me to meet a few Owen descendants who were wealthy, urbane, and industrious. But rich or poor, well- or ill-educated, atheist or devout, most of them were kind and generous beyond their means: givers, not takers. Of the hun-dreds of Owen descendants I have met, some were very creative, none were mentally deficient, and only two, alas, were mean. Not a bad average.

My first visit to New Harmony ended with humor and a new acquain-tance I made at the tollgate of the bridge that would launch us across the Wabash on our long drive to Houston (see area map). Horace, the bridge's defender, and Kenneth had received their early schooling in New Har-mony and were delighted to see one another.

"By the way, Horace," Kenneth asked, "does anyone swim in the river these days, as we used to?"

Horace kept us waiting for a moment of reflection, while my husband looked anxiously in my direction.

"No, not no more, Kenny. Since the gravel diggers caused suction holes, it just ain't safe for swimming. But come to think of it, there was a lady in there yesterday afternoon. Sure was a lady because she undressed behind that bluff over there, and I couldn't see a thing."

The restored fossil fish. *Photograph by Darryl D. Jones, 2009.*

Kenneth gave me a sly wink, for the day before I had begged him for a baptismal dunking in that turgid, silt-heavy stream; he had grudgingly consented and followed me into its waters.

The Wabash was no ordinary baptismal font but a river fraught with history. Willows still line both banks, vigorous descendants of those the Indians used for their baskets. La Salle might have grasped the topmost branches of cottonwoods and sycamores when the river's current swept his canoe too swiftly four centuries ago.[6] A devout Roman Catholic, La Salle would have rejoiced that French apostles of religious education followed in the wake of his canoe a century and a half later. Mother Theodore Guerin traveled past New Harmony and up the Wabash to Terre Haute in 1840 to found the Sisters of Providence of Saint Mary-of-the-Woods. Two years later, six brothers of the Holy Cross took the same water route on the final stage of their journey to South Bend, where they laid the foundation for the University of Notre Dame. According to Carl Sandburg's *Abraham Lincoln: The Prairie Years,* a young Abe ferried passengers from Illinois to New Harmony. And George Rogers Clark waded up to his shoulders along its swollen banks, keeping his musket dry and his ragged army poised to raise the siege of Vincennes. Lesueur swam in its summer waters and felt for *Unios* (freshwater mussels) and other shells with his feet. Men and women of courage and imagination had traveled that waterway long before the advent of Harmonists and Owenites and long before my own total immersion. Heroic men and women had become my touchstone, as Kenneth's signet ring had been his at a crossroads of his life.

Fields of tall corn on either side of the highway fueled Kenneth's plans. "Just look at that healthy corn, Jane. We're going to grow our corn on the Indiana side of the river. Great-grandfather Richard was also a farmer and as precise about farming as he had been about geology."

Kenneth's blue eyes softened. "We once owned thousands of acres south of town. The highest part of it was called Indian Mound because prehistoric Indians had mounded their spent mussel shells. I intend to buy most of that land back and call on Purdue's agricultural expertise to revitalize the soil. We'll need to grow our own hay."

"Do you mean to raise cattle?"

"Yes, of course there'll be cattle. White-faced Herefords and golden Guernseys."

I was warming to his dream.

"I'll be a farmer's wife and yell out the window when you come home, 'Leave your muddy boots on the front porch!'"

The closer we came to Texas, the more our thoughts turned back to New Harmony. "Richard and his brother had a horse farm, as almost every landowner did in those days." Kenneth's voice quickened and his eyes sparkled. "Some of their horses competed in harness races around the county. I'll show you the old fairground when we return (see area map on front endpaper). I haunted it as a boy with a savvy old horse trader called Truman."

I sensed that Kenneth was adding Standardbred colts and fillies to his wish list and shuddered at the thought of a racing stable in our family and an absentee husband. Where would he be when the children we hoped to have needed us both? Off to the races! What would happen to the covenant we had formed with the derelict fish above the Laboratory's tower? Perhaps his oil and gas interests in his Houston office and a young family would divert him from harness horses. Perhaps not.

Whatever the future might hold for us, there was more joy than fear in my heart as we headed southwest to the Gulf Coast. On the outskirts of Houston, however, we became bewildered by its size. The contours of this gung-ho metropolis had expanded during our three-month absence. Houstonians of vision and generosity were proving equal to their city's physical growth and worthy of their inheritance from "wildcatter" ancestors, bold men before whom I still stand in awe. They birthed a giant industry that in the short course of forty years brought Houston into the pantheon of urban gods. Revenues from that industry would create a world-renowned medical center, universities, museums, theaters, parks, operas, a ballet, and a symphony. Inheritors of oil wealth also built places of worship and eventually the Jung Center to answer the spiritual and psychological needs of Houstonians.[7]

How could anyone of sound mind leave a city teeming with such energy and promise? How could I, a descendant of families who had found

William Thomas Campbell.

Blaffer-Owen family photograph.

Sarah Jane Turnbull.

Blaffer-Owen family photograph.

their fortunes on the expanding Texas star, a star called "Spindletop," hanker after another star? My pioneer maternal grandfather, William T. Campbell, and my father, Robert Lee Blaffer, were in the forefront of my mind as Kenneth and I drew closer to Houston's sleek buildings of competitive heights.

Grandfather Campbell emigrated from his native England as a young man, worked as a reporter for the *Cincinnati Enquirer,* and married Sarah Turnbull of Middleport, Ohio. But he remained a true son of empire and envisioned the oil fields around Beaumont, Texas, as a new country to explore, colonize, and conquer. He left his news desk, sold his printing press, brought his young family to Waxahachie and set off for Spindletop in 1901.

My father belonged to a third generation of public-spirited New Orleanians. He cared for his city and its traditions, but the Queen City of the South had lost her crown in the Civil War and, apart from the entertainment of Mardi Gras, had not regained her kingdom or replaced cotton and sugar cane as her source of wealth and revitalization. When news of

Robert Lee Blaffer, his father,
John August(e) Blaffer, and
my elder brother, John,
as a baby, 1913.
*Blaffer-Owen family
photograph.*

Sarah Campbell Blaffer
with John, 1914.
*Blaffer-Owen family
photograph.*

the bountiful gusher in Beaumont reached Lee Blaffer in the teller's cage of his uncle's Hibernia Bank, he lost no time in exchanging a safe monotony for the unpredictable life of a wildcatter in East Texas. He brought more than an adventurous spirit with him to Beaumont; he brought a small library of history books. During the dreary months of waiting for a well to "blow in," Daddy spent his evenings reading Gibbon's *The Decline and Fall of the Roman Empire.* Had he been a senator in pre-Augustan Rome, he would have distrusted the imperial ambitions of any Roman citizen and opposed his election. Despite Daddy's distaste for empires, he and William Campbell became friends. My father fell in love with the Englishman's beautiful daughter. I became the second child of the bipartisan and felicitous marriage of Lee Blaffer to Sarah Campbell.

Kenneth's voice interrupted my reverie: "Why are you so quiet? Aren't you excited about being back in Houston as a bride of almost a month?"

I reached for the fingers of the strong hand on the steering wheel.

"Of course I'm glad we'll soon be living in our own home. But I can't help imagining the day in 1909 when my newly married parents arrived here, after their two-month honeymoon in the capitals of Europe. They intuited Houston's great future. Surely their spines tingled with anticipation before an evolving city where they would invest their energies to improve it economically and culturally. I am also grateful to their contemporaries, men and women who also believed in the future Houston. Nothing was impossible or unbearable for them."

Kenneth eyed me quizzically. "I'm not hearing your spine tingle."

"Not above this traffic noise while stopped at the one-hundredth red light that seems to have been added since we left three months ago. But you'd hear it on the Indiana farms you plan to buy. Remember, there's only one overhead traffic light in New Harmony, and its skyline is formed by the trunks of the tallest and most leafy-headed maples I've ever seen. Let's hope that the gnarled roots of the sturdy trees can keep the poor, malnourished houses from falling until you can take me back!"

Kenneth squeezed my hand. "Thank you for your loyalty to a town most people consider a lost cause, especially your mother. I'd like to spend more time there, too, but I have to make a living in Houston; you don't. You'll find plenty to do here and perhaps think more kindly about cities, which are as necessary as farms and country towns." His words echoed those my father had once spoken to me: "You make money in the city so you can spend it in the country."

Kenneth drove beyond downtown, toward my parents' home in Shadyside, where we would stay until our rented house was ready. I couldn't help but notice the ostentatious automobiles—Cadillacs, Lincolns, even a Rolls-Royce—encircling the Museum of Fine Arts as we passed. With triumph, I pointed. "Look! Houston is teeming with generous benefactors; I won't be missed here. But in New Harmony . . . " My voice became inaudible as my thoughts turned inward.

Cities are good for commerce, the presentation of fine art, education, advancement, and the intermingling of peoples and races. Yes, they can even be explored, but not as we explore oceans. Persistent daydreams of New Harmony intruded upon my civic efforts. I imagined myself as if on the bank of a great but as yet unexplored river, exhilarated as surely as Magellan had been when he first beheld the unlimited body of water that he named Pacific.

An ocean prompts us to dive below the surface, not to look above unless to navigate by the stars in the night sky. It invites us to sail beyond the horizon of our perceptions. The very uncertainty of what I would find scanning the horizon or discover beneath the surface, treasure or terror, was part of the spell New Harmony had cast over me. Cockeyed or sacrosanct as my daydreams might appear to my family and friends, I felt with all my heart that New Harmony would be my gateway to ocean depth.

Humility, that low, sweet root,
From which all heavenly virtues shoot . . .

—Thomas Moore, *The Loves of the Angels*

CHAPTER 2

Indian Mound

My fears about a racing-stable absentee husband began to dissipate. In the first year of our marriage, Kenneth began necessary improvements to the Laboratory residence and purchased a large portion of Robert Owen's original holdings, rolling farmlands that culminated in the highest point on the Wabash River for many miles, a rise known as Indian Mound (see area map). Archaeologists called it a midden, a deposit containing refuse indicative of an early human settlement; this one was created with mussel shells discarded by prehistoric Native Americans. But generations of townspeople had other names and softer feelings for this ageless place. Indian Mound became for Kenneth and me (and later our three daughters) a refuge from the rattle of trucks along Church Street, heat, and concerns. The greatest reward for climbing that far, however, was the expansive view of Cut-Off Island, belonging half to Indiana and half to the nearby fertile, flat plains of Illinois, still innocent of factories and housing developments on the other bank of the Wabash (see area map).[1]

Kenneth planned to grow corn and soybeans on his newly acquired Indian Mound Farm and sought expertise from members of Purdue's agricultural department concerning how best to reinvigorate the land that had lain fallow for many years (see area map). As a young boy, he had picked corn on the gentry farm on the Old Plank Road for a dollar a day. His agricultural instincts were sound, but he needed professional advice. Fences would be built and hay sown before purebred Herefords could graze on well-seeded fields.

Heeding Louis Bromfield's advice that the best manure is the owner's foot tracks, we headed for the farm soon after our return to New Harmony from Houston in the late spring of 1942.[2] I was several months pregnant with our first child and eager to have the unborn Owen accompany us on our excursions to Indian Mound. We passed Sled Hill, so called because it is steep enough for sledding in winter, which I've done by starlight (see area map). We walked beyond the dairy barn and continued through catalpa trees, which showered us with orchid-like blossoms, to reach the broad back of the hallowed mound.

The sound of whirling blades assaulted our ears. A small but deadly machine, like an armored knight, was waging war against my husband's invasive enemies, the thorn trees that grew on land intended for pasture. The stump remover was winning the battle, and Kenneth was buoyant. Whatever hindered the best use of the land was abhorrent to him, a splinter in his flesh, for land to my husband was what it had been to the Woodland Indians, his other body. He grinned broadly, having slain his dragons for the day.

Regaining our breath after the brief climb and filling our lungs with the clover-fragrant air, he turned to me, for I had lagged behind.

"I don't know how you feel about Indian Mound, but I know that we don't really own it. Time does. Let's never build here or allow a paved road to come anywhere near."

"I love you, Kenneth, for thinking this way. We'll let nothing rob eternity of its foothold on this place. Unless . . . ," I added timidly.

"Unless what?" came his no-nonsense reply.

I became silent because unpredictable emotions were rising from many leagues below the level of my conscious mind, claiming my complete attention.

Abraham, patriarch of our Jewish-Christian-Muslim faith, a historical figure whom I was not expecting, seemed to have a message for me.

View of New Harmony and the Wabash River on the
horizon from Indian Mound, January 7, 1936.

*Don Blair Collection. Courtesy of Special Collections,
University of Southern Indiana.*

Although not a biblical scholar, I was familiar enough with the Book of
Genesis to know that I could not easily brush Abraham aside. I was remembering that the old patriarch had dutifully changed his name from
Abram to Abraham, a sign that the mission of his life included more
than he had previously realized. The God whom he worshiped had
said: "Get thee out of thy country, and from thy kindred, and from thy
father's house, unto a land that I will shew thee" (Gen. 12:1).[3] As a
young bride, I had changed my name, and as a social malcontent, I had
yearned for a new country and a new way of life. In obedience to his
Lord, Abram had "removed from thence unto a mountain on the east of
Beth-el, and pitched his tent . . . , and *there he builded an altar unto the
LORD,* and called upon the name of the LORD" (Gen. 12:8, emphasis
mine).

A pragmatic Hoosier sun did not dispel Abraham's insistent presence on the hilltop or his companionship on the homeward walk. From an ancient mound an ancient prophet had communicated, not in an audible external voice but rather through an inward discernible intention. The implications of Abraham's presence on the highest point above New Harmony were unmistakable: the buried treasures in the village below would never be fully discovered and shared until every endeavor was consecrated to higher purposes than mine. Had not previous plans of well-meaning people who had wanted to restore New Harmony always come to a standstill?

With unabashed self-righteousness before the entrance of Abraham, I had believed that the Lord would hear and bring to immediate realization my list of priorities, such as:

Buy and rehabilitate every available Harmonist house
Remove the Standard Oil filling station and reactivate the well nearby
    that had supplied water to the town in Father Rapp's day
Keep after Kenneth to secure options on the old Granary and the
    Rapp-Maclure-Owen House on his block
Provide classes in dance, crafts, and especially ceramics
Make it possible for art, religion, education, and economy to join
    hands and encircle our town

The jealous God of Abraham must have desperately wanted to widen and deepen my worthy but egocentric plans for the future, because He had chosen the right place and moment to do so. I was thoroughly shaken by the time Kenneth and I reached the Laboratory. Mighty chords of the Old Testament were ringing in my ears; listening, I knew I would have to reset my course and make myself very small before goals and thoughts higher than mine could flow into New Harmony. In good Texas vernacular, I had to be a pipeline, not the fluid.

Another Old Testament prophet, Malachi, also had advice for me: "'Bring ye all the tithes into the storehouse, that there may be meat in mine house, and prove me now herewith,' saith the LORD of hosts, 'if I will not open you the windows of heaven, and pour you out a blessing, that there shall not be room enough to receive it'" (Mal. 3:10).

Trusting both Abraham and Malachi, I believed that, in time, there would be an altar acceptable to the Lord of Hosts, and once it was consecrated, blessings would "pour" into the village and beyond its borders. I was confident in a brief moment of certainty that I would be led to people who would help me keep the covenant with Abraham I had made on Indian Mound. Blind faith, yes, but not the wide-eyed faith that sees and counts solely on human blueprints and financial resources.

My nascent humility was tested a few years later, in 1948, when an undernourished but self-confident French intellectual stayed briefly at my first Harmonist house as a writer-in-residence. Not unreasonably, Dane Rudhyar voiced concerns about my endeavors and cautioned me like a policeman about to arrest me for driving without a license.

"Surely, Madame Owen, you have a master plan for the renewal of New Harmony?"

I cleared my throat to answer with minimal emotion but not glibly. "No, I do not have such a plan. I once made a list of needs for New Harmony, but I laid that list aside on Indian Mound during the spring of 1942. There is, however, a master plan in the mind and power of our Creator. If I stand still long enough, I can comprehend a few fragments; if I shut my eyes, I can catch glimpses."

Many years later, I read Walter Nigg's interpretation of words preached by the twelfth-century Cistercian St. Bernard of Clairvaux, which reaffirmed to me the need for balance:

> For to him [Bernard], action and contemplation were not two contrary, mutually exclusive operations; they were organically linked together, like the flower and its stem. Contemplation that cannot be expressed in action is a self-consuming inwardness; action that does not flow from contemplation becomes a breathless driving that destroys the soul's life. A man therefore must be truly penetrated with Christianity before he should think of throwing himself into active works. "Why do you act so hastily? Why do you not wait for light? Why do you presume to undertake the work of light before the light is with you?" And again, in another sermon: "If then, you are wise, you will show yourself rather as a reservoir than as a canal. For a canal spreads abroad water as it receives it, but a reservoir waits until it is filled before overflowing, and thus communicates, without loss to itself, its superabundant water. . . . Be thou first filled, then pour forth with care and judgment of thy fullness."[4]

Thomas Kelly said it best, as indeed St. Thomas Aquinas before him: "Humility . . . rests upon the disclosure of the consummate wonder of God, upon finding that only God counts, that all our own self-originated intentions are works of straw."[5] My unearned income and unmerited grace were joined atop Indian Mound.

But since everything living strives for wholeness, the inevitable one-sidedness of our conscious life is continually being corrected and compensated by the universal human being in us, whose goal is the ultimate integration of conscious and unconscious, or better, the assimilation of the ego to a wider personality.

—Carl Jung, *The Structure and Dynamics of the Psyche*

CHAPTER 3

The Sixth Generation

Our first daughter, Jane Dale, arrived prematurely on September 30, 1942, at Toronto General Hospital. Had she come on schedule, in late October, my delighted father would have not been able to hold her in his arms or bring a crib to my hospital room filled with convalescent port for me and champagne for his granddaughter's christening. Daddy had brought his gifts to my hospital room himself. The exertion had taken its toll, for he had not fully recovered from a prostate operation earlier that summer.

After resting awhile in the armchair near my bed, he rose and declared with his old exuberance, "Jane, you're not returning to Houston in an ordinary way. I am going to the train station to exchange our return tickets for a private Pullman car to take us all home."

He embraced his granddaughter and me with tenderness, then took up his cane and gray felt hat. I never saw him again. He died of a blood clot to his great heart on the sidewalk outside the train station. The loss of my father on October 22, 1942, was my first experience of grief, a profound and prolonged mourning for the kindest man I would ever know.

Robert Lee Blaffer, 1941.
Blaffer-Owen family photograph.

The joy of caring for and nursing my firstborn gradually comforted me, and my thoughts returned to Indian Mound. My mother believed that I was captive to a lost cause. She could not fathom why anyone would trade "boom town" for "doom town," but added, "If you are still determined to pursue your damn foolish dreams in New Harmony, Jane, you will need the help of George and Annie Rawlings." Wiser advice was never given.

When I first met George, he was a master gardener on a Canadian estate that I had visited before my parents acquired our summerhouse Ste. Anne in 1939.[1] My days at Hamilton House were spent more happily at the Rawlingses' cottage than at the manor house, where no laughter was permitted from the kitchen wing.

George's wife, Annie, was an ornithologist without knowing the meaning of the word; she would recognize native birds by their calls before sighting them "in the feather." I can still see her clearly, the delicacy of her features and her luxuriant red-brown hair neatly gathered in a knot at the nape of her neck. She and George, both Yorkshire-born, had immigrated to Canada after successive crop failures in that land of bleak moors. "Speak Yorkshire for me, Annie Rawlings," I would beg. Her sharp brown eyes softened as she gave me a few words of caution: "Don't fall in a slap-hole and get in a blather"—Yorkshire for falling in a puddle and getting wet and muddy. Several years would elapse before George and Annie came to my aid in New Harmony.

On July 22, 1944, Kenneth and I were blessed with the arrival of a second daughter, Caroline Campbell. She was born six weeks prematurely, almost in the car that rushed me to the small hospital in Cobourg near my parents' Ontario farm, which we visited annually in summertime. Thanks to prayer and the wits of a country doctor, Carol, fragile and exquisitely formed, won her battle for life. She became for her family (and for all who define love as the total giving of self without expectation of reward) the embodiment of love and concern for others.

Carol's first love was for Janie. We owe the closeness that our daughters enjoyed throughout their years together to the wisdom of their English nurse, Joyce Isabella Mann, who came to assist me in December 1943. "Ninny" (never "Nanny" to rebellious Texans) charged Janie with the responsibility of introducing her sister to all worshipers at the egg-shaped crib that had rocked their father. The pride and pleasure this assignment gave an elder sister left no room in her heart for jealousy or fear of replacement in parental affection.

When Janie turned seven and Carol five, we remained in New Harmony for the fall of 1949, rather than returning to Houston. We were reluctant to leave New Harmony's golden yellow maples, the scarlet oaks, and the campfires that warmed the hands and coffeepots of my husband,

Jane Blaffer Owen with Janie and Carol, 1946.
Blaffer-Owen family photograph.

his posthole diggers, and fence builders. We enrolled Janie and Carol in the K–12 school across Church Street from David Dale's Laboratory.

Our daughters would be taught, although briefly, in New Harmony, though not in the same building where Kenneth and his contemporaries received their first schooling. That fine brick 1874 Harmonist building was demolished to make way for an undistinguished structure in 1913 (9 on town map). While we mourned the loss of a building of good architecture and Harmonist origin, we could rejoice that sixth-generation Owens would be classmates of children whose ancestors had arrived in the early nineteenth century.

Their first playmate would be Albert Hodge, whose ancestor was the renowned Pestalozzian teacher Madame Marie Duclos Fretageot. Other young friends or classmates included Claudia Elliott and Tommy Mumford Jr., whose forebears had come in 1825 and 1828, as well as Johnsons, Fords, Stallings, six Wilson boys, and an Alsop, who, with several Hardys, were descendants of late nineteenth-century colonists.

Eugene Bishop "Bish" Mumford, Tommy's grandfather, had left New Harmony to pursue a successful medical career in Indianapolis, but he would bring his only son, Thomas Frenzel, on holidays to stay in the log cabin built by the first Mumford to leave England for Indiana. Young Tom, enamored of fertile ancestral land, dreamed of restoring the log cabin and raising a family there. Toward that end, he took his agricultural degree from Purdue and brought his beautiful, vivacious wife, Letitia Sinclair, from Indianapolis to New Harmony. His most constant refrain, "I am the luckiest guy in the world to have a city girl share a life on the farm with me," evolved as he became a father: "Tish has provided us with six children—one daughter and five sons for farmhands." Their only daughter, Liz, is a nationally respected painter and watercolorist on Cape Cod. A younger son, another Bish, manages the family farm on the hills above the small town of Griffin. History and families sometimes move in orderly procession.

John Elliott, a fifth-generation New Harmonist, earned a degree in archaeology at the University of Chicago, where he met his brilliant wife, Josephine Mirabella, who earned undergraduate and graduate degrees in Romance languages and education. John taught at the University of Kentucky until called back to New Harmony by an aging father who could no longer manage the family farms. Their only child, Claudia, a classmate of

Janie's, became a lifelong friend of hers and mine. Josephine later earned certificates in library science from the University of Evansville and Indiana State University. She became not only the pillar of our Working Men's Institute and the editor of the Maclure and Lesueur papers but also a living encyclopedia of the history of New Harmony (10 on town map).

But these events lay in the future; suffice it to say that few towns in America can claim a similar unbroken human chain of being and becoming.

We are creatures identified by what we do with our hands.

—Frank R. Wilson, *The Hand: How Its Use Shapes the Brain, Language, and Human Culture*

CHAPTER 4

Harmonist House

A Standard Oil of Indiana filling station stood across Church Street from the Lab and the Rapp-Maclure-Owen House, darkly foreshadowing the challenges of the journey on which I was embarking to reinvigorate New Harmony (11 on town map). Trucks roared noisily along Church Street, Highway 66, on their way to or from Illinois (see area map). This shining white station with its red, blue, and white torch, an ersatz imitation of the torch that ancient Greek athletes carried before their Olympic Games, bluntly proclaimed: "I am the only real thing in this town; I give gas and cold drinks to truckers all day and night, and they adore my Muzak." There was no possibility of a full night's sleep in the Lab.

Fantasy kept pace with my indignation: "Even with your imitation torch, you're not the truth and reality of New Harmony but rather a servant that pretends to be more important than the geologists who once lived across the street. Were it not for their intellect and devotion to geology, you might not even be on this corner." My anger was not directed at

33

Standard Oil Company gas station in 1930, a decade
before my arrival in New Harmony.

Don Blair Collection. Courtesy of Special Collections,
University of Southern Indiana.

the attendants. The filling station itself repre-sented, for me, Prospero's servant Caliban, of Shakespeare's *Tempest,* who stoked the fire and brought the water. All went well on the island until Prospero imprisoned Ariel (a spirit of imagination and of art), an act that elevated Caliban's ambi-tions. Matters could not be righted until Caliban resumed his rightful place and Ariel could be set free and given liberty to create. I never doubted that the filling station would someday, somehow, disappear or that the aspirations of earlier gen-erations would find contemporary expression.

Kenneth and I were unable to negotiate with the owners of the Standard Oil Company gas sta-tion; the asking price exceeded the resources at my disposal. The gas station remained for decades, an abomination and a gadfly to my efforts. From that day onward, I opted for the greater reality of the faded old houses and half-ruined Granary.

Setting my sights on what could be achieved in 1946, I bought a Harmonist house three blocks southeast of the Lab on Steammill, so called be-cause the Harmonists had built a steam-powered factory on that street to manufacture shingles and weatherboards for the wooden houses of what his-torians now refer to as their middle period (12 on town map). The idea of creating a tranquil escape hatch for my family excited and challenged me.

Years earlier, nomadic Indian tribes across the plains had hunted animals and stretched their hides for tepees. Later, Eu-ropean pioneers supplanted them and cut down trees to build log cabins. In my time, I too would forage for building materials to repair and restore a house that would be as protectively mine as were those earlier shelters for my forbears. Notwithstanding my husband's plea to friends—"If you see Jane with a hammer, for God's sake, take it away!"—I persisted.

I loaded my tools in the pickup truck of a local contractor, Fred E. "Silo" Cook, who knew where to find old barns and abandoned farmhouses

Interior of my Harmonist house No. V on Steammill, late 1940s.
Blaffer-Owen family photograph.

with weathered siding, ripe for my plucking. We pried loose old planks and a stable door; we gathered fieldstones for future garden paths. The joy of a hunter returning home with a bag full of fresh game would not have exceeded mine as we brought the quarry of my first expedition to Number V or "No. V," my name for the Harmonist house on Steammill.

A word of advice to young couples, wherever you live and whatever your budget for building your first home: don't let it reflect solely the expertise of an architect or a decorator, however considerable their talents. Abandoned barns and derelict houses may lie beyond your reach, but not urban warehouses filled with seasoned lumber and fixtures from dismembered houses. Paint at least one room of your house with your own hands! Such physical involvement won't tire you as much as three sets of tennis. Yes, your hands will ache after using a wire brush to clean old barn wood, but you'll feel pride with the end result and unexpected joy.

I respectfully disagree with the authors of the Declaration of Independence, who gave us the freedom to pursue happiness, because I never find happiness by pursuing it. For me, happiness is an untamed creature that comes unexpectedly from behind and licks a tired elbow after a long day of work. I have heard its sound in the song of a bird that has brought twigs and feathers to a nest.

Harmonist house No. V holds some of my happiest memories. My husband took refuge there from the truck stop noises that assailed the Lab, where his aunt still resided. Our daughters Janie and Carol could play at No. V without disturbing Auntie Aline's prolonged naps and celebrate their birthdays. In July 1949, while preparing for Carol's fifth birthday, I asked whom she wanted to invite to her party. Her quick response was indicative of her noble nature and my concept of society, "Mother, please invite everyone who can hear us having a good time."

Our first Thanksgiving in No. V during 1948 brought an unexpected reason to be thankful. I had hired Ott Conner to fire my furnace. Ott's former boss, a farmer who placed little faith and no capital in modern farm machinery, had employed Ott to harness a reluctant mule to an ancient corn rake to harrow or harvest the farmer's corn, a partnership that lasted until the mule decided to make a sudden bid for freedom, taking his entangled muleteer over rough territory with him. The odd accident had left Ott with a permanent limp and the inability to maneuver stairs in a straightforward manner, so he worked for me only irregularly. However intermittent his days in my employ or daunting my cellar stairs, Ott never mentioned his infirmity and always arrived with a cheerful smile.

Preparations were well under way on the eve of Thanksgiving. I had just purchased a bushel of apples and pears from Ollie, one of the Hardy brothers who owned orchards in the Hardy Hills, east of town. I was eager to try the recipes a neighbor on Steammill Street had given me for apple butter and pear honey. I put Janie, age seven, and Carol, age five, to work in the kitchen, white aprons tied around their necks, stirring fruits in iron pots. The delicious aroma of cloves and cinnamon filled the air of the barn-like central room when Ott tapped gently at the front door.

He declined to enter, not from timidity, but because he wanted me to hear his truck's motor running outside my gate, the heavy breathing of the horsepower that had brought its rider with an urgent message. The messenger was not exactly standing upright in my doorway, for a crooked right leg tilted his long, lean body sideways. But his invitation was whole-bodied, his self-worth intact. "I'm on my way to Carmi for Thanksgiving, Mrs. Jane," he said. "I've got a quart of ice cream and a whole chicken in my truck, and I wish to God you were coming!" I was thankful that humble Ott had extended a firm hand of friendship to me, as I was still considered an outsider by some in town.

While No. V holds good memories, my first Harmonist house also reminds me of my early reckless approach to restoration. My partners in crime were teenage schoolboys: Donald "Donnie" Hatch, the Travelstead brothers, and a smattering of Russells and Brands. They wanted money for bicycles and Scout uniforms. I needed their young muscles and laughter. The walls of No. V were an easy prey for male-hunter instinct as they attacked wallpaper and flaky plaster with crowbars and victorious cries. My own murder weapon was a rotary sander with a seven-inch sandpaper disc, which quickly but inexpertly removed thick layers of paint from overhead beams. Circular marks on finely ground, honey-colored poplar wood are now less visible than in those scarlet-letter days but still remain.

I found an adult carpenter to install in the downstairs bedroom paneling made from wide planks that Silo Cook and I had taken from an old barn. Thin and long-faced Mark, a somber figure as if from Picasso's Blue Period, arrived one morning more taciturn than usual.

"What's wrong, Mark?"

After a few minutes of silence, he blurted out accusingly, "You're teaching my daughter to dance."

Janie and Carol sitting on the stairs of
No. V in their white aprons, 1948.
Blaffer-Owen family photograph.

I was unprepared for this outburst of undisguised rage. I had studied
dance as a student at Bryn Mawr with Josephine Petts, who learned the
Duncan method of dance. It helped orient me to nature and improved my
posture, for sisters Isadora and Elisabeth had taught pupils to walk so the
sun could touch their chests. I wanted to pass on what I had learned to
anyone who wished to attend my classes in the Ribeyre Gymnasium (13
on town map). More than a dozen girls came, including my carpenter's
daughter.

"But Mark, the girls love their classes. They walk out holding their heads high and shoulders straight; surely you've noticed a difference in Mary." I then made an unforgivable mistake, for I pointed to the barn siding, which Mark was applying to the wall, and traced with my finger the meandering path a famished termite had left on one of the boards. "See, even termites dance as they eat their way through wood."

Mark was too angry to speak; he left the house and never returned. This was my first but not my last encounter with what seems to me a rigid, joyless way of viewing religion, a view I have never shared.

I found other, more congenial workers. The most memorable was Harvey, an African American brickmason from nearby Princeton. He tenderly fondled one of the old firebricks I had collected. "These are from a slow-fire, wood-burning kiln, Miss Jane. I like them. I'll take the job. If you let me sleep here at night, I can finish the whole wall and the chimney in a week."

Harvey was provided with a cot in the unfurnished house, and I brought his meals to him. He pretty much kept to himself because, in those days, blacks had to be inconspicuous in the all-white community of a small southern Indiana town. I spent my mornings admiring the artistry of his masonry; when he inserted an occasional black brick among the pinkish red and coral ones, the gesture seemed symbolic, reminding me that racial prejudice could infect northern communities as easily as those in the South. The town had disregarded Robert Owen's belief that the role of rational religion in society was "in promoting, to the utmost in our power, the well being and happiness of every man, woman, and child, without regard to their class, sect, sex, party, country, or colour."[1]

I found other employment for my child-labor gang: they followed me with my seven-inch disc sander to my next operation, at the house of George and Annie Rawlings, who had arrived from Ontario by 1950 (14 on town map). The boys helped me clean old bricks for the foundation of a modern greenhouse that George was supervising (16 on town map). We gathered the bricks from the town dump, where they and other objects worth salvaging had long ago been heedlessly discarded. The discovery of a limestone plinth was significant.

Students of our architectural history believe the plinth was once part of the Harmonist brick cruciform church. In the future, the plinth would

The hearth of No. V photographed by my friend
Sibylle de l'Épine when she visited in 1950.

Blaffer-Owen family photograph.

reside at the center of the St. Benedict Cloister Garden near the New Harmony Inn (17 on town map). From the former site of the dump, Richard Meier's glistening white Atheneum would rise in the mid-1970s as an orientation and education center for visitors (18 on town map). Fellow preservationists, don't overlook the middens of your historic districts, and take with you eager scavengers like the boys who enlivened my excursions.

After loading our discoveries on my golf cart, the boys would wave, like heroes in a ticker-tape parade, to pedestrians we zoomed past. They were proud passengers on the only golf cart in town, and they had a mission. Donnie Hatch's wide grin shone through the brick dust on his face as he called out to passersby, "Hey, you guys, New Harmony is going to have a greenhouse!"

I shared his enthusiasm, but for a different reason. On the site where the Lab now stands, Father Rapp's followers had built a marvelous greenhouse on rollers (to facilitate adjustment to weather changes) to house his orange trees. No records exist indicating that David Dale removed it to make way for his laboratory. Whatever the cause of its demise, I decided that a new greenhouse, albeit one without wheels, would serve a Harmonist tradition and protect potted plants in winter.

Donnie Hatch's excitement, I think, came from an expectation of future amenities too long absent from New Harmony. A few years later he watched and welcomed the bittersweet advent of the first swimming pool in town, added behind No. V. It would be essential for Janie to exercise her polio-affected legs in water, but her primary thoughts were for others: "Oh good, Mother! We can teach everybody to swim!" It was equally important that New Harmony children have swimming lessons. Recent gravel digging in the Wabash had created dangerous eddies. The river where Kenneth's generation had learned to swim was no longer safe, and too many local boys had drowned. My friend Don Blair, an engineer, agreed wholeheartedly with me that swimming classes were necessary; he supervised and recruited teachers to give lessons to all the children who wanted to learn. That first summer, Flossie Tanner, an Owen descendant and beloved civic leader, inspired by Janie's outreach, initiated professional classes and taught for almost a decade. Other dedicated instructors followed Flossie and have for more than fifty years kept New Harmony boys and girls from drowning in the Wabash.[2]

Donnie rejoiced in learning to swim. But his hopes for a new school far from the heavy traffic of Highway 66 and with room for an athletic field, though legitimate, were premature.

Nevertheless, there were some instant gratifications for those of us who were learning that removal was as necessary as preservation. Between two Harmonist houses on Granary Street stood a decrepit barn, no longer a storage house for grain but a community center for rats. The low brick columns that supported the barn were high enough for people to throw garbage underneath. Providence alone spared New Harmony a bubonic plague. I finally managed to buy the barn and, with the deed fresh in my pocket, called my young friends to watch a tractor demolish the dismal eyesore. Their loud hurrahs buoyed my spirits. In fact, they still do. Whether clown white from falling plaster or dirt brown from planting squares of zoysia grass on the lawn of No. V, whether silent or cheering, my child laborers bolstered my sometimes insufficient faith. As much as the poetry of Gerard Manley Hopkins does, they taught me to believe that within each battered Harmonist house and "deep down" in each weed-filled vacant lot or ill-used parcel of land lay the "dearest freshness" and wellsprings of new life waiting to be tapped.

Why did I call my first Harmonist house No. V? There are several reasons for the numbered name of the house that strained my muscles but brought me freedom. Richard Smoley, in his excellent book *Inner Christianity,* reminds us that the human body is based on a five-fold pattern or pentagon. Leonardo da Vinci confirmed this geometric fact in his drawing of a man measured in ratios of five. Can we, then, with Smoley's friend Aleister Crowley, dare to believe that not only the famous but also all human beings are stars? Not every child who learns to swim in No. V's pool or learns the names of flowers in its garden will shine like a planet, but there is reason to hope that each of them may offer pinpricks of light in a darkening world.

And I devoutly hoped that the boys who attended our swimming classes, as they grew into their teens, would remember other lessons from No. V, in particular the difference between clenched and unclenched hands. It may seem necessary sometimes to tighten a fist to punch an adversary; but certainly not in New Harmony, or any town, should fists be permanently clenched. Released and splayed outward, the five fingers of either hand can wave hello to friends or strangers alike. Esther de Waal once told me, "If you want to keep your head, use your hands." More recently, the Rev. Martha Honaker's image of stewardship for her parishioners at St. Stephen's Episcopal Church in New Harmony strengthened my case for relaxed and open hands: "When our fingers are tightly closed around something, they are unable to receive anything else."

May all young graduates from our high school never forget that beyond New Harmony's soup kitchen, which feeds hungry families of Posey County, too many empty and open hands, each with five fingers, reach out for food to sustain life. If No. V, the victorious firstborn of my New Harmony houses, has a message for the youth of the world, it is: "Watch your hands!"

The pool at No. V is ready for swim lessons offered through the
Robert Lee Blaffer Foundation, summer 2014.

Photograph by Janet Lorence.

For a path to become a road, it is not enough that one person travels it, opens it. The traces of those steps would be erased immediately if other persons did not gather the signs, did not step into the same footprints, did not make the path just traced more passable by their traveling it.

—The dedication from the booklet honoring Maria De Mattias on the fiftieth anniversary of her beatification, October 1, 2000[1]

CHAPTER 5

Harmonist Church and School

K enneth and I were not alone in our respect for the achievements of New Harmony's founding fathers and mothers and in our love of the land. Thomas Mumford and John Elliott, whose New Harmony roots reached back as far as my husband's, also returned to land their ancestors had farmed. Consciously or not, these descendants of British citizens who had arrived in New Harmony in the 1820s were reenacting the early American tradition of sons who worked their ancestors' land. This custom decreased during the transition from an agrarian economy to an industrial one. Sons left family farms for cities, and small towns withered. The story of human erosion is well known. We are less aware of exceptions to this pattern.

These three public-spirited and well-educated men returned as farmers and civic leaders. They were not bedazzled by utopia, like the members of two previous societies. They had no thought of holding their goods in common, as did the Harmonists, or of realizing Robert Owen's ambitious plan for a quadrangular Phalanstery for communal living. Each one brought his city-bred wife, who also embraced the town and its history.

The regeneration of New Harmony resumed in the 1940s with the friendship and collaboration of the Owen, Mumford, and Elliott families, a nucleus for unfolding events. I thank heaven that we newlyweds did not enter a vacuum of nonremembrance. A small, caring minority of towns-people, who were aware of the unmined gold that lay beneath their feet, welcomed us. They had lacked the means and the youthful energy to bring these riches to the light of day, but they had tried and in significant ways succeeded. Mary Fauntleroy, for instance, saved the Harmonist Commu-nity House No. 2 from demolition (19 on town map).

Laura Corbin Monical was my nearest neighbor and first friend in New Harmony. This extraordinary "widow lady," the local title for women who had lost their husbands, lived in her parents' home, the fad-ing, white-pillared Rapp-Maclure-Owen House, across the lawn from the Lab. Miss Laura spent her mornings removing cobwebs from the fourteen-foot-high ceilings of the old house. Her cleaning tool consisted of two broom handles joined together and topped with dust rags. For this daily ritual, Miss Laura covered her red wig with an eighteenth-century ruffled linen cap and enveloped her short stature with a wide apron. Her words of friendship to me were, "If you see me in the morning, Jane, don't speak because I will be very busy. Do drop by later in the day for a cup of tea." Traces of beauty remained in her aged face; I could easily believe that a member of Indianapolis's Fortune family had once sought her hand in marriage.

My husband started his schooling in a building across Church Street from the Corbins' house and the Lab (9 on town map). He and genera-tions of schoolchildren since 1874 had entered their classrooms through a door designed by Frederick Rapp, sometimes called the "Door of Prom-ise," that had once been the principal entrance to the brick Harmonist church. I prize a photo of Kenneth's grandmother and mother in a horse-drawn carriage before that handsome building.

A brief history of the brick Harmonist church will be helpful. In 1822, the Harmonists began construction of a large brick church (on the west side of their original wooden church) that was finished not long before

Robert Owen purchased New Harmony (20 on town map). The impressive church was one of the most significant buildings on the American frontier during the first quarter of the nineteenth century. During and after the Owen/Maclure Experiment, the cruciform church was unfortunately converted to secular purposes as New Harmony's multipurpose hall. The east arm of the cross was used for dancing, the south arm for a theater, and the other two for libraries (the original location of the Maclure Working Men's Institute). A clutter of shed-like wooden structures had been added later for pork packing.

Rumors of this desecration reached the devout Harmonists now living in Economy, Pennsylvania. They were understandably disturbed. Consistent with their practice of bringing important matters before the entire community, prayer sessions were held in their church in Economy. With characteristic dignity and liberality, the Harmonists selected Jonathan Lenz, son of David Lenz, to return to New Harmony in 1874 in order to purchase and demolish the church. The sum of two thousand dollars and a sufficient supply of bricks salvaged from the old church were given to the town for a cemetery wall (22 on town map). The plans were drawn by a student of Frederick Rapp's architectural school, hence its superior character. This enclosure was for the Germans who had died in New Harmony and been placed in unmarked graves alongside those of the Woodland Indians, who were likewise unidentified except by low, grass-covered mounds. Both the Indians and Harmonists, despite their dissimilar cultures, believed their departed dead did not need individual markers on Earth, because they were already known by the Spirit of God. With the remaining bricks, a school was built in 1874 that also incorporated from the cruciform church the Door of Promise with its golden rose and a puzzling quotation attributed to chapter 4, verse 8 of Micah incised in the pediment above: "Unto thee shall come the golden rose."[2]

In 1913, the town fathers made the unwise decision to raze the 1874 brick school, on the pretext that it was unstable, to make way for a new school. Fortunately, Miss Laura was on the scene at the time of the school's demolition. Righteous indignation still throbbed in her voice as she recounted the story to me in the early 1940s: "It took a mule team three days to pull down each wall; but the most wicked thing of all was

School built in 1874 with bricks from the demolished
Harmonist cruciform church.

*Photograph by Homer Fauntleroy, March 21, 1905. Don Blair Collection.
Courtesy of Special Collections, University of Southern Indiana.*

when the men in charge carted that door with its golden rose of Micah to
the dump. I gave them a big piece of my mind, and they brought the door
back." After she notified the mayor about the Door of Promise, the architect and contractor were obliged to incorporate it into the 1913 school
building. The Women's Library Club members approved Miss Laura's
motion that they assume responsibility, with the community, for restoring the door, which became the west entrance to the 1913 school. Miss
Laura was the first to confront an enemy of preservation.

I view Miss Laura's rescue of the consecrated church door as a decisive
factor in the ongoing battle between the secular and the sacred for the
physical heart of New Harmony. As much as I admire Robert Owen,
the lessons of history do not support his stubbornly held theory that education alone, without the complementary discipline of religion, would
prevent the human race from suicide. I never questioned Owen's heart.

Above.
School built in 1913 with
the saved Door of Promise
(photograph taken in 1919).
*Don Blair Collection. Courtesy
of Special Collections, University
of Southern Indiana.*

Left.
Door of Promise, 1959.
*Photograph by John Doane.
John Doane Collection.
Courtesy of Special Collections,
University of Southern Indiana.*

He labored throughout his long life for the betterment and happiness of mankind, achieving those goals in New Lanark, Scotland, but falling short of them in New Harmony.

About six hundred years earlier, another ardent reformer, St. Bernard of Clairvaux, had also acted from purity of heart. In launching the Second Crusade from the hilltop Cathedral of Vézelay in 1145, his sole and passionate desire was to reconquer Jerusalem and Palestine to gain access to the sacred sites of Christ's birth, life, crucifixion, and resurrection. Legend tells us that Bernard accented his rhetoric with tattered pieces of his cloak, scattering them among the multitudes who had come to hear this charismatic saint. Inevitably, only a few shared St. Bernard's zeal. The vast majority who joined this disastrous crusade went for plunder.

Similarly, Chuang Tzu, the Taoist sage who lived in the fourth and third centuries BC, understood the paradox: "When justice and benevolence are in the air, a few people are really concerned with the good of others, but the majority are aware that this is a good thing, ripe for exploitation. They take advantage of the situation. For them, benevolence and justice are traps to catch birds. Thus benevolence and justice rapidly come to be associated with fraud and hypocrisy."[3]

Apart from the educators, scientists, artists, and teachers, many of those who followed Owen and Maclure to New Harmony came for free meals and board. Summital thinking can prevent highly placed individuals, even saints, from reading the thoughts and intentions of those in the valley below.

In 1988, Historic New Harmony received permission and funding from the State of Indiana to remove the unremarkable 1913 school with its cluster of tacked-on buildings and to create in its place what is now known as Church Park. Many of us considered this an act of redemption. Others, especially those who had been taught there, thought it a desecration. Some townspeople considered ways the outdated school building could be given new life, but they did not prevail. No one regrets, however, the present-day one-story, handicap-accessible, energy-saving replacement school on twelve acres of traffic-free land southeast of town made possible by the Lilly Endowment (21 on area map).

Church Park was dedicated April 18, 1997. Townspeople and visitors can now enter through a brick and limestone arch that replicates the original Harmonist portal. The fragile Door of Promise, which for so many years received the touch of the hands of pious Harmonists and New Harmony's schoolchildren, is safely stored. Well-trimmed hedges recall the cruciform shape of the brick Harmonist church; they reach out from a central circle into empty space, thirsty for the *Fountain of Commitment,* which I gave in memory of my husband. Water flows from the sculpture of interlocking bronze and glass circles by Don Gummer.

Fountain of Commitment in Church Park.

Photograph by Darryl D. Jones, October 2009. Courtesy of the artist,
Don Gummer, © 2001, cast bronze, 77 × 32 × 26 inches.

The moral outlook of a community can be shown to be closely connected to its history, geographical environment, economic structure.

—C. S. Lewis, *Miracles: A Preliminary Study*

CHAPTER 6

Acquiring the Granary
and Mansion

Beginning in the 1940s, Kenneth and I had agreed that his efforts would stretch southward to reclaim ancestral farmland, while mine would extend northward to restore historic Harmonist homes. We would meet in the middle of New Harmony and branch out from the David Dale Owen Laboratory. Kenneth's first priority was overseeing the restoration of his childhood home, accomplished through the skills of Fred E. Cook. Auntie Aline's memorabilia were reduced and organized, which allowed for the addition of lovely furnishings. Most important, the fossil fish, which became for me a symbol of hope and renewal, was restored. The Lab had awakened from its slumber.

The publication of Marguerite Young's book *Angel in the Forest* in 1945 piqued the interest of staff at *Life* magazine, who visited New Harmony to prepare an article. The caption of the feature photograph describes the Lab as a "fairy-tale castle." In another photograph inside the Lab, Auntie Aline sat reading beside the open shutters of a bay window shedding light on a bust of Robert Owen.[1] We were no longer concerned about the home leaving family hands, as the wartime years slowed outside interests in acquiring our historic properties.

Kenneth concentrated his energy on Indian Mound Farm.[2] My focus included more than my well-intentioned but novice attempt at restoring No. V and offering dance classes in the Ribeyre gym. Remembering my mother's stories about growing up in Lampasas, a small Texas town without access to the arts, I wanted to provide cultural opportunities here in New Harmony. My friend Alberta Sandefur, known as Amy, was a brave soul and a fine pianist. She gave piano lessons for a living and cared for a difficult, aged father. On the rare occasions when our daughters sighted him down the lane, they would sing, "There goes a crooked man with a crooked stick, walking a crooked mile." Her father, mercifully, was deaf.

I invited David Nixon, a violinist from New Orleans, to share his considerable talents with the community. I rented Murphy Auditorium for a concert on Thursday, June 20, 1946, when children would be out of school and around the time when our family would customarily transfer from Houston to New Harmony (24 on town map). David, a recovering alcoholic, was addicted to sweets, particularly chocolate ice cream sodas, and could be found each morning at our local Ramsey pharmacy, which, in the 1940s and '50s, was the town's social center, its ice cream parlor, and its dispensary. In the evenings, he would play his violin on the streets of New Harmony for whoever wished to listen. His audience kept increasing and, I believe, would have followed its Pied Piper into the Wabash had he led them to it. There was no need to hire a professional to bring an audience for his concert later that month. I had doubts, however, about David's intentions to present only the music of Bach and his contemporaries.

To David's "We'll pack the house," I replied, more soberly, "People here won't sit through an entire evening listening to seventeenth- and eighteenth-century music. Please throw in a little Victor Herbert or Cole Porter, who is a native of Peru, Indiana."

David would not budge. "There'll only be Bach and his contemporaries or no concert. By the way, I'll need an accompanist. Is there anyone here who can play Bach, et cetera?"

Amy consented, with misgivings at first, but within a week she mastered the difficult scores David placed before her. Shabby old Murphy

Auditorium was filled to capacity that evening, adults at fifty cents each and for children only a quarter. The response to the concert exceeded all expectations. The applause was long and vigorous. Children, accustomed to juke boxes and Muzak, stood up and cheered; parents sat still, quietly moved. That night empowered my future decisions. I would never underestimate the capacity of human beings to ingest and recognize quality. Talk up, not down.

When our valiant neighbor Miss Laura was nearing the end of her long life in late 1947, speculation about the disposition of the Corbin property dominated the conversations of coffee drinkers at Richard's Cafe, reviving concerns from a decade earlier.[3] Miss Laura had apparently been "put out" with the state's overtures for the properties in the late 1930s, and some townspeople believed she had held firm at the end of her life.[4] Others thought she had been swayed by "recent comings and goings" at her home.[5] Kenneth had stronger ties to the Corbin family than anyone else but tactfully had never questioned Miss Laura about her will. He also possessed the patience to wait for substance to replace rumors. Miss Laura died April 21, 1948.

The arrival in New Harmony of a large black limousine with an Indiana "official" license plate put an end to speculations. Representatives of the legislature had arrived at Miss Laura's funeral not to mourn the passing of a valued citizen but to declare themselves the front-runners in the race for part of her estate.[6] We soon learned that the State of Indiana had been granted a first option to buy both her house and the Granary. The beneficiary of Miss Laura's will was her nephew Robert Heinl Jr., but the house and Granary remained with all the siblings, Helen Corbin Heinl et alia, through the John Corbin estate.

The idea that officials from the state would be moving in and out of the Harmonist Granary and the Rapp-Maclure-Owen mansion did not sit well with many in the town, my husband, or me. Helen Heinl, an accomplished pianist, and her son Robert would have been heartily welcomed as residents. People were proud that a hometown girl often accompanied the Navy band in the nation's capital. As a Texan, I was still considered an outsider by a majority of the townspeople; some of them were even more suspicious of the state legislators, who were considered analogous to aliens from another planet.

An unexpected reward for my six-year overtures of friendship with townspeople arrived one afternoon shortly after Miss Laura's funeral in the person of Walter Finnell. Walter, a native son, was an honorable citizen. He, his wife, Mildred, and his old father ran the town's only grocery store, which was located in a small brick building they had covered with bright aluminum paint to attract customers. He also drove the school bus, cleaned still-extant privies, and collected Owen baggage from the Mount Vernon train station, some fifteen miles south of town (see area map).

Keystone to the arch over the Lab doorway of a trilobite, 1959.

Photograph by John Doane. John Doane Collection. Courtesy of Special Collections, University of Southern Indiana.

I was standing in the doorway of the David Dale Owen Laboratory one early June afternoon. Teachers and students of geology had once entered the Lab through that same southeast door from under its honeysuckle-covered verandah. The cast-iron replica of a trilobite, one of the earliest forms of life, still crowns the pediment of the entrance that leads to the room where Kenneth was born and which had become our room. I was trimming back the vines from the wrought iron railing when Walter Finnell hailed me from the sidewalk.

"I've got something to tell you, Mrs. Jane. Have you a minute?"

"Of course, Walter, but let's step inside. It's hot and noisy out here."

"No, thank you. I'd rather sit right here on Kenny's front steps."

I sat down beside him, wondering what he had come to say. But he was silent as he scratched the back of his cropped gray hair. A minute or so passed before he blurted out, "Jane, we've decided we like you."

He had dropped my local title of "Mrs. Jane" in his haste to deliver what had been for him a heavy package, carried for many years. Could the burden he laid at my feet have been an apology for having misread my intentions? I believe so. He left with a lighter step and I with a sigh of relief and gratitude.

I did not have long to savor the sweetness of my improved social status or to ponder the freshly demonstrated truism that acceptance, much less

An early 1919 photograph showing the relationship
of the Laboratory to the Harmonist Granary
(sometimes called the "old Rappite fort").

*Don Blair Collection. Courtesy of Special Collections,
University of Southern Indiana.*

popularity, could not be easily gained in small-town America and never bought. I could hear Kenneth swiftly approaching from around the corner and called to him, "What has happened?"

"Happened?" Kenneth responded. I could hear his ire rising to fever pitch. "Why, everything has gone to hell. Come look what our Granary Street neighbor has planted in her backyard overnight—four prefabricated cabins for tourists. An insult to the town! And Amy Sandefur is *your* friend" (23 on town map).

"Didn't Amy implore you to buy her house months ago, and didn't you refuse?"

"Yes, of course I remember. Big mistake. But I'll buy her lot and house tomorrow."[7]

"At a higher price," I muttered softly to myself. "Good for Amy."

"And our front lawn will soon be invaded by legislators from the state."

By midsummer, we were hearing more rumors than facts about the state's plans for the Corbins' home and the Granary. While Kenneth waited to learn something credible, I began to realize how strongly he felt about the home that had been in his family for generations.[8] David Dale Owen had worked for many years in the Granary, and he had died in 1860 in the home that was now part of the Corbin estate. Kenneth's great-grandfather Richard Dale Owen spent his final years there, dying from an accidental poisoning in 1890. Upon Kenneth's broad shoulders rested the weight of reversing the family fortunes, not only on behalf of his mother and sister but also for future generations, which had undoubtedly motivated his determination and success as a young man. He remained silent and strong until he could wait no longer.

The loud slamming of brakes and hooting of a horn from the driveway behind the Lab alerted me that my husband was back from the farm. My suspicion that something was amiss in his world was correct. An angry man was still honking as I turned the corner of the stone Granary.

"Will you *please* get in the car?" Kenneth insisted. "We are driving to a telephone booth in Mount Vernon. I'll explain why when and if you get in the seat beside me. Now hurry!"

Kenneth's explanation came through clenched teeth. "I'm damn tired of waiting for the state to make up its mind. Helen Heinl and I have always liked each other. She'll listen when I offer to buy the Granary and the Corbins' house. I don't want the whole town listening in; that's why we are driving to Mount Vernon."

Dial telephones had not yet been installed in New Harmony. The two-story building that housed Miss Reeney's switchboard was in the center of town and had a large window. From such a vantage point on the corner of Main and Church, she could see who had left their offices or homes and would advise her customers to try calling again later.

Kenneth's conversation with Helen Heinl was not overheard in New Harmony and was only gradually relayed to me, waiting impatiently in his parked car. I watched him close the door of the telephone cage and walk toward me with his familiar assurance. He only lost his temper when confronted with stupidity, whether his own or someone else's. He started the motor calmly, with an ever-widening smile.

A curt note came from the sculptor's own hand, his round letters billowing from their page as though to soften their hurtful content, indicating that he had nothing suitable for my "garden party." My disappointment turned to anger. Jacques Lipchitz would hear from me, for I was anxious to dispel what seemed to be his preconceived notion of an indulged woman with a checkbook. Still believing something was being withheld from me, I overcame my hesitation to intrude on the privacy of a serious artist.

Lipchitz was currently completing a commission, a bronze carving of Pegasus for Blanchette Rockefeller. According to Greek mythology, the hooves of that winged horse ploughed the earth to give birth to the Muses. Lipchitz was mounting this large semi-bas-relief *Birth of the Muses* over the fireplace of the Rockefellers' New York City guest house, one of Philip Johnson's most imaginative designs.

Dr. Frankfurter had given me the telephone number of that pavilion of delight. I dialed the number and waited while one, two, and finally ten rings passed. Common sense advised me that no one was there. Intuition and desire spoke otherwise. A scaffolding had, undoubtedly, been erected above the fireplace to enable the sculptor to continue his work on Pegasus, and however reluctant he was to leave his lofty bench, he would have to climb down to silence the ringing telephone either by hanging up or by answering me.

He chose to speak. "Who are you and what do you want?" came the weary, exasperated voice, straining the black leash of the cord that connected us.

I spoke quickly before he broke away. "Oh, this is Jane Owen. My borrowed sculptures and Maypole ribbons are simply a means, a *moyen*," for I had started to speak in French about Indian Mound and New Harmony. "There is a holy hill that must receive an altar before the visions and the intellect brought to a small village in the valley below almost two centuries ago can flow into it again. Two societies came here, one after the other, with open hands to give. I sense that you have in your studio or in your head a creation that could express such generosity. Didn't Abraham teach us about faith thousands of years ago?" I paused, breathless, waiting for "Abraham" and "holy hill" to penetrate.

His voice came slowly and also in French, the language he used to express his deepest emotions. *"La colline sacrée—les bras étendues"* ("holy hill—arms extended"), he repeated. "I am beginning to understand. You are partly describing a small white plaster model I wish to give to a Catholic church in Assy, France."

"Could you send it to me for my celebration?"

"Ah, no, madame, my sculptures are my children. They are as yet too fragile to travel alone. I'll send you a photograph."

Shortly after this conversation, our daughter Anne Dale arrived prematurely on April 25, weighing a mere three pounds. More fragile than a sculpture, she was tenderly placed within the first incubator in Houston. Lipchitz's promised letter and photograph of the model of *Notre Dame de Liesse* (Our Lady of Joy) reached me in the hospital while I convalesced.[9] The force of the figure that reached out to me from the photograph at my bedside, with arms extended and palms open, stunned me. At first glance it appeared the work of a nameless twelfth-century artisan who would have used broad chisels and not sought to imitate nature. Such works, however crude, can breathe with a vital life that is often denied more polished art.

Five years later, on St. Columba's island, Iona, I would learn that early Celtic artists had the wisdom and humility to avoid lifelike representations of persons or animals, believing that the Creator had designed them more perfectly. It was for them presumptuous to rival nature.

Closer survey of the photograph, in the days that followed while in the hospital, altered my initial impression. Lipchitz was a master of composition and technique. Flowing lines descending from the beak of the dove led my eyes where the artist had intended, to the heart-shaped mantle. No visual surprise or pleasure was accidental. The Virgin was upheld by cherubim and seraphim in this initial rendering. I had been wading so far, but with Lipchitz I was submerged in deep waters. The almost simultaneous arrival of Annie and the photograph of the Virgin seemed more than a mere coincidence; for me it was semimiraculous.

Facing.

Jacques Lipchitz, *Study for Notre Dame de Liesse*, 1948, Bronze Edition of 7 (33 × 18 1/8 × 16 in.)

© *The estate of Jacques Lipchitz, courtesy Marlborough Gallery, New York. Photograph by Reto Rodolfo Pedrini.*

I wrote to Lipchitz from Hermann Hospital on April 29 with an out-
pouring of my feelings, impressions, and hopes:

> *Maître,*
>
> It was a very moving experience for me to receive your "Descent of
> the Holy Spirit," for your beautiful conception of the virgin so
> crowned with the dove obliges me to give it that name, a few days
> after the birth of my daughter Anne. Thank you for the inspiration
> you have given me and for your offer of the third version, which
> I am seriously considering.
>
> For many years I have thought of building a very simple shrine
> on the highest hill of my husband's farm in New Harmony, Indi-
> ana. The site overlooks the Wabash River and, beyond that, the
> fertile plains of Illinois. I would like to have spiritual leaders from
> different faiths hold services there from time to time, while the
> listeners sat outside, under the Lord's blue sky (their automobiles
> would be left on the road, and the twenty minute or so walk
> through the fields should, to my mind, make them more receptive
> to religious services and thinking than an entrance through a
> parking lot and traffic jam). You may have read or heard something
> about the history of our village—it has been a battleground for two
> Utopias, and my husband's ancestor Robert Owen was a contender
> in the first quarter of the last century. But that is another story. I
> mention this because I feel that where so much human aspiration
> has watered a particular area, there must surely, someday, spring
> rich spiritual fruit. I have tried various social experiments in the
> village at the foot of the hill for the last eight years, and while I am
> not discouraged, none have matured as I would have wished. It may
> be that the first step must be the dedication of the shrine I have
> mentioned. Of course, it will be less ambitious than the church of
> Assy in its physical plan. In fact, so far, I can see nothing but an
> arch overlooking the western view I have briefly described (and no
> coloured glass could compare with our sunset colors there!) and a
> simple altar. Now—can you imagine your "Descent of the Holy
> Spirit" on that altar within that arch? Also bearing in mind that the
> woods on either side are constantly murmuring with the sound of

mourning doves? By this time you may think me completely mad, so I will close. But write me at your convenience your reaction to this "Shrine of the Holy Spirit" and your perfectly honest thought of the appropriateness of your figure there. Also, the inevitable question of price.

May Day, thanks to my sisters and friends, and because everything was planned before my sudden departure, will go on, and I will be home to watch from my bedroom window. They say May wine is good for mother's milk, so I shall surely drink a cup to you.

With profound admiration of your both bold and delicate piece, believe me.

Sincerely,
Jane Blaffer Owen [10]

His immediate affirmation buoyed my spirits:

Dear Madame,

Thank you for your nice letter of April 29. I am very touched by your writing me from the hospital and delighted to know you have a new baby girl, since I too have a new little girl, now a year and a half old. I hope you and the child continue to be very well.

What you tell me about the Shrine is very interesting indeed. It seems to me too that "The Descent of the Holy Spirit" as you so beautifully call my madonna, would be inspiring in an outdoor setting such as you write me about. I would be very pleased if you could send me a photo of the country you describe.

The statue as it is to be executed for the church at Assy is to be 7 feet, 5 inches high. In the church it is to stand on a baptismal font which I have designed.

Set out in nature as you conceive it, would be very fine and very pleasing to me, since many of my large sculptures have been set in nature and are there most beautiful. In that case, I would design a pedestal at the right height to overlook the country.

Will you write me as soon as you can telling me what you think of the size of the sculpture and how high you think the figure should stand with its pedestal? We can then discuss all the further details as to price, etc., etc.

I am sending you my best wishes for your and your baby's health and good fortune.

Sincerely
Jacques Lipchitz[11]

Kenneth and I began to adapt to having tiny Annie cared for by medical experts in the hospital. Our first priority was for our newborn's continuing growth and development. Her anticipated early release from the hospital in late May did not materialize.[12] In between visits to the nursery with Ninny, I distracted myself by writing to Lipchitz about his sculpture and its symbolism.

> I must make sure that it cannot be interpreted as the Immaculate Conception of Mary. . . . The whole idea behind this outdoor shrine is to emphasize Christian unity and the importance of spirit as against the trend toward division and materialism. The common denominator of the Holy Spirit should be the extent of the theology involved. As I understand your symbolism, and your placing of Mary on her Old Testament tripod of Cherubim and Seraphim, it appears universal rather than doctrinaire. I know that we can not expect all individuals to respond alike. . . . I agree with George Sand who considered the sky alone as an appropriate roof for the Lord's Temple.[13]

I was not prepared for the astonishing response and reassurance from Monsieur Lipchitz, which conveyed more than I had hoped for or imagined possible:

> Thank you for your kind letter of May 12. I understand perfectly well your scruples, since it is really a very important and responsible undertaking. As you know, I am not a Christian. When Father Couturier asked me to make the Virgin for the Church of Assy, I made one condition: to avoid any confusion the following inscription has to be put on the back of the statue: "Jacques Lipchitz, juif, fidèle à la foi de ses ancêtres a fait cette vierge pour la bonne entente des hommes sur la terre afin que l'esprit règne."

I think this will answer your question. My statue really represents a dove who has in his beak three parts of the sky which form a mantle from which the Virgin emerges, her hands generously opened for all humanity. All that is supported by three cherubim. Now you can judge for yourself if this statue is what you would like to have. I am looking forward to receive your photographs and have the pleasure of your visit. I will be at this time in New York.

Very sincerely,
Jacques Lipchitz[14]

Jacob Lipchitz, Jew, faithful to the religion of his ancestors, has made this Virgin for the better understanding of human beings on this earth so that the Spirit may prevail.[15] Lipchitz would later confide to me that he had kept these words and an early sketch of the Virgin in his breast pocket on his return to America after he revisited France following the war and received the commission for *Notre Dame de Liesse.* (He had fled from the Nazis in occupied France.) My written reply could only inadequately communicate the profound impression his words would have on me and in the future upon many others:

I am once again deeply moved by the powerful beauty of your imagination. It was also gratifying to learn that my first impression of your virgin was correct, for I intuitively felt her transcendental quality, and it was only when the worldly portion of my mind reasserted itself that I began to question your symbolism. Nothing could be more universal than your idea of the dove holding Mary's sky mantle, or more important to all mankind than the hope expressed in your inscription. In fact, it is not an inscription, but a fervent prayer.[16]

Our daughter Annie eventually gained enough weight to leave the hospital almost three months after her birth. She came safely home and settled with her family and Ninny. Anne's courageous spirit of survival continued as she developed into a strong and determined woman, which can be attested to by her husband, Hal Pontez, and daughter, Abigail.

Carol, Anne, and Jane with "Ninny," Joyce Mann, in 1950.
Blaffer-Owen family photograph.

I had tried for months to arrange a time to meet Lipchitz at his studio, which was not an easy matter. I had wanted Kenneth to come with me while we were near New York en route to Ste. Anne's, where my mother expected us to join her as usual, or on our return. After several failed attempts, however, I traveled from Canada in September to stay at my sister Titi's apartment, for my first visit.[17]

Here, then, "in the heart of the United States," Owen proclaimed, "the Power which governs and directs the Universe and every action of man . . . permits me to announce a new empire of peace and goodwill to men."

—From Robert Owen's 1825 address to the U.S. Congress, in Frank Podemore's *Robert Owen: A Biography*

CHAPTER 8

Lipchitz

When I at last knocked on his studio door at Twenty-third Street in September 1950, Lipchitz opened it himself, a courtly gentleman despite his working clothes. I felt like a small child in *The Nutcracker* ballet entering the magical world of the Snow Queen, for he was leading me into the wonderland of an artist's powerful creation, filmy from the fairy dust of white plaster and dried clay; I have never shaken off that which fell on me.

I proceeded straight to my reason for coming, and we soon reached an agreement about Our Lady, *Notre Dame de Liesse*.[1] He asked me to approve the casting of three identical figures: one for New Harmony and one for himself in addition to the commission for Église Notre-Dame de Toute Grâce du Plateau d'Assy, a Catholic church in the small town of Haute-Savoie, France, known at that time principally for its tuberculosis sanatoriums. Former patients who had been cured wished to help build a church where they could bring their gratitude and prayers that others might be healed, and current patients wanted a place for worship. I mention this because the subsequent and justly deserved fame of the church has sometimes obscured the reason for its existence. We also tend to forget that the star-studded cast of artists—Matisse, Léger, Lurçat, Richier, Vuillard, Rouault, Chagall, and Lipchitz—had not yet been represented in a church. When two remarkably enlightened Dominicans Marie-Alain Couturier and Jean Devémy asked Lipchitz through an emissary in 1946 (during Lipchitz's return to France) if he would create a Virgin for their baptismal font, he reminded them he was a practicing Jew. According to Lipchitz's account, they replied with a tolerance not always exhibited by church fathers: "You are the best sculptor for this. If it doesn't disturb you, it doesn't bother us." I had heard of Père Couturier's ecumenical zeal that included those of the Jewish faith through our mutual friends Jean "John" and Dominique de Menil.

I had learned of Assy through them and later through publications. I felt privileged to consent to an agreement that would enable Lipchitz to give his time freely to such an endeavor.[2] Unlike the other artists, who had contributed their works without requesting a fee, he had to rebuild his financial house. Lipchitz had arrived in this country with only his genius and his courage. Yet he had been as unwilling to exhibit his design for Assy as I had been reluctant to seek a dealer. Two hesitations and two deeply felt needs were meeting. The realization of this sculpture depended on a commission from outside Assy.

We reached our "formal" agreement without attorneys or extra copies (in those pre-Xerox days), simply exchanging two pieces of brown wrapping paper with handwritten notes and our signatures in pencil.[3] Before leaving, I added a condition of my own. If two of the castings were destined for sacred places, Assy and Indian Mound, I did not wish the other, which he held in abeyance to benefit his daughter, sold to a museum or private collector. It must likewise occupy a site where spiritual values were strong enough to overcome pride of ownership and divisions of race, color, and creed. He gladly consented to this amendment.

There were hurdles ahead, however, which neither Lipchitz nor I could clear without help from my husband. Indian Mound—or, as Lipchitz usually called it, la colline sacrée (holy hill)—belonged to Kenneth, not to me. Believing that two intelligent and charming men would come to an agreement if they could meet face-to-face, I began plans for their encounter. I asked Lipchitz to hold the first week of October in reserve and called my husband in Lexington, where he customarily entered a trotter in the Kentucky Futurity. I asked him to meet me in New Harmony when the races were over. After Kenneth answered that he could manage to arrive on the twelfth, I at once advised the sculptor in New York via telegram.[4]

In those days, Lipchitz did not travel by air, stating as his reason that it was too costly to insure his life, so I waited for him at the Evansville train station. I can still see him as he stepped down from the train. Deliberate in his movements, he had the confident bearing of an emissary from a foreign court, except that he wore a beret instead of a homburg, and his credentials consisted of an oversized roll of black drawing paper, which he carried like a stovepipe over his shoulder, and a message from a Spanish poet.

We were scarcely settled in the car for the thirty-minute drive to New Harmony when my distinguished guest addressed me with formality. "Madame, I bring a message from a dear friend, a Spaniard living in New York, Juan Larrea. A scholar and a poet, he was for many years a principal interpreter of Picasso. Their collaborations ceased when Picasso joined the Communist Party." Lipchitz paused a moment for a deep sigh. "Ah, what an intelligence. A marvelous man." The word "marvelous," as it rolled slowly from his lips, freed me from the familiar mooring of Highway 66 and carried me to a plane of being where I could breathe a more rarefied air.

With visible excitement, pressing his fingertips to his forehead, Lipchitz continued: "When I informed Larrea, quite casually, that you had asked me to come on the twelfth day of October, I was not prepared for his expression of complete astonishment. He could not speak for a few minutes. Then came surprising words: '*Mon petit Jacques,*' as he sometimes calls me, 'you have no idea what this date means or what you have been asked to do. You will be arriving in a place close to the physical heart of America on the anniversary of the day Columbus discovered the New World!'"

As we moved along, Lipchitz shrugged. "As for me, madame, I know little of such matters. *Je ne suis qu'un simple ouvrier* (I am but a simple worker). And it suffices that I am here to meet Mr. Owen, see *la colline,* and begin work. Larrea, who has studied and thought much, possibly sees further than we do. I feel obliged to repeat his emphatic words: 'We must remember, Jacques, that America has not yet been discovered!'"

Later that day, Kenneth and Lipchitz talked amiably as they walked through fields and low hills to climb the back of the mound. While my husband unlocked the cattle gate, Lipchitz whispered to me: "Beneath

Monsieur's pleasant smile, I sense an opposition to our designs. Never will we have *la colline* for *la Madone*."

He was quick to add with his measured, beautiful laughter: "I have Monsieur's permission to return in the morning and gather all the walnuts I can carry home." I still see Lipchitz in my mind's eye as he left us, rejoicing in a heavy burlap bag slung over his shoulders, a benevolent Santa Claus.

I did not fully understand Juan Larrea's message for mid-America until I met him several months later at Lipchitz's studio. He had the look of a cloistered monk, with dark eyes set back below a high forehead and a thin face. The loss of most of his family, his homeland, and his considerable fortune in the Spanish Civil War had not embittered the man or diminished the smile with which he greeted me.

Larrea gave me a copy of his book *Guernica* and pulled out the folded page that reproduced the whole of Picasso's anguish over the bombing of the small Spanish town, which gave its name to the painting and the book. Larrea's finger traveled slowly from the right side of the page to the upper left, where Picasso had sketched a small map of his country, smaller and paler than the choking dove on the table below the map. "See, madame, the bird of peace struggles to leave Spain, as do the other persons of the Trinity, however unusual their presentation!" With his finger pointing to the promontory of Galicia, Larrea summarized his philosophy in words that I found again in the text of *Guernica*:

> This group seems about to slip out of the picture, toward Life, through the tiny gate in the West where, if the earth ends there, Heaven or Paradise begins. . . .
>
> For beyond the end of the world of the ancients there looms a New World, that is, behind all those space-time symbols there looms, in real and vital concreteness, America, the natural Beyond of the Spanish Finisterre.[5]

Picasso, like every Spaniard before him, knew the legend of Santiago de Compostela, the "Field of the Star." He remembered the war cry that had expelled the Moors and recognized "the natural Beyond of the Spanish Finisterre," toward which the admiral of the *Santa Maria* had set his course. Picasso might have professed Communism with his lips and denied religious content to *Guernica*, but he remained a son of Catholicism in his symbolism, according to Larrea. In perhaps the most significant painting of the twentieth century, he painted the crucifixion of his beloved country.[6]

The unsentimental dove was still the Holy Spirit and the Comforter as it fled from a nation that no longer sought its guidance and from a Europe that was to go up in man-ignited flames. Without Larrea's explanation, I would only have seen the chaos in *Guernica* and missed the winged hope that looked to America not for money, munitions, and troops but as a refuge from horror.[7]

I was no longer baffled by Larrea's ecstatic reaction to Lipchitz's arrival in New Harmony on Columbus Day. I was willing to believe that Europe's exiled bird of peace could settle in a town founded by George Rapp, who early in the nineteenth century had left a war-weary Württemberg for America. I needed the reassurance of that visit with Juan Larrea because Jacques and I would eventually lose our case with the legal owner and guardian of Indian Mound, my husband.

As Lipchitz had predicted, Kenneth Owen had no intention of giving us space for a statue, although this reality did not emerge until later. For my husband, Indian Mound was sufficiently sacred, and he was right. In seeking to impose my own will, I had forgotten my earlier agreement with Kenneth never to build there. I had also forgotten my own lament over the gap that too often exists between orators on hilltops and the people in the valleys below who either cannot or will not hear those who speak with authority from higher ground. I began to question the validity of my encounter with Abraham. Had that experience been a self-induced illusion or had it come to me unbidden, as when the first sickle of a new moon surprisingly appears from behind a cloud or a tangle of branches? Whichever the case, I realized—or it was revealed to me—the sober fact that Lipchitz's Virgin, her dove, and the winged cherubim had, as yet, no place to land from their heavenly flight.

I was slower than Lipchitz to regain my fighting spirit and to seek alternatives; time alone would teach me the rightness of my husband's decision and the truth of a Portuguese proverb, "God writes straight with crooked lines." If ever a commissioned work of art had a circuitous and difficult journey, surely it was that for Our Lady, *Notre Dame de Liesse.*

I reminded myself that *Notre Dame de Liesse* means "Our Lady of Joy" and that she was giving her creator Lipchitz an increasing measure of it as he brought his image closer to realization. I also knew that the joy she could bring others would depend on finding for her not just any place but a special place, and that I would have to find it.

I must confess that I have not learned from any theological book as much as I learned from these pictures of the great modern artists who broke through into the realm out of which symbols are born. And you cannot understand theology without understanding symbols.

—Paul Tillich, "Existentialist Aspects of Modern Art"

CHAPTER 9

Enter Paul Tillich

Meanwhile, work on the sculptural front progressed: Lipchitz began the enlargement of the small plaster model.[1] He permitted me to watch his progress, and I loved observing the sculptor cut away at malleable clay with sure, unhesitating strokes of his scalpel. I also relished the intervals of rest, when he would speak of the artists whom he had known when he lived as a young man in the Montparnasse section of Paris.

Lipchitz brought to life for me the period of artistic creativity between the two world wars. He might just have had an absinthe with Picasso or recently have received visits from Soutine and Modigliani, two of his closest friends, both less worldly than the more successful Spaniard. Lipchitz rarely laughed, but he chuckled when he remembered Soutine's behavior after making his first sale to the eccentric but highly perceptive art collector Dr. Albert C. Barnes of Philadelphia.

"Unaccustomed to having money in his pockets," Lipchitz said, "the poor fellow was almost out of his mind when he broke into my studio.

'Look at my Charvet tie, Jacques!' he announced to me. 'It cost me five hundred francs. See my taxi outside your window? The meter is still ticking. I'm on my way to Nice.'"

Stories about Modigliani were legion. "Undernourished and poor, like Soutine, Modi was a proud man and an intellectual. He would often drop in on Berthe and me in the middle of the night and recite from Dante's *Inferno.*" These recollections of famous artists, though enjoyable, had no bearing on New Harmony.

One of Lipchitz's recent experiences, however, would have a profound and lasting effect on New Harmony and me. I recall that particular Wednesday afternoon when Lipchitz's alert and often intense persona was in a state of delirious excitement as he opened the studio door for me.

"Monsieur," I greeted him, for I never called him Jacques and he always addressed me formally, "whatever has happened?"

"Ah, Madame, yesterday, at the Jewish Theological Seminary, I met the most marvelous man!" Sighing deeply and lifting his eyes heavenward, as if in thanksgiving to Yahweh, he continued, "We artists are invited to exchange ideas with theologians of different faiths." His blue eyes were ablaze again. "You have no idea what it means to find a theologian, yes, a *théologien,*" he emphasized in French, "who understands what we artists are trying to do." Lipchitz lifted a clay-wet hand in a gesture to remembered misunderstandings. "He understands modern art perfectly! He sends his students to look for works of art that do not seem to have a religious subject. Art that goes below the surface.[2] He and Père Couturier think alike."

The modest and insightful priest Père Couturier was responsible for bringing authentic Christian art back into Catholic houses of worship, but the great stride of this Colossus had taken place in Europe, not in my country.

"Oh—oh!" I said. "A theologian exists who cares as much about art as he does about religion? Who and where is this phenomenon?"

"He is Paul Tillich, now teaching theology at Union Theological Seminary."

As I listened to Lipchitz's rapturous account of Tillich, I sensed that here in New York City I had discovered another Colossus, a person essential to my hopes for New Harmony and a catalyst for the reunion of art and religion on this side of the Atlantic. And I believed that Lipchitz and Tillich together were art and theology.

There was a way for me to meet Paul Tillich, who stood with one foot in both theology and philosophy and the other foot in culture, including art of the twentieth century. Since my boarding days at the Ethel Walker School, I had known and loved the Thomas J. Watson Sr. family. Jane, the eldest daughter, was one of my closest friends.

Thomas J. Watson Sr. was a trustee at Columbia University, and he appreciated my respect and need for people of heart and genius. He knew why I had sought them for New Harmony and agreed with me that a town once envisioned and inhabited by extraordinary men and women would require such people again for its rebirth. Bricks, mortar, funding, and community would follow in their wake.

A visionary himself, Tom Watson, the founder and first president of IBM, a significant pioneer of the computer age, believed in the importance of the Midwest. He had once explained to me how the population center of our country fluctuated up and down the Wabash and Ohio Rivers. He insisted that whatever happened in this heartland could affect for good or evil every state in the Union. Moved by this awesome prophecy, I did not hesitate now to recruit Jane to ask a favor of her distinguished father. (Jane and I referred to her father's IBM office as "Uncle Tom's Cabin" because I used the term of endearment "Uncle Tom.")

"Please, dear Jane, I must meet Paul Tillich at Union. Ask your father to find a way."

I learned from Uncle Tom that Tillich also lectured in philosophy to graduate students at Columbia and that a close relationship existed between the seminary and the university. He reassured me, saying, "I'll pick up the phone and see that you meet him."

My request was honored not only with computer speed and efficiency but also with the warmth characteristic of the Watson family. I could attend Dr. Tillich's lectures and have occasional short visits between classes whenever his schedule and mine permitted. Randolph H. Dyer, comptroller at the seminary, escorted me to a classroom where Tillich was teaching.

The subject of the first lecture I attended was salvation. I felt uneasy among seminarians who had earned their admission without benefit of powerful friends and was awed by the international renown of the man whom I had been both eager and afraid to meet. Moreover, the room was hot and airless. Halfway through his explication of the difference between *kairos* (vertical or fulfilled time) and *chronos* (horizontal or measured time), and speaking in a thick but soft German accent, Professor Tillich addressed the student seated nearest the window: "For our immediate salvation, vould you pleeze open ze vindow."

The intellectual giant—who had defied Hitler from the pulpits and lecture halls of Germany in the early 1930s—suddenly became a human being. He was now a professor with a sense of humor, tousled gray hair, and a rumpled, ill-fitting suit. As we left the classroom and sat on a bench in the corridor, he was someone whom I could now face comfortably.

"I am a friend of the sculptor Lipchitz," I began boldly. "He was excited to meet a theologian who knows and cares about modern art."

The man who exemplified his own "belief-ful realism" looked at me as the bearer of great news; his weariness vanished.

"What a truly remarkable artist, and he seems so young for all he's been through. An exile from his country, as I am."

"Lipchitz also spoke of your own youthful energy."

Not since my father's face had I seen such kindness in a human countenance or heard laughter as joyful. I had not expected to be at ease in his presence and had only brought a copy of *The Courage to Be* for his autograph.[3] The bell rang again. I spoke hurriedly: "I could bring you a photo of the model of the large sculpture Lipchitz is working on for New Harmony." I expected and received a positive response. Dr. Tillich invited me to bring my photograph to an evening class the following week.

How glad and grateful I was for that invitation! I became familiar with Tillich's general theory on art, namely, that a true work of art does not merely represent what meets the eye but also points beyond itself to a higher—or, as he preferred, a deeper—dimension of reality, which neither human hands nor words can fully capture or define. I was not prepared, however, for the new criterion for judging art that he gave me when I asked, "Would you care to comment on the symbolism of Lipchitz's statue?"

After slowly analyzing the photo of the sculpture, Tillich replied, "The symbolism of any valid work of art is inexhaustible."

Whether a question came from a student, from Henry Luce, the man who dominated American journalism for decades, or from an art enthusiast like myself, Tillich unfailingly gave his questioners more than they asked for. So it was that Our Lady of many titles acquired a new one, "Our Lady of Endless Possibilities." I was jubilant. But sensing that even immortals can tire after long hours of teaching, I excused myself with, "Only please remember having met me, when I invite you one day to my beloved New Harmony."

Little did either this powerful, sought-after theologian or I suspect that Our Lady would eventually lead him to New Harmony. Even so, and however determined she was—for I had come to believe that Lipchitz's Madonna might have her own agenda—she would need human agents to carry out her wishes.

The greatest miracle of Lourdes is the look of resignation
on the faces of those who are not healed.

—Fulton Oursler, *The Happy Grotto*

CHAPTER 10

Polio Epidemic

A severe polio epidemic tore into Houston early summer of 1952, and, like a merciless hurricane, it crippled and killed.[1] Each of our daughters succumbed, but our eldest daughter Janie, aged nine, was most seriously affected.[2] Customarily, once school was out, we left for "up there," as Janie and Carol, their forefingers pointing north, called New Harmony. This was the year, however, of their first private swimming pool and of relocating from our home on Shadow Lawn Street to a house that Kenneth had purchased in a then-wilderness area of Houston along Buffalo Bayou.[3] Our daughters were loath to leave this unexplored wonderland and its nearness to adored cousins Joe and Lee Hudson, whose parents' house was not far from the oyster-shell road that connected our Pinewold Lane with South Post Oak Lane.

We were caught by a life- and limb-threatening epidemic that unalterably changed the patterns of our lives. Kenneth and I lost a united family, and Janie lost the use of her legs. Hermann Hospital and Hedgecroft Clinic treated poliomyelitis patients in Houston. Sister Kenny's techniques of heat therapy for six months and massages morning and night at home lessened pain and brought comfort for Janie but did not strengthen the muscles that would enable her to walk.

Grieving parents often ask God to heal their child, and we laid siege at heaven's door. Fulton Oursler's book *The Happy Grotto: A Journalist's Account of Lourdes* taught me that prayers for the healing of loved ones are seldom, if ever, answered precisely as we word them. Oursler tells us that many who come for immersion in the waters of Lourdes but are not cured of their illness or physical handicaps nonetheless achieve emotional healing and the power to live comfortably, joyfully, and even creatively with their infirmities.

My faith in the Almighty's long view and Janie's unfailing courage carried me through that first dark year and its quarantine, for no children were allowed to visit a property that health authorities considered infectious. Kenneth and I felt deep parental pain. Janie's often futile efforts to handle the crutches, with her legs in steel braces that caused her to fall, were agonizing for us.

Well-meaning friends came to express their sympathy for her illness. Janie's heroic ability to soar above the storm that had knocked her down is best summarized by her response to her visitors: "Thank you for coming. I'm okay, but my legs have had a hard time. I call the weak one 'Pansy,' the strong one 'Peter.' He'll have to learn how to handle his poor sister." Our brave daughter clearly had no intentions of remaining in a wheelchair the remainder of her life, and it behooved her parents to look beyond what Houston, at that time, could offer.

Heaven's gates were slowly opening: we learned through friends in New York of two exceptionally skilled therapists Klaus and Josephine Schmidt, a Dutch émigré couple. We flew east to meet them. We read kindness in their faces and decided to place Janie in their professional care. We had already chosen faithful Emma Lafanet as Janie's housekeeper. Janie and Emma relocated to the Stanhope Hotel in 1954. A brown French poodle, Cappy, would be a surrogate sister. I would learn to be a cross-country mother: one month with Carol and Annie in Houston, the alternate one in New York City, with my occasional stops at New Harmony, including annual summers there and at Ste. Anne in Ontario with all three daughters.

The Schmidts never promised us that massage therapy would enable Janie to walk without crutches, but they did hold out hope that operations could make walking much easier. Their faith in the ability of a skilled father-and-son team Philip D. Wilson, MD and Philip D. Wilson Jr., MD to achieve this goal was implicit. We decided that these orthopedic stars of New York's Hospital for Special Surgery should begin their series of successful operations. They fused the knee of Pansy, the useless leg. Peter, the stronger leg with its flexible knee, aided by crutches, would eventually enable Janie to go wherever she wanted. Adapting skillfully in the years to come, she went on to marry a fine man, to bear and raise two wonderful children, and to participate fully and generously in the life of her community. Her former husband Per Arneberg and her children, Ingrid and Erik, have seldom seen her in a wheelchair and never in steel braces.

There were some benefits to being in New York: the city's theaters and museums compensated for the proms and athletic events her former classmates were enjoying at Houston's Kinkaid School. Janie carefully scanned the *New York Times* for reviews of current plays and exhibitions and would have a list of suggestions for my cultural nourishment awaiting my arrival from Texas.

One particular evening of theater remains bittersweet for me. The celebrated actress Katharine Cornell had met my daughter at my parents' summerhouse in Ontario, Canada. Miss Cornell's aunt Lydia, a friend and neighbor of my parents', had brought her famous niece to tea at Ste. Anne. Impressed with Janie's zeal for the legitimate stage and moved by her brave spirit, Miss Cornell invited Janie to come backstage after her performance in Christopher Fry's *Tiger at the Gates.* "I'd love to have your honest viewpoint of the performance, Janie," she said. "Do come see me in my dressing room after the play."

To a stage-struck girl of thirteen, this gracious invitation from a phenomenal actress was manna from heaven. I booked reservations well in advance for *Tiger at the Gates.* Finally the long-anticipated evening was at hand, and we were soon immersed in Fry's dramatization of the Greek and Trojan War. Halfway through Cassandra's prophecies from the walls of Troy, Janie turned to me. "Mother, this is really deep. Miss Cornell is awesome. I can't wait to tell her what I think of the play. Remember, she asked me."

The last curtain calls over, we began our slow but determined way to the backstage door, where an usher was waiting for us. But, alas, when he opened the door to the dressing room area, Janie and I encountered a steep

Sarah Campbell Blaffer.
*Courtesy Sarah Campbell
Blaffer Foundation, Houston.*

flight of stairs without railings, impossible for anyone in a wheelchair. Sadly, we turned away toward the nearest exit, not daring to look at one another because of the disappointment we would find on each other's face.

An unexpected telephone call from Katharine Cornell awakened us the next morning. Having forgotten about the stairs and not knowing where to reach us, she had called her aunt Lydia in Buffalo for Mother's telephone number in Houston in order to apologize to Janie in New York. Some great actresses are also great ladies. We eventually met her.

Janie's exile from Houston and my migratory life brought support from two devoted and irreplaceable grandmothers who were alive and well in Houston, my mother, Sarah Campbell Blaffer, and Kenneth's mother, Lucille Eagle Owen, respectively known as "Ma" and "Gaga." Kenneth's mother and his sister, Frances, would return to their hometown, New Harmony, with us each summer.

Lucille Eagle Owen, 1941.
*Blaffer-Owen
family photograph.*

Last but not least, we relied on our English nanny, Joyce Isabella Mann, a graduate of the Princess Christian School of Nursing for Genteel Ladies. Her first employers were Prince and Princess zu Wied, who had needed an English governess for their children. The Wieds had lived in Norway during World War I, as the Prince had been the ambassador there from Germany.

Ninny was sequestered with the Wied family throughout the long war years. "Never once were the Wieds so tactless as to mention the war," she told me. On the subject of tact, I recall her saying to me shortly after taking on our girls in 1943, "The only reason I decided to accept your position, Mrs. Jane, was that you reminded me slightly of the Princess Wied."

But her snobbery did not run deep; she was devoted to all the children of New Harmony and would have given her life to save any children in danger, regardless of their race, creed, or financial status. Ninny later resided with Auntie Aline in the Lab as her full-time companion until Auntie's death in 1960. Miss Mann bequeathed her substantial life savings to New Harmony's Working Men's Institute. Anyone interested in learning more about this worthy representative of the British Empire in New Harmony can locate *Wings of the Morning: Memoirs of Joyce Isabella Mann* in the library of the Working Men's Institute and admire a large photographic likeness of her on the west wall of its reading room.

Murphy Auditorium to the left of the Working Men's Institute, 1920.

Don Blair Collection. Courtesy of Special Collections,
University of Southern Indiana.

If you think there's such a beast
as a war horse, walk up to my
Belgian and look straight in
his eyes.

—Susan Wunder, "If You Think"[1]

CHAPTER 11

Sir George MacLeod

Since there was no land as yet available for Our Lady and her "Descending Dove of Peace" in New Harmony in 1953, I decided to search elsewhere, as far as our nation's capital. In Houston I had recently met the Reverend Francis Sayre Jr., dean of Washington National Cathedral. Impressed with his warmth and intelligence, I felt he would understand my views on war and peace. Since he was the grandson of Woodrow Wilson, who had fought for his belief that there would never be another war after establishing the League of Nations, surely Dean Sayre would be my ally in bringing the "Dove of Peace" to Washington. I had even ventured to express to him my conviction that it is powerful men in the capitals of nations who start wars, not men in small country towns. Perhaps Lipchitz's sculptural ambassadress for peace was needed more in Washington, D.C., than in New Harmony, Indiana.

Dean Sayre was receptive to my offer to place *Notre Dame de Liesse* with her "Dove of Peace" on the cathedral's grounds, and he invited Lipchitz

and me to Washington. He envisioned an appropriate site outside Bethle-
hem Chapel, though he warned us that the cathedral's trustees would
have the final say. As the dean had feared, the trustees refused my offer,
and he shared my disappointment.[2]

Ironically, James Sheldon's will funded a heroic statue of George Washington, which was accepted later by the cathedral. The work by Herbert
Haseltine, who created the sculpture of the racehorse Man o' War, seemed
to celebrate the father of our country on horseback as "first in war." We as
a nation seem to have forgotten that our founders also deemed Washington to be "first in peace." When we remember that the Korean and Viet-
nam Wars followed after the installation of the statue in 1959, one could
say that my wounded "Dove of Peace" had been trampled by the hooves of
that unwilling, misnamed "warhorse." There was small comfort in com-
paring myself to Cassandra, whose prophecies from the walls of Troy
were rejected by the Trojan people.

My disappointment over not having a habitation for *Descent of the Holy
Spirit* endured. A panacea finally came in the late summer of 1954 at Ste.
Anne's when I met again a friend since the early 1950s, who was lecturing
in Ontario.[3] I told her about the rejection of Our Lady and her "Dove of
Peace" in Washington, D.C., laying bare my hurt. Dr. Gladys Falshaw
advised me to take a week in New York City at a convent school. The Rev-
erend Mother Ruth, a biracial nun originally from Harlem who studied in
Canada to escape prejudice, had founded a religious order for Anglican-
Episcopal women, the Community of the Holy Spirit. Initially, Reverend
Mother Ruth and two sisters had received a calling to take the Word of
God to remote parts of Canada, which explained their description as "bush
nuns." She received a second call to establish a school in New York City
and in 1950, together with Sister Edith Margaret, founded St. Hilda's,
close to Columbia University and Union Theological Seminary.

Trusting the logic that often resides under the surface of the improba-
ble, I decided to take Dr. Falshaw's advice. Washington's rejection of Lipchitz's emissary of goodwill had left me feeling empty and unequal to the
fulfillment of the mission I had undertaken. I saw myself as no more than
the handle of a fork, its prongs badly bent and incapable of serving either
my family or the always-endangered cause of peace.

I told Janie I would be away for an unworldly week at St. Hilda's House convent and asked Emma Lafanet not to forward mail or telephone messages. Carrying a tote bag of bare essentials, I hailed a taxi and asked its driver to take me to West 113th Street.

I knocked several times before one of the resident nuns opened the somber door of the narrow brownstone house where her fellow teachers both lived and taught. There was a similar brownstone next door that housed classrooms for older students and, if I remember correctly, the chapel. Sister Catherine's face was a network of fine wrinkles, campaign ribbons from her mission work in England. The broad smile with which she welcomed me, however, returned youth and beauty to the face of this intrepid nun.

We crossed a dimly lit, commonplace entry hall and climbed a steep, enclosed stairway. Sister Catherine reached the second floor before I did and, addressing me once again with a radiant smile that dispelled any notion one might have of a withered, wasted nun, she pointed to a closed door and said, "Mother Ruth is expecting you."

The foundress of St. Hilda's, clothed in a floor-length black habit, her face framed by a starched white wimple, reminded me simultaneously of a rubbing of an abbess from a medieval tombstone and of an enthroned monarch. Except for the softness of Mother Ruth's voice and the kindness in her brown eyes, her appearance was intimidating and prepared me for the regime she expected me to follow: prayer services morning, noon, and night in the small chapel; silent meditations; and lean fare in between. To these austerities I should add sleepless nights, for St. Hilda's was located in an impoverished neighborhood where unemployed Puerto Ricans slept during the day and partied at night.

As an indulged southerner, I was unaccustomed to physical discomfort or to three prayer services daily. After the first four days, my zeal for spiritual nourishment and direction was ebbing. But whenever I passed Mother Ruth in the narrow hallways or the chapel, a message of "hold on" beamed in my direction, and so I plodded onward.

On the fifth day I was summoned to the office. Reverend Mother greeted me with one of her rare smiles. More empress than abbess, she asked me to take a seat. "Our school has just been visited by the very distinguished Sir George MacLeod," she began crisply. She then gave me an account of the Scottish theologian and minister, also a former soldier in World War I now turned pacifist, and founder of the Iona Community.[4]

As the first Harry Emerson Fosdick Visiting Professor at Union Theological Seminary for the 1954–55 academic year, Sir George was staying in New York along with his wife, Lorna, and children Mary and Maxwell for eight months. "Furthermore," Mother Ruth continued, "he recently walked over from Union in a blinding rain to enter his children at the best school in the neighborhood, which is our own." (Ultimately, her prophecy about St. Hilda's & St. Hugh's was fulfilled. It became, indeed, one of the best schools in New York City.)

"Jane," the Reverend Mother concluded in a no-nonsense voice, "I have a strong feeling that Sir George could be a help to you. You must manage to meet him." The right suggestion had not fallen lightly on my hearing. She glanced at her watch, then, giving me a brief smile and a nod, said, "It's time for vespers." That was the end of our meeting and the beginning of one of the most exciting and rewarding adventures of my life. Events from that afternoon onward began to move swiftly, as when the albatross fell from the neck of Coleridge's ancient mariner and water spirits guided his ship to safety.

The path to George MacLeod would be the same one that had led me to Paul Tillich. When I shared with Jane Watson Irwin my wish to meet George MacLeod, she did not need to go through her father because her husband, John, was now serving on Union's board of directors. A dinner honoring the first recipient of the Harry Emerson Fosdick Chair would take place before my return to Texas. She invited me to the dinner and promised that she would arrange for me to sit at her table the evening of Sir George's inaugural address.

Listening to one of the most inspiring speakers of the twentieth century, I sensed that the twice-rejected *Descent of the Holy Spirit* would find a home on St. Columba's holy island, Iona, where George MacLeod had restored an ancient abbey and changed the lives of his co-workers.

At the request of John N. Irwin II, a meeting with MacLeod was arranged for me early the following day, before classes began. Randy Dyer, the obliging comptroller at Union, again led me through labyrinthine corridors, this time to the door of a classroom where my future co-conspirator was standing, tall and almost menacing, more like a warrior than a man of the cloth. Such a commanding presence would on an ordinary occasion have intimidated me. But this, as we both suspected and later acknowledged, was a providential encounter, and I did not hesitate to state boldly my mission and to describe Lipchitz's *Notre Dame de Liesse* and her descending dove. Sir George's first response was a chuckle. "I hear that Picasso has turned the dove of peace into a chicken," he said. "What is your position?"

Mortified, I stood my ground and replied, "That, I believe, Sir George, is a Communist attempt to make Picasso's art adhere to their ideology and can be discounted. In any case, Lipchitz is not a Communist, and the dove I am offering Iona is not a chicken."

By then we were both laughing, as Sir George had probably intended. Our interview ended with an invitation to visit Iona during the following summer and to present my proposal to his trustees. Immediately upon my return to Houston, I booked passage on the *Normandy* for my daughters Janie and Carol and our Cajun nurse, Emma, who would be needed to assist Janie on the journey.[5] Although that indomitable young girl of twelve had learned to walk with crutches, a wheelchair would be needed for our travels. The strong arms and infectious good humor of Emma Lafanet were also essential.

It is only after a pious journey to a distant region, in a strange land, a new country, that the meaning of the inner voice guiding our search can be revealed to us.

—Heinrich Zimmer, *Myths and Symbols in Indian Art and Civilization*

CHAPTER 12

Iona

In midsummer 1955, we sailed out of New York Harbor, landed in England, and from London took a train to Oban, the Scottish port of departure for the Outer Hebrides. Our adventures now began in earnest.

At Oban, we boarded a small but stout boat commonly at the service of travelers bound for the inner and outer Hebridean Islands. They were known as Puffers because of the billowing smoke clouds that issued from their steam-powered engines. The Puffer pushed fearlessly through the rough waters of the Hebridean Sea to the slim island of Mull. Here we transferred to an antiquated bus for the last land leg of our journey on a narrow, uneven road leading to Fionnphort, Mull's embarkation port for Iona. The faded, frayed velvet seats of our conveyance and the weathered mail pouch our driver tossed out to waiting villagers along the way remain solely in my memory, for like the audacious Puffers, this vintage bus no longer serves passengers.[1]

The only vessel in sight at Fionnphort was a sizable rowboat. With some anxiety, I arranged for the owner to take us across the sound to Iona. Perhaps Kenneth's dim view of my itinerary and what he called a "wild-goose chase" was correct and more prophetic than either of us realized, for we were not aware that the rebuilders of Iona had renewed an early Celtic association of a wild goose with the Dove of the Holy Spirit.[2] It is possible that invisible stout and broad wings hovered over us as our obliging oarsman loaded our bags, Janie, her wheelchair, Carol, Emma, and me into his shallow boat for what became a turbulent and wet crossing.

When I, a repentant and foolish mother, told George MacLeod of the risks I had taken in the small boat and of our near escape from drowning, he comforted me with one of his cardinal articles of faith, a one-size-fits-all response to seeming obstacles and danger: "If our deepest intent is acceptable in the sight of God, He will take that intent, run with it, and carry it further than we could ever imagine." He left no doubt in my mind that the oarsman who had steered us safely across the estuary separating Mull from Iona had been the recipient of extraterrestrial help and that my heart's intent had found acceptance.

One doesn't arrive in a rowboat at an island three and a half miles long by one and a half miles wide without attracting attention. Moreover, we had been expected. Our host had posted scouts—one of whom was the watcher Charles Turner, a six-foot-four retired English general and volunteer assistant to Sir George—to be on the lookout for errant Texans. Charles Turner served as an essential bridge between sacred and secular worlds. The gentle giant waited on the white shell beach to greet and lead a wet and weary group to the St. Columba Hotel.

No idle talk intruded as we washed away the dust from our journey with two pitchers of hot water left outside our door and prepared for bed in our unadorned room. I took Janie and Carol's silence to be a veiled reproach to the hardships I had brought on them. Quite the contrary, as I tucked them in for the night, they embraced me with more than their usual warmth and thanked me for the "explorations." In 1955 Disneyland had not yet captured the imaginations of American children, but I was confident that were my daughters ever to visit lands of make-believe, they would be able to separate fiction from fact, entertainment from nourishment.

The first day, our lordly host MacLeod stood in a posture that reminded me of the bronze effigy of Archangel Michael on the entrance wall of Basil

Spence's rebuilt Coventry Cathedral. Like St. Michael, Sir George fought with the flaming sword of the Spirit. In his own assessment of the archangel, MacLeod writes: "Michael must come back into our consciousness (not just our intellects). Angels must become our consciousness again . . . not floppy damsels in their nighties, but dynamic forces in their serried ranks . . . 'the whole company of heaven.'"[3]

But the resemblance to the archangel was not exact: Sir George Mac-Leod carried a shepherd's crook, not a spear, and wore a dark blue shirt, not chainmail. A well-worn tartan was sufficient shield from possible enemies and the intermittent rain that had already descended upon us. "Here we live peacefully in the rain," he announced cheerfully. "I hope you like it too."

Reassured that it would be a soft rain and not a Texas gully-washer, we followed our unapologetic leader to St. Oran's eleventh-century chapel and its cemetery, called Reilig Òdhrain. Kings from Scotland, Ireland, Denmark, and Norway were brought here for burial centuries ago because, whatever their earthly sins, these powerful but credulous monarchs believed Iona would show them mercy and provide access to heaven. It continues to be regarded as "a thin place" by those who seek peace there, so called because of the "thin as gossamer" veil that separates Iona from the next world.[4] Islanders believe the body of the Scottish king Duncan lies here, close by that of Macbeth, his murderer and usurper.

Carol was not drinking in Scottish history as thirstily as her older sister, Janie, but I was unprepared for her sudden disappearance. Our quick-eyed host settled my fears: "Your lively Carol asked me if there are any hills to climb. I told her about Dùn Ì, behind the abbey. I believe you'll find her there."

I hurried toward the island's solitary hill. Distances not being vast on Iona, I soon reached the base of the hill that Carol had so eagerly sought. Dùn Ì was not too high for me to discern her lithe figure in its belted navy blue raincoat or to marvel at the beauty of her exquisite features, profiled against a freshly washed blue sky. There was music and joy in the voice that called out to me.

"It's stopped raining, Mother. Please come up! You'll see everything from here, even the sheep Sir George calls Iona's lawnmowers!"

Whether it was the tallest tree or the highest hill, Carol always sought heights. She was like a kite caught in the current of strong winds, tugging for release from the human hands that held her slender cord.

Mercifully, on that unforgettable day on the heights of Iona, I had no foreknowledge of Carol's early, tragic death. Years later, by which time she was the wife of a beloved and loving husband, James Coleman, and the mother of a healthy, alert, and handsome son, Jamie, Carol could no longer bear the pain and darkness of an encroaching and incurable illness. Mistakenly believing she was a burden to her family, she pulled herself free of all strings and earthly moorings.

On that glorious day on Iona, for her and for us together, there were no shadows, only fullness of life in the present moment, which Paul Tillich speaks of as the "Eternal Now."

"Sure," I called up to her, "I'll climb to you, Carol, but only if you promise to join your sister, Emma, and me for vesper services in the Abbey Church at five o'clock."

Carol did not keep us waiting at the vaulted entrance of the twelfth-century St. Mary's Cathedral, beautifully restored in the early 1900s.[5] The invincible will of George MacLeod led the restoration of the abbey's domestic buildings through the combined efforts of priests and seminarians who were learning to use their hands and of skilled artisans who were learning about prayer.[6] MacLeod's cry had been effective: "We ministers don't know how to use our hands for labor, and you workers want to know how to pray. Let's learn from each other."

At the doors of the Abbey Church, tall iron candleholders stood sentinel on either side of the entrance corridor. Their candles glowed from the base of intersecting arches, and above each transparent sphere were the winged insignia of air force pilots shot down in World War II. My eyes were moist as we took our places on rush-bottomed wooden chairs.

A bouquet of flowers, gathered by the village postmistress, graced the altar, and above the shallow apse rose a large five-light west window with a view of the sound we had crossed. There was healing in the bluish light that came from this opening, healing in George MacLeod's rich-toned homily, and a sense of shared sacrament as small squares of bread and communion vessels were passed from hand to hand. The chalices were of clear Bristol glass, gifts from Sir Stafford Cripps. Verses from scripture were etched along their brims, and each was covered with the sheerest linen I had ever touched. Later, when I asked my host if Iona's spiders had woven them, he replied, "No such airy-fairy nonsense, Jane. They were my grandmother MacLeod's often-washed handkerchiefs."

General Turner was waiting outside the abbey by St. Martin's Cross to escort us to dinner in the recently restored refectory, originally built by St. Margaret of Scotland's Benedictine monks in the twelfth century. Sir George stood on its threshold to welcome my valiant little troupe, not in an abbatial robe but in his customary navy blue suit and shirt. We were seated at the high table on a raised platform, which alternately served as a podium for lectures.

Seated at tables below this dais were jovial, loquacious young men and women, some in blue jeans and turtleneck sweaters, Asians and Europeans, all of whom alike had come to this timeless small island to work, worship, and learn. Would the tonsured monks of St. Margaret's day have been shocked or pleased? I could not tell from their imagined shadows flickering on the stone walls.

As an aspiring preservationist, I was eager to learn how and when the medieval refectory had been rebuilt. A German Granary in New Harmony was waiting for its resurrection, and here in Iona, I was the guest of an indefatigable rebuilder. I needed to learn from him while I had the chance.

Today, visitors to New Harmony's Rapp-Owen Granary will find a bronze plaque on a wooden support column with the names of the workers who rebuilt its massive walls, timbered ceilings, and stairways. It bears a benediction from Iona's master builder:

> Wherever there is good craftsmanship,
> there is the Hand of God;
> Wherever there are good thoughts,
> there is the Spirit of God.[7]

With his customary relish in the telling of a good story, my host gave me a lesson in the ways of Providence. "A distinguished group of Norwegian businessmen, primarily ship owners, were visiting Iona a few summers ago. 'What,' they had asked, 'is a huge pile of stones doing on an otherwise tidy terrain?' To which I replied, 'You are looking at the remains of the Benedictine refectory your Viking ancestors demolished on one of their frequent raiding expeditions. A great pity!'"

The Norwegians echoed their host's lament and asked for forgiveness. The canny Scotsman knew how to console them. "Never mind, my friends. You and your fellow Viking descendants can put this venerable ruin back together."

Not surprisingly, beautiful Norwegian timbers arrived from church and business leaders alike the following year. Angus Robertson, a proud Scot, not to be outdone by Norsemen, contributed seven thousand pounds toward the reconstruction.

There have been varying and incomplete versions of the agreement reached that night in the candlelit and laughter-filled hall where Sir George, having left the high table, entertained us with a hilarious performance on the piano. In writing now, I feel obliged, while still in possession of my faculties, to give an accurate account of our covenant, particularly as it would be yet further evidence of George MacLeod's prophetic powers. Whatever this extraordinary man envisioned usually came to pass.

He foresaw that the third casting of Lipchitz's *Descent of the Spirit* would, sooner or later, reside squarely in the center of the unrestored medieval cloister.[8] With equal clarity, he anticipated the formidable roadblocks that Scottish anti-Catholics would place before the sculpture's arrival at Iona. But, he must have reasoned, had there not existed greater obstacles to his vision of Iona as a safe haven for physical and spiritual renewal in the 1930s? If he had been able to keep his dreams for Iona whole throughout the tragic years of World War II and without the support of his own Church of Scotland, no one and nothing would prevent him from planting a Jewish quasi-Catholic Virgin on Presbyterian Scottish soil.[9]

In fact, a plan had already formed in his mind: "Jane, you could give the sculpture, and I would find an equivalent sum for her dowry." I readily agreed with Sir George's decision and offered to provide funds for the purchase of the third casting.[10] He, in turn, would find Scots donors to match my payment to Lipchitz, believing that a so-called dowry would help her gain acceptance by staunch Presbyterian islanders. I experienced the intensity of their anti-Catholicism the very next morning.

The ruined walls of the convent that St. Margaret of Scotland had commissioned for her nuns were an easy walk from our inn and an enticement to my daughters. They had never touched stones that old and asked permission to follow those that had fallen into the meadow, wind-polished and scattered like giant unstrung beads.

Some years later, Sir George illustrated a universal concern for balance when he wrote:

There is a carved Pre-Christian stone strangely set in the Nunnery Wall. It is a "Sheila nan Nigg" stone and has its counterpart in Poland and elsewhere. It is the figure of the "Mother of the Dawn God." She is the Mother of the Sun. She has no breasts, for to suckle the Sun would be to give her the pre-eminence. She has no arms, for to cuddle the Sun would be to give her superiority of the origin of Light. Yet Maternity must have its place. Such was the pre-Christian seeking.[11]

After the girls left with Emma, I settled into a niche in the nunnery wall and began reading my copy of George MacLeod's *We Shall Rebuild*. A villager carrying an egg basket passed by, and I asked her with feigned innocence if she knew of plans for rebuilding the convent. She laid down her basket and hammered the air with both fists. Her voice was harsh and angry. "There'll be no nunnery on Iona never again!"

A few years later, the fervent feelings of this islander on Iona were echoed in a leading Glasgow newspaper when the editor learned that a fruit freighter, on its way around the world, had picked up at New York's harbor, in mid-December 1957, a statue of the Virgin Mary bound for Iona. One headline accused the Iona Community of being a "Jesuit Movement in Disguise." These speculations traveled down to the dockworkers at the port of Oban, where the freighter was expected, by chance or by fate, to arrive on Christmas Day 1958. The stevedores had been instructed by the anti-Catholic hierarchy not to put a pagan idol on a ferry to Iona.[12]

But the conspirators had not counted on the wizardry of George MacLeod. Forewarned of their plans, Sir George had enlisted his own rumormongers: "It nae be the Virgin Mary in that box," they proclaimed with vigor, "it be Rabbie Burns." As it turned out, 1959 would begin the year celebrating the bicentennial of the poet's birth, which of course made MacLeod's rumor easily credible. *Descent of the Spirit* arrived safely on Iona with the new year.

Thus was the dreaded image of the Mother of Our Lord smuggled onto the unsuspecting holy island, and there she resides to this day, centered in the garth of the abbey cloister, fully and beautifully empowered with "dowry" funds supplied by generous and faithful friends of Iona, Sir John and Lady Lena Mactaggart.

The placement of *Descent of the Spirit* in the abbey cloister allows viewing from multiple perspectives, including the reverse, which features Lipchitz's inscription in a field of stars.

Photograph by Margaret Woodson Nea, 2011.

CHAPTER 14

Kilbinger House

The first reborn of my adopted family of Harmonist houses was No. V on Steammill Street. Kilbinger House, on the southeast corner of Main and Granary, became my second child and, like its sister, a hungry orphan (25 on town map). An arm could reach through a wide crack in the brick of its west wall. If these bricks could be carefully reknit, the state might be shamed into doing necessary repairs to its building next door, Harmonist Community House No. 2, an approach I called "whitemail," as it encourages positive action by example rather than coercing by extortion. Missing roof shingles from the Kilbinger house invited rainwater. The house, built in the 1820s, tottered on the brink of the same steep cliff that New Harmony has hovered upon since its inception and from which it has been, so far, consistently and mercifully rescued.

The last owner, Mary Catherine Kilbinger, affectionately known as Miss Mamie, had been custodian of the state-owned Community House No. 2, also called the Dormitory, while residing in the adjacent family

Kilbinger House, after initial exterior repairs, and adjoining
log room, 1959. Harmonist Community House No. 2 to the right.

Photograph by John Doane. John Doane Collection.
Courtesy of Special Collections, University of Southern Indiana.

home all of her life. She, like other genteel ladies in town, had lacked the wherewithal to stitch cracks that scarred and endangered the Kilbinger House walls. The safest Harmonist room was its log cabin annex, one of only two remaining log structures in town (26 on town map). I have left Miss Mamie's rocking chair by the south window, where the good woman read her Catholic Bible or sewed. A large cast-iron Harmonist cooking pot is still imbedded in the brick grate, its slanting flue intact, a reminder to present-day architects that straight chimneys invite downdrafts and dampen fires.

After Miss Mamie's death in early 1951, I eventually bought the Kilbinger House from the heirs of her estate for two thousand dollars.[1] Seeing the dire condition of the house, I realized more slowly and soberly that my exuberant play days with restoration were over. I clearly needed professional and costly help. Heeding the counsel of my New Harmony friend Ena Long, I contacted the National Trust for Historic Preservation in Washington and its gracious first director, Fred L. Rath Jr. Wisely and generously, he dispatched his right arm, Helen Duprey Bullock, to my aid.

I shall never forget this remarkable woman's entry into my life through the doorway of my No. V and into its large, barn-like room. The ceiling at the lower end was left unplastered to expose the mud-covered and straw-wrapped wooden bats the Harmonists had used for insulation and to which I would point when curious visitors asked me, "Who lives here?" I would answer, "Can't you see it's a horse? His hay is up there." Placing a hand on the faded red door that I had salvaged from an abandoned stable, I would add, "He goes out through here," and then, indicating a venerable poplar column that stood midway in the room, "And there is his hitching post."

For cold-weather guests, I kept a fire going in the ample hearth, which Harvey had built with red and black brick. Into this hybrid space, Helen Bullock was blown in by a gusty wind one wet night and headed straight toward the fire, which fresh air had bellowed into a sudden burst of flame.[2] She stood silently, an indecipherable dark mass, until she lifted the hood of her rain cape, uncovering a cheerful countenance that did not fit my preconceived image of Williamsburg's first historian, the author of its cookbook, and the principle troubleshooter of an emerging National Trust for Historic Preservation. Every feature of that red-cheeked, rain-soaked face was circular: the rounded small nose, the dancing gray-blue eyes, and the pursed lips that parted easily and often for laughter. I helped my

long-awaited guest remove her cloak and led her toward one of two small rocking chairs opposite the hearth, where we could both rock and talk.

She began in her soft, musical voice, "How good to be here, Jane Owen, and not where I've been. After a horrendous flight from Washington to Indianapolis, I was told that the commuter plane would not leave for Evansville until the weather cleared the next morning. Guess what happened?" Exuberant laughter inhibited further explanation. I handed her a Kleenex to wipe her tears.

"I can't guess, Helen. Tell me."

"There were no vacancies at the airport hotel or anywhere else, for that matter." More laughter erupted before she resumed her outrageous tale, with ill-concealed delight. "Mistaken for a twentieth-century Wife of Bath, I was dropped off at a bawdy house, where I spent a restless night."

Soon Helen's mood shifted from impiety to reverence. With hands folded demurely on her lap, she began to speak worshipfully about Thomas Jefferson, and knowledgeably, for she had been present at Monticello with Carleton Sprague Smith of the New York Public Library for the opening of the Jefferson papers.

My own interest in Jefferson had begun when, in my twenty-seventh year, I read a marvelously written book *My Head and My Heart,* the poignant story of Jefferson's love for an Italian beauty and gifted musician and painter, Maria Hadfield Cosway. They had fallen in love during his ministry to France. Sadly, he had promised his wife on her deathbed never to remarry. Maria was the wife of a British miniature painter, the foppish Richard Cosway. Neither broke their vows, their heads overruling their hearts. Jefferson returned from France to father the University of Virginia. Maria returned to Italy to found a convent school for girls at Lodi.

Enamored of their story, I had memorized a portion of his May 21, 1789, letter to her: "Be our affection unchangeable, and if our little history is to last beyond the grave, be the longest chapter in it that which shall record their purity, warmth and duration."[3] I had, however, forgotten the author's name.

Facing.

One of the two oldest remaining Harmonist
log structures, with Miss Mamie's rocker, is attached to Kilbinger House.

Photograph by Darryl D. Jones, 2013.

The Harmonist kitchen, with its welcoming hearth, became a tavern during the Owen/Maclure period. The downstairs room as it now appears.

Photograph by Darryl D. Jones, 2013.

"Helen, surely you would know who wrote *My Head and My Heart*?"

The round bun on the nape of Helen's neck stopped bouncing, and with lowered eyes she answered almost apologetically, "I wrote it."

My preoccupation with the rechanneled love between Jefferson and Maria Cosway was extinguished with the wood ashes I heaped on the embers of the dying fire, a ritual the Irish call "smooring."

A historical romance did not figure in the meat-and-potatoes assessment of the severely wounded Kilbinger House the following day.

Helen Bullock promptly advised me to secure the services of Nicholson & Galloway, a
New York firm that excelled in the reknit-
ting of cracked walls.[4]

"There'll be plenty for their skilled masons to do," she told me. "Let's look at the
injury inflicted on a defenseless house by post-
Harmonist owners." Clearly, someone had
replaced a Harmonist window with a very
ordinary door on the north wall. "That wrong
door will have to become a window, and
precise masonry and carpentry will be required for the operation."

My alert mentor also rightly surmised
that the first-floor rooms, including the log
annex with its iron kettle, had served as a
kitchen for the brethren of Harmonist Community House No. 2, the adjacent building.
She made other revelations and issued orders that I promised to obey.

West of the log Harmonist room that had
kept Mamie Kilbinger warm in winter are
two downstairs rooms with an interesting
history. Judge James O. Wattles and his wife,
Deborah, had converted the room with a
hearth (where Harmonist women had once prepared meals) and the adjacent room into a tavern for travelers in the Owen/Maclure period. Prince
Maximilian zu Wied-Neuwied, the celebrated naturalist of his day, and
Karl Bodmer, the painter of his expeditions, would have dined there during their sojourn to New Harmony in 1832–33.[5] I wish their dinner conversations with resident naturalists and scientists—Lesueur, Say, and the
Owen brothers—could have been recorded. John Kilbinger, Miss Mamie's father, had acquired it for a home, returning the building to its original use as a Harmonist home.[6]

The second floor honors the lives and accomplishments of two of my
most important mentors. The room east of the stairwell became the
Helen Duprey Bullock Book Room (later renamed Memorial Library), a

repository of books on preservation, many from Helen's own collection. Brochures on historically significant towns and buildings in America can also be found there, including material on World Heritage sites and UNESCO.

The room to the west is dedicated to Paul Tillich and accessible to scholars and students who have "ultimate concerns." Early on, the Society for the Arts, Religion, and Contemporary Culture held the Paul Tillich Commemorative Lecture in New Harmony May 16–19, 1968. Amos Wilder delivered the lectures, and thirteen ARC fellows attended as well as members and the general public. The North American Paul Tillich Society held its international meeting in New Harmony in June 1993 and returned in 1999. Each time members were invited to this room and its archive. Added to its collection of books, essays, personal belongings, and correspondence are several unpublished photographs.[7] The most moving of these was taken of Tillich when he was still a chaplain to German troops in World War I, his haggard face haunted by the memory of dying soldiers. A few years later, he sat for another photograph, this time in civilian clothes at his desk, a serene young poet-scholar. The tragedy of two senseless wars had not defeated his love of life or dimmed his powerful intellect. Nor need today's wars and recessions defeat us at New Harmony. Let us preempt despair by adding the name of Paul Tillich to our pantheon of the valiant men and women who have preceded us here: the Harmonist builders; the Scottish, Welsh, and French scientists and educators; early and contemporary philanthropists. Their life stories should inspire us to balance the courage to be—to borrow the title of one of Tillich's most seminal books—with the courage to do.

Facing top.
The Helen Duprey Bullock Book Room was dedicated in her presence on October 23, 1967.
Photograph by Darryl D. Jones, 2013.

Facing bottom.
The Paul Tillich Archive with his favorite chair in the corner.
Photograph by Darryl D. Jones, 2013.

In the mid-1960s I asked Helen's advice about attaching a new wing to the historic log cabin of the restored Kilbinger House as a place of retreat and recreation for guests. This modest space would be dedicated to Mother Ruth, as Mother Superior House (27 on town map). I could not forget my debt to her for having repaired my own fractured self, for I had come to her convent feeling incapable of nourishing myself or anyone else. Mother Superior, her sisters, and my ordered, prayer-filled days had renewed my spirit and directed me to Iona. My gratitude was greater than my monetary gift to St. Hilda's School could express. Mother Ruth came to New Harmony only once to enjoy the room I had prepared for her, but it contains her prayers. Her presence remains in my inward eye: I see her, even now, seated in the tall woven-straw niche of a hooded Orkney chair or a regal silhouette in her black habit standing before the canopied four-poster bed, curtained in white wool, thin as nun's veiling.[8]

I have not returned the rooms of this multifaceted house to their original purpose or furnished the ground-floor rooms with replicas of Harmonist rope-webbed beds. Had I done so, the house could not have provided comfort and repose to distinguished guests. Brother Patrick Hart, former secretary of Thomas Merton and editor of his journals, was an early guest. After his first stay, Brother Patrick called Mother Superior House "another hermitage" and told his abbot Timothy Kelly that it was sufficiently distant from Gethsemani for him to retreat there upon occasion.[9]

Recipients of Mother Superior's hospitality have included leaders of New Harmony's Benedictine retreats and Sister Élise of St. Hilda's & St Hugh's School and convent, as well as four authors of spiritual classics: Esther de Waal, Joan Chitister, Cynthia Bourgeault, and John Philip Newell. Weekend hospitality is extended to clergy from the Episcopal Diocese of Indianapolis who come to preach at St. Stephen's across Granary Street, including Bishop Cate Waynick, Bob Gianini, and Kate Clayton.

African American high school students from gang-infested areas of Chicago have also been sheltered here. May streams of priestly and fecund visitors continue to flow through the doors of Mamie Kilbinger's once-battered house, freshening and renewing our community.

Mother Superior House.

Photograph by Darryl D. Jones, 2013.

That which is most perfect and most individual in each man's life is precisely the element in it which cannot be reduced to a common formula. It is the element which is nobody else's but ours and God's. It is our own, true, uncommunicable life, the life that has been planned for us and realized for us in the bosom of God.

—Thomas Merton, *The Sign of Jonas*

CHAPTER 15

Poet's House and Beyond

In the summer of 1958 the first Magi to arrive bearing gifts for the Poet's House, the third of my rescued Harmonist dwellings, were my Irish friend Professor Walter F. Starkie and his lively Italian wife, Ita, who came for a month's residence (29 on town map). Walter had grown up largely near Dublin because his father had served there as the last resident commissioner of national education for Ireland under British rule at the turn of the century. Walter often stole time from his studies to explore less frequented paths and the brightly colored wagons where Tinkers lived. (Tinker was the Irish name for Gypsy.) He was more attracted to their music, however, than to the pots and pans the Tinkers made and sold for a living. From them he learned how a fiddle could cast a glamour, or spell, upon whatever needed recovery or repair, be it a lost sheep or a broken heart. Romanichals also taught an eager Walter the folk songs of middle Europe while he remained in Italy following World War I. He once made a bet with a former Trinity College classmate that he would be awarded free meals and lodging from

Gypsies outside Budapest or Prague once he had played for them the old songs and tunes that he still remembered. Starkie won his wager.

Back in Dublin, Walter resumed visits to the famous Abbey Theatre. He was familiar with its writers and actors from his youth and subsequently became its director, forming a close friendship with Ireland's greatest living poet and playwright William Butler Yeats. They worked

Jane Blaffer Owen welcomes Dr. Walter and Ita Starkie to Poet's House, 1958.

Photograph by John Doane. John Doane Collection. Courtesy of Special Collections, University of Southern Indiana.

Professor Starkie performs for a rapt audience in Murphy Auditorium, 1958.

*Photograph by John Doane. John Doane Collection. Courtesy of Special
Collections, University of Southern Indiana.*

passionately to prevent the partition of Ireland, believing rightly that a
shared pride in their creativity and art could unite Catholics and Protes-
tants and forestall the devastating religious wars that followed the golden
years of the Abbey Theatre.[1]

Walter's Irish Catholic heritage and aspirations for peace, however, did
unite and delight some New Harmonists. Children gathered regularly after school on the lawn between Poet's House and the Rawlingses' house
to listen, spellbound, as Walter played his violin. And after supper, the few
parents who cared about theater and I would sit quietly outside while he
read from Yeats's collected plays. Little did Professor Starkie realize that

he was preparing us for the return of theater to New Harmony.[2] (Twenty-five years later, drama graduates and directors from the University of Southern Indiana and the University of Evansville, as well as Actors' Equity Association professionals, would bring workshops and performances to our community. But let's not preempt the future.)

In its long history, Poet's House has nurtured many visitors of renown—scholars, writers, poets, musicians, and artists—who have in turn nurtured New Harmony's townspeople.[3] In the fall of 1988, Poet's House welcomed the artist John Hubbard, who came at my invitation to capture New Harmony's indwelling spirit. Hubbard's eye and hand offered a reality outside the confines of the brick, wood, and limestone surfaces of New Harmony. The etchings that evolved from the charcoal drawings he made during the time he and his wife, Caryl, spent there justified my initial faith in his sensitivity and skill.[4] His rendering of the Poet's House is tender and devout, as were the Harmonist hands that built it.

May all houses that have been physically restored heed the counsel Sir George MacLeod gave me after his first visit to New Harmony in 1962: "Look upon each house as a birthing cradle for vigorous, fully awake babes. Don't put waxed dolls in them." Poet's House, in particular, remains such a place for poets, artists, and writers in need of the profound stillness that fosters creativity.

During the mid-1950s, while Lipchitz continued progress on *Notre Dame de Liesse–Descent of the Holy Spirit,* I continued to apply myself to the earthier demands of locating a site for his creation in New Harmony. I owned no property other than a few small lots with erstwhile "beat-up houses," as one of the boys who worked with me called them, and so my nose for nature led me from the center of town to its street farthest north. A mishmash of tumbledown houses and privies lined both sides of North and Main Streets, and an oil field tank yard dominated the area. The brutal pounding of hammer on steel was almost continuous, so I called that lot the "machine-gun nest." But past this war zone lay quiet meadows and lush woodlands. The Harmonists had cleared nature's wilderness to create a town, and latter-day "harmonists" would have to clear away the "wilderness" that man had made. My first lieutenants in this effort were George and Annie Rawlings.

George Rawlings was my first New Harmony gardener but became a clandestine real estate agent on my behalf. Thanks to the affection and respect with which the Rawlingses were soon and always regarded, slowly but surely parcels of land were acquired. George's father had been a shepherd in Yorkshire and had given his son some ancient horticultural secrets. George's roses were larger and redder than those of his neighbors for the simple reason that he mixed the blood of pigs with their roots.

George also knew with whom to share his garden lore and how to seal an agreement. A retired farmer by the name of Chester Wellchance owned a small vacant lot essential to a project devised by Tom Mumford, the National Society of Colonial Dames of America in the State of Indiana, and myself. The Mumford family owned a Harmonist house on Church Street that the Colonial Dames wished to move to a quieter street and restore. Another farsighted couple, Jane and Harry Wade of Indianapolis, agreed to pay for the transfer of the Mumford house, thus prompting an endless chain of philanthropy. I had also promised to give the Colonial Dames a portion of adjacent land. George Rawlings, knowing of Chester's weakness for cabbages and fresh asparagus, saw that the best of both found their way from his garden to Chester's door. We were able to purchase this lot in time to save the giant sycamore that now shades the David Lenz House; George poured truckloads of leaf mulch over the long-exposed roots (30 and 31 on town map). He was also concerned over one of the last remaining elms on land between Poet's House and the house where he and Annie lived on Granary (32 on town map). We purchased those several lots so George could fill the hollow trunk of that magnificent specimen with three sacks of concrete. Saving the sycamore and elm became his lasting legacy, for George would not live to see the Harmonist house moved in 1958 to the lot he had helped secure.

Joe McCrudden, Kenneth's manager of Indian Mound Farm, endeared himself to me when he chose to nurse George Rawlings through his last illness during the winter of 1957. Joe would lift George tenderly when he changed his sheets, just as he would lift a sick calf to freshen its straw. On the night shifts, if Joe was unable to drive down from the farm, one of Kenneth's post-hole diggers would keep vigil with Annie Rawlings. These selfless acts in the interior of our small village encouraged me to believe that the upland hill-country folk who tended Kenneth's cows and built his fences could bond lovingly and creatively with the valley people who worked with me.

The lawn between Poet's House and the Rawlings House has been the site of many gatherings throughout the years. The Rawlings greenhouse is at right. Behind the giant elm, Bradford pear trees shade Carol's Garden. The 1840 Garden House sits to the left.

Photograph by Darryl D. Jones, October 2009.

Had Joe McCrudden's selfless charity set an example for Kenneth and me? That question, sad to say, would remain unanswered throughout the 1960s and '70s, decades in which I indulged myself in the rescue of battered houses, the creation of a church accessible alike to angels and mortals, the launching of restaurants and modern dormitories, and on and on, all the while laboring under the illusion that I had been divinely ordained to reestablish Father Rapp's earthly paradise and Robert Owen's as yet unrealized "empire of peace."[5]

Little wonder that my husband decided to leave these quirky departments entirely to his wife. Unintentionally, I had diverted his attention from the goals we had pursued so passionately in the first decades of our marriage: the restoration of David Dale's Laboratory, the purchase of the Granary and Rapp-Maclure-Owen House, the enrichment of Indian Mound pastures, and the rearing of our three beloved daughters. In retrospect, I can understand Kenneth's need to distance himself from my missionary zeal and seemingly inexhaustible bank account.

His question—"Jane, have you married Robert Owen or me?"—was more legitimate than humorous. My inability to provide an honest answer to that question sent him not to the nearest bar but to the yearling sales of purebred harness horses in Lexington. Never a gambler, he employed his keen eye and scientific mind to size up future champions for breeding, and he began buying them. He became part owner of a horse farm in Versailles, Kentucky, to breed and train trotters and pacers. His next breeding farm was farther away, close to Harrisburg, Pennsylvania. When the house there was being decorated, I brought some antiques and contemporary art from shops along Church and Main Streets to add to it. Kenneth was surprised at their quality. I answered, "If you'd spend more time in New Harmony, you would see for yourself."

His breeding farm in Pennsylvania had a private training track and a large stone barn, which he proceeded to restore, to my sorrow. Our New Harmony Granary was still a storehouse for derelict farm equipment and an incestuous breeding ground for stray cats, quite a contrast to Kenneth's immaculate New Oxford stables. Pricey, well-groomed stallions waited in their stalls to mate with eligible fillies, whose royal lineages were as carefully researched as those of their prospective bridegrooms. Kenneth's good horse sense and sportsmanship earned him a place in the Harness Racing Hall of Fame in 1987. I should have been the first to ap-

Kenneth Dale Owen with Noble Victory, the 1964 Two-Year-Old
Trotter of the Year, who was trained and driven by Stanley Dancer.
Blaffer-Owen family photograph.

plaud his induction but, sad to say, was not. Still unaware of my responsibility for the reversal of Kenneth's priorities, I hurried headlong into my
projects, increasing my emotional and financial investment in a place I
thought my husband had deserted.

Laetare! Rejoice!

—The incipit of the introit for the Fourth Sunday
of Lent, "Mothering Sunday"

CHAPTER 16

Violets Down the Lane

My month with Janie almost over in March 1957, I booked a return flight to Houston. Taking leave of my daughters, particularly of Janie in New York, always tugged at my heart. The French proverb *Partir c'est mourir un peu* (to leave is to die a bit) spoke to my condition but did little to improve it. Solace, once again, came from Reverend Mother Ruth. Knowing that I faced another separation, she had asked Sister Élise, a teacher at St. Hilda's and a tutor "on loan" for Janie, to give me a verse from an old English book of carols to read on the plane. It began: "She who goes amothering shall find violets down the lane." I hummed this comforting line in the taxi to LaGuardia.

My spirits were lifted again on the plane when I recognized a friend seated across the aisle from me: Jean "John" de Menil, an enormously charming and cultivated Franco-American. He and his brilliant, trail-blazing wife, Dominique, were both aware that the casting of the Lipchitz statue intended for New Harmony was still landless and homeless. Disregarding the Madonna's present poverty, Jean foresaw a turn of her fortunes

145

and suggested that Lipchitz's Lady would one day require an architect and a dwelling worthy of her status.

Skilled in the art of persuasion and with a voice like Charles Boyer, Jean launched again into high praise of Philip Johnson, the architect who had built his Houston house. The home would sustain five de Menil children and, as their parents became increasingly involved in the cultural life of their adopted city over the next decades, would also eventually welcome artists of distinction and heads of state, among them His Holiness the Dalai Lama and former president Jimmy Carter.

The single-story, boxlike but well-tailored house still lies half hidden from the street and gives no hint of the old and new art treasures behind its brick walls. This understated Johnson house, sad to say, was not the norm in an affluent neighborhood conspicuous for its *m'as tu vu* (have-you-seen-me) houses.

I could identify with this restrained approach to domestic architecture, for I had grown up in a house almost completely covered with fig ivy. A passerby peering through its penetrable privet hedges might well have been disappointed and walked quickly on. By night the warm glow of candlelight from tall downstairs windows might have aroused a sense of wonder in the onlooker but surely not envy. Nor would he or she have hazarded a guess at the market value of such a house. My wise parents had taught me to look for interior riches, whether of people or of houses.

Such remembrances prepared me for Jean de Menil's evocation of Philip Johnson's many gifts. "His background is as much in art history as in architecture," he told me. "You would find Philip very sensitive to your most unexpressed wishes. I would go so far as to call him clairvoyant. He'll be returning to Houston soon for the AFA convention." The upcoming American Federation of Arts convention, which I also would be attending in April, was of great interest to art patrons.

On the freeway home from the airport, my thoughts outraced the speeding cars. They flew back in time to my vow to build an altar in my adopted town and forward to the present, where my vow, though unfulfilled, stood at a threshold.

John Bunyan's *Pilgrim's Progress* bequeaths us a classic prescription for jump-starting creativity. He said that the impulse for writing that immortal book came from his heart; from there it traveled to his mind, and "thence into [his] fingers trickled." Fingers, hands, and skills other than mine were required, and because of that fateful flight with Jean de Menil, they were drawing closer.

My taxi turned onto the feeder lane that would connect with our drive- way, the last leg of my journey home. I expected a hushed house, for it was past Carol and Annie's bedtime, and Kenneth was away at his horse sta- bles. Carol, however, had heard the crunch of car wheels on the driveway and was awaiting my arrival outside the front door in her scanty pajamas. She threw herself into my arms, and I soon held her head in my hands. I tilted it away for a closer, longer look into the most jewel-like eyes I had ever seen. I had once called them "twin amethysts," but from that night onward, they would always be "violets down the lane."

Three slender things that best support the world:
the slender stream of milk from the cow's dug into the pail;
the slender blade of green corn upon the ground;
the slender thread over the hand of a skilled woman.

—*The Triads of Ireland*

CHAPTER 17

Enter Philip Johnson

n November 1956, the de Menils had asked me to accompany them to the University of St. Thomas for the presentation of Philip Johnson's plans for additions to Houston's fledgling Catholic university.[1] I had eagerly accepted their invitation in order to make my own assessment of the renowned architect they both admired so fervently. I wondered if out of airy nothingness Philip Johnson could extract a habitation for my homeless advocate for religious tolerance, *Descent of the Holy Spirit*. My heart was beating fast as I took my front-row seat between Jean and Dominique.

Pencil thin, wearing a close-fitting dark suit, Johnson had approached the lectern with rapid strides and just as quickly drew back from it to address his audience informally. I could now observe the essential lines of his expressive face; they were as if incised on metal rather than as drawn on paper or canvas. Energy sprang from him, as when a tightly coiled wire is suddenly released. The dos and don'ts of his architectural credo followed in rapid succession with precision and wit.

One commandment, however, I should have taken with a large measure of salt: "When a client asks me how much per square foot a building or a house will cost, I have no answer to that question. I should either simply roll up my sleeves and build a work of art that pleases me or else look for a client who cares more about beauty than about concrete and dollars." A decade later I learned that aesthetic concerns, sound engineering, and economic sanity could coexist as equal partners and not as unrelated entities.

On that evening of new possibilities, I had resonated more closely with Johnson's deep commitment to art, quality of material, and right proportions than with his reference to cost per square foot. It was exhilarating to discover an architect who appeared capable of understanding my unorthodox hopes for an altar that was not an altar and a church that was not a church. This Houston visit, primarily for the St. Thomas presentation, however, was not conducive to sharing my inward thoughts.

My hopes resumed in March 1957, when Jean de Menil informed me on the flight from New York to Houston that Philip Johnson would attend the upcoming American Federation of Arts convention in early April.[2] My longtime friend Preston Bolton, one of the local committee chairmen for the AFA and a Houston architect working with Johnson, invited me to come along when he went to pick up Philip at Hobby Airport for the first evening's activities—a cocktail reception and buffet dinner in the Emerald Room at the Shamrock Hilton before visiting the Museum of Fine Arts' exhibit "The Three Brothers," featuring the work of Marcel Duchamp, Jacques Villon, and Raymond Duchamp-Villon.

The next day, Thursday, April 4, Philip Johnson introduced the notable art critic Meyer Schapiro, who gave the keynote address, "The Place of Painting in Contemporary Culture." During a break, I made my way forward to where Johnson was seated with the de Menils. Halfway there, I stood still, one foot on terra incognita, the other on familiar, safe land. How could I present my obsession—for an altar within a walled but roofless church—to an urbane, successful architect without appearing naked to myself and totally vulnerable, even ridiculous, in the eyes of a man I admired but hardly knew?

I had underestimated Philip's ability to intuit what others were thinking and needing. Sensing my hesitation, he rose from his seat, took my

Jane Blaffer Owen, Bernard J. and Becky Reis in the audience at
the American Federation of Arts convention held at the
Shamrock Hotel (*second from left to right*).

*Photograph by Henri Cartier-Bresson, April 1957. Gelatin silver print,
9 1/4 × 13 7/8 in. (23.5 × 35.2 cm). The Menil Collection,
Houston. Henri Cartier-Bresson/Magnum Photos.*

arm, and led me from the green glare of the Shamrock Room to the shelter
of an alcove within the Cattleman's Club, a quiet place that served to ne-
gate the logo placed above the bar: "Rattle, rattle, here come the cattle."[3]

My inhibitions dissolved and a torrent of long-considered thoughts tum-
bled out. My attentive listener caught them skillfully and gave them form
and substance. Although he possessed a vast knowledge of art and architectural history, he addressed me without a touch of the schoolmaster.

"What do you know about Norwegian stave churches?"

"Nothing whatsoever."

"They date from the tenth century, when Norway was Christianized, and
were wonderfully shingled outside and timbered within. Some reminders
of pagan worship remained. Statues of Christ and His mother replaced

Philip Johnson and James Thrall Soby at the American Federation of
Arts convention held at the Shamrock Hotel.

Photograph by Henri Cartier-Bresson, April 1957. Gelatin silver print.
9 1/4 × 13 1/2 in. (23.5 × 34.3 cm).
The Menil Collection, Houston.
Henri Cartier-Bresson/Magnum Photos.

those of Odin and Thor for the most part, but wisely, I think, those erstwhile Viking raiders didn't altogether banish carvings of dragonheads on
the rooftops. Otherwise, an infidel like me would never have entered."

Having clarified his position as a non-Christian, he paused long
enough to gauge my reaction. I did not wince, and he continued: "What if
we follow a precedent from these old Norsemen and place a shingled dome
over the altar you want?"

His clairvoyance took my breath away, for I had not yet described my
efforts to find sculptures of pre-Christian goddesses of spring and rebirth
and their successor, the Virgin Mary. By drawing my attention to a place
of Christian worship retaining pagan elements, he had reinforced my perspective, however unwittingly. Philip Johnson had won me as a client.

"Yes, of course, we'll borrow from the old Norse churches and fish awhile in their waters. But how soon can I expect architectural prints?"

My impatience and my confidence could best be expressed by these lines from T. S. Eliot:

Quick now, here, now always—
A condition of complete simplicity
(Costing not less than everything)
And all shall be well and
All manner of thing shall be well.[4]

My faith in Philip Johnson's ability to interpret my Abrahamic imperative was shattered following our conversation in the Cattleman's Club. After a week of eager waiting, I found the drawings submitted from the Johnson offices profoundly disappointing. Philip's proposal for a canopy lacked the warmth and buoyancy of a Norwegian stave church. It stood heavy-footed, unredeemed by a single gracious, curving line. "The earth is round," I muttered angrily to myself, "and people don't worship gods, goddesses, or God with their elbows. And, as for the stone plinths which support your canopy, they look like Egyptian coffins!" End of soliloquy and start of a cooling-off period.

"Philip," I began a few days after my disappointment, "you have designed a charming, accordion-pleated dome for the nuclear power plant you have been commissioned to build for Israel. Send your drawings there because they are entirely unsuitable for New Harmony."

With unaccustomed humility he answered, "What do you propose that I do?"

"I suggest you take a look at the lay of the land in southern Indiana. It is not a desert."

To his credit, and in the interest of an as-yet-unrealized Roofless Church, Philip did not disconnect the telephone but agreed to meet me in New Harmony a few days before Easter.[5] Shortly after Philip's arrival at my Harmonist house No. V, I recommended a survey of my husband's land with the Scots manager for Indian Mound Farm. Joe McCrudden was a big-boned, big-hearted man with a thick lock of white hair that swept halfway across his forehead. He swung his sizable frame from left to right when he walked, a gait he had doubtless acquired from tending my husband's purebred, white-faced Herefords. Joe endeared himself in many ways to both man and beast. Telluric Joe McCrudden would introduce my guest to the hinterland of the southwest corner of Indiana.

The bed of Joe's farm truck was filled with fragrant hay; Philip and I clambered in with laughter and high hopes, both of us believing that our tour would influence a new and appropriate shape for a church canopy. Once past Maple Hill Cemetery, the road began to rise (see area map). Beyond wooded hills, it brought us to freshly tilled and gently rolling fields, unlike the flat plains of Illinois across the Wabash. Kenneth's farmlands were curving, feminine, and soft.

Philip left me with his assurance that by the time I rejoined Janie in New York he would have plans for a new canopy. I had not hoped in vain for a revision of Philip's original concept for the Roofless Church (33 on town map). The drawings he presented to Lipchitz and me in Janie's apartment proved he had learned Mother Nature's lessons well. Sharp, angular openings were replaced with round arches; their limestone supports became oval and less like coffins. Reaching heavenward fifty feet, the canopy itself was no longer segmented but a seamless whole. It billowed like the spinnaker of a sailboat.

Lipchitz spoke first, but softly, as though we were already in a cloistered space. "Why, Philip, you are building a haystack." With one of his rare smiles, Lipchitz reached over to my daughter's desk, removed an inkwell, and placed it at the center of Philip's design. "Here, at last, madame, is a house for my *Vierge de Liesse* and your *Descent of the Holy Spirit*"[6] (34 on town map).

We three—architect, sculptor, and client—shared a moment of intense joy. The ascent had been difficult to the plateau, where we now stood in perfect accord. Even so, I had other concerns, for instance, the unacceptable south entrance in the surrounding walls.

"Philip, your entrance is simply beautiful. The recessed wood panels on either side echo your taste for Japanese architecture. But should this opening be as tall as the twelve-foot enclosure wall? Human beings will be entering, not giraffes."

He accepted my critique with grace. Taking a pen from his pocket, he reduced the giraffe door down to human scale.

Philip Johnson had the gift of accepting input from others. He readily accepted the challenge posed later by my close friend Millie Johnstone, an accomplished needleworker, when she saw the plans and asked him able in the late 1950s; a brilliant engineer in Johnson's office, unaided by computer science, had eventually resolved their configuration with precision and, I believe, considerable passion.

I quickly forwarded these printed and persuasive harbingers of a new era for New Harmony to the trustees who held the purse strings of the Robert Lee Blaffer Trust. My esteemed advisors were not architects, and only one, Don Blair in New Harmony, was an engineer, but none had reason to question the soundness of Philip Johnson's plans. His architectural reputation rivaled that of his mentor Mies van der Rohe, and Johnson was the darling of New York's prestigious Museum of Modern Art (MoMA). He had, in fact, recently built the brick walls of the Modern's Abby Aldrich Rockefeller Sculpture Garden, their design like those for the walls I was submitting to my trustees. We had no cause for concern, other than the question of dates for construction.

Given my large appetite for rituals and festivals and the rites of spring, I hoped that a cornerstone could be dedicated on May 1, 1959. The contractor reviewed the plans for the Roofless Church and assured me that the northeast corner of an emerging foundation would be far enough along. Brimming with joy, I alerted family members to reserve that date, and in frequent dialogue with Helen Duprey Bullock in Washington and Sister Élise of St. Hilda's in New York, plans for the blessing and fiesta were set in motion and invitations extended to all residents of New Harmony.

And did the Countenance Divine
Shine forth upon our clouded hills?
And was Jerusalem builded here
Among these dark Satanic Mills?

—William Blake, "Jerusalem"

CHAPTER 18

Cornerstone Dedication

T he verse from the prophet Micah
that had captured my imagination would be inscribed under my father's
name on the cornerstone of the Roofless Church, as it exemplified
Lee Blaffer's belief in the fulfillment of dreams if the dreamer worked
hard enough and with constant integrity. Back in 1822, Father Rapp
had chosen for the pediment over the entrance door of his brick cruciform church "Unto thee shall come the golden rose," from chapter 4,
verse 8 of Micah.

My own King James Bible reads "first dominion" instead of "golden
rose":

> And thou, a tower of the flock,
> The stronghold of the daughter of Zion
> Unto thee shall it come the first dominion.

Neither is there any mention of the golden rose in other translations of
the Bible that I had consulted, from Roman Catholic to contemporary

Lutheran. I was puzzled for many years, and no one I knew could provide a clue.

One day in the late 1940s, I received a letter from an old gentleman in Maine who wished to sell some articles that had descended to him from Harmonist relatives at Economy, Pennsylvania. He had heard that people were beginning to care about New Harmony on the Wabash, and he hoped I would be interested. Indeed I was, for among the objects, he listed a nineteenth-century German Bible.

The Bible arrived in an old shoebox, not wrapped neatly in tissue paper but within two oversize silk handkerchiefs, one imprinted with "George Rapp," the other with the name of his adopted son, "Frederick Rapp." The other treasures—silver coin spoons with long handles and a coiled-straw circular bowl, called a dough basket—arrived in a larger box. I made haste to locate the verses from Micah and someone to translate the German into English:

> And thou, Tower of Eden, a stronghold of
> the daughter of Zion
> Your golden rose will come, the former
> dominion,
> The kingdom of the daughter of Jerusalem.

I was particularly grateful to have a Bible with Father Rapp's version of the golden rose, which I learned came exclusively from an early Martin Luther translation. For Father Rapp, the golden rose of the millennium was also an emblem of quality for goods manufactured in his three separate but similarly inspired colonies. Pieces of woven cloth from a Harmonist loom, whether silk or linen, that did not meet Father Rapp's high standards would not be stamped with his chosen imprint. A pound of butter, a sack of potatoes, or a case of "high wine"—the Harmonist euphemism for whiskey on its way to New Orleans—would bring better prices if they were stamped with the golden rose of quality.

Perhaps any close-knit group intent on perfection leaves some of its energy behind. The artifacts with genuine Harmonist fingerprints reinvigorated me. The discovery of the original passage from a Rappite's own, well-worn German Bible gave me the nod I needed to continue my efforts in New Harmony. It also provided me with an honorable retreat from the maze of historical research, for which I was not trained. I have a reverence for scholarship and for those who wear its gown with humility, but buried

Above. Blessing the cornerstone of the Roofless Church, 1959.
Photograph by John Doane. Robert Lee Blaffer Trust Archive.
Courtesy of the Robert Lee Blaffer Foundation.

Facing. My brother, John, and I acknowledge the placement
of the plaque honoring our father, May 1, 1959.
Photograph by John Doane. Robert Lee Blaffer Trust Archive.
Courtesy of the Robert Lee Blaffer Foundation.

I was, therefore, not surprised that John had canceled a business trip to Washington in order to stand beside me. Friends and neighbors gathered with us to witness the placing of the plaque onto the northeast corner of an emerging limestone foundation, as Father Lloyd blessed the cornerstone. The brief ceremony was a promise, not a fulfillment, like an engagement before the full-scale wedding; the dedication of the Roofless Church would be May 1 of the following year.

John felt the moment as intensely as I did, but our private thoughts dif-
fered. I was thinking of Lipchitz's Madonna, her arms extended to people
of different faiths and beliefs, and of her future canopy, which could alternately represent a full-blown rose for Christians and Jews, a lotus for Hin-
dus and Buddhists, a rounded mosque-like dome for Muslims, or simply
an architectural attraction for the nonreligious or "infidel," as its architect
had once referred to himself.

My brother was thinking of our grandfather John A. Blaffer, who had
fought with Lee's Army of Northern Virginia.[4] After the Civil War, he returned barefoot to New Orleans to start his brick factory, begin a family,
and name his second son, our father, for his beloved commander.

Father Lloyd had no sooner turned over the building site to the tender
mercies of our Creator than John leaned forward to me, saying with considerable passion, "Thank God the Blaffer name is on Northern territory."
While my brother's remark was not surprising from a man never at ease
with piety, it was sincere and added missing directions to my compass for
New Harmony. If the Roofless Church sought common ground with different religions, pointing east and west, New Harmony's weathervane
should also pivot north and south to honor the reunion of Confederate
and Union soldiers.

Facing top.
Trustees of the Robert Lee Blaffer Trust: Philip Johnson, architect;
Helen Duprey Bullock, National Trust for Historic Preservation;
Sister Élise, CHS (aka Zoe Euverard); Don Blair, chairman;
and Ora V. Howton, treasurer/secretary, 1959.
Photograph by John Doane. Courtesy Working Men's
Institute Archives, New Harmony.

Facing bottom.
Annie Rawlings and Philip Johnson in her house after the
cornerstone dedication and festivities, May 1, 1959.
Photograph by Don Blair. Robert Lee Blaffer Trust Archive.
Courtesy of the Robert Lee Blaffer Foundation.

Who had persuaded me that God preferred four walls
and a roof to wide-open spaces?

—Barbara Brown Taylor, *An Altar in the World:*
A Geography of Faith

CHAPTER 19

May Day Dedication of the Roofless Church and Barrett-Gate House

O n the northeast corner of Main and North Streets, across from the freshly blessed cornerstone, stood a dilapidated barn and a rusty, retired gas pump. Luckily, the lot and barn belonged to close friends Mildred and Dorothy Donald, who once lived nearby. I never see their former home without remembering their story of the days preceding the birth of their brother. "Our parents never told us how babies came into the world," they half whispered to me. "So by way of explanation, they placed stork feathers on every windowsill the day that our brother was born."

These delicious spinster sisters, retired teachers, quickly understood my reasons for wishing to acquire their property and wanted me to have it for a token sum. I now would have a strategic location for conjoined houses that Carl and Laura Barrett had offered me: an early Harmonist two-story log house with a mid-nineteenth-century addition attached to its entire east wall. The relocation was in line with a plan Tom Mumford and I had conceived in the late 1940s. Aware that we lacked resources to restore every vintage house in the village, we decided to concentrate our efforts on North and Granary Streets, saving donated houses through relocation there when we could. Tish and Tom Mumford had already given their Church Street Harmonist house to the Colonial Dames.

Now genuine Harmonist houses would orbit around the central planet of the Roofless Church, an enclosure where all people—of any denomination, any religion, or none—would be welcome. Or would the Church be more like baker's yeast, an active, essential ingredient in the heavy dough of our humanity? Regardless of how the future would answer the question, construction progressed on the burgeoning Church.

Practical matters across the street at the newly acquired lot required immediate attention. I asked Joe McCrudden for a bulldozer and farm crew to remove the sagging barn and level the land. I again sought advice from Don Blair, the engineer who had supervised the construction of the bridge built in 1930, connecting us with Illinois.[1] He had fallen in love with both New Harmony and a winsome New Harmony girl, his future wife, Bettie Frances Hooks. Don was an enormous help in the relocation of the glued-together houses—a lengthy process, for they had to be moved separately. No one seemed to mind that power lines would be down during the day, interrupting cake and bread baking. In fact, a holiday spirit took hold. People gathered on sidewalks half a block east of the only traffic light on Church Street and one block north on Main to cheer the houses on wheels as they rolled past.

"History is on the move!" someone shouted.

I shouted back, "And we'll be making history too!"

Once he had reunited the houses on the Donald sisters' erstwhile lot, Don Blair proved to be an inventive ad hoc architect. He designed the two-story bay window in the rear of the joined houses to form a passageway between them and converted a dry sink into a wet one between the kitchen and dining areas of the nineteenth-century house.

I am responsible for the choice of French tiles on the floor of the addition to the original log structure, as I wanted a reminder of childhood summers in France. The floors in the adjoining Harmonist log house did not require replacing: their wide poplar boards responded gratefully to gentle sanding. A carpenter, whom we called "T" because of his tall and thin frame, arrived out of nowhere to make the kitchen cabinets and the paneling around the fireplace.

Oval limestone supports for the canopy were lowered into position by crane; walls rise around the framed classical balcony in the distance.

Photograph by Don Blair, June 29, 1959. Robert Lee Blaffer Trust Archive. Courtesy of the Robert Lee Blaffer Foundation.

The Barrett House being moved to its new location across from the Lipchitz gate, 1959.

Photograph by Don Blair. Robert Lee Blaffer Trust Archive. Courtesy of the Robert Lee Blaffer Foundation.

Throughout my endeavors, the right people arrived when they were needed, bolstering my belief in a master plan that exceeds what any of us might envision for New Harmony. When I came as a bride, three elderly ladies, Mary Fauntleroy, Ena Long, and Laura Corbin Monical, gave me motherly guidance and a lasting legacy. Encouraged by their example, other preservers followed them: the Mumfords, the Elliotts, the Blairs, the Fords, the Stallingses, the Tanners, the Donalds, the Glumps, the Couches, the Menkes, Linda Sue Alsop, and others. These, my earliest role models and co-believers in the worth of New Harmony, gave freely of their time and their various gifts.

I do not regard them or myself, however, as entirely autonomous individuals. I continue to believe now, as then, that we are actors in a play written by an omniscient Playwright who prefers to remain anonymous but whose identity I suspect. We sometimes flub or forget our lines. We debate, often hotly, who is hero or villain. But however inadequate our performances, we follow willy-nilly the script and keep together as an actors' company. Those earlier years were Act I of a play I like to call *A New Harmony in the World or Chaos*. Other acts shall follow, other voices heard.

The Barrett-Gate House would itself have a central role for May 1, 1960, the date chosen for the dedication of the Roofless Church (36 on town map). Dr. Pitney Van Dusen, a brilliant orator and self-styled "ecumaniac," then president of Union Theological Seminary in New York, had accepted my invitation to preside over the occasion and to lead representatives of major religions through the ceremonial gates. He and Mrs. Van Dusen would be the first to stay in the newly restored Barrett-Gate House. Elizabeth Van Dusen was responsible for initiating religious drama at Union.

Facing top.
A bay window joins the two houses
on the north side.
Photograph by Darryl D. Jones, 2013.

Facing bottom.
An early Harmonist log structure is the
southwest side of Barrett-Gate House.
Photograph by Darryl D. Jones, 2013.

Descent of the Holy Spirit awaiting the arrival of geraniums for the planter beneath it, spring 1960.

Photograph by Don Blair. Robert Lee Blaffer Trust Archive. Courtesy of the Robert Lee Blaffer Foundation.

Ribs of the emerging canopy are visible beneath the polyurethane that provided a shelter not only for workers but also for a grieving architect.

Photograph by Don Blair, March 1960. Robert Lee Blaffer Trust Archive. Courtesy of the Robert Lee Blaffer Foundation.

I asked my daughter Carol, then fifteen, to wait for the arrival of the Van Dusens and to show them to their rooms on the second floor, which had been vacated only a few hours before by plasterers and painters and where Carol had used her hairdryer to dry still-damp walls.

Philip Johnson had arrived earlier, depositing his narrow black suitcase in the downstairs bachelor's room. He soon joined Annie Rawlings in planting red and white geraniums under the canopy of the Roofless Church and in the flowerbeds that circled Lipchitz's sculpture, where Philip lost his broad horn-rimmed eyeglasses among the flowers.

This was not Philip's first experience with our geraniums. A few months earlier, in late March if I recall correctly, he telephoned to tell me of his father's death. He began in a voice that lacked its customary authority: "We were not a church-going family. There was not a word spoken over Father's grave, much less a blessing."

Sensing his sadness, I offered to arrange a memorial service in the unfinished church under its skeleton canopy, which was draped with a polyethylene shroud, enabling construction to continue during the winter. Greenhouse geraniums would temporarily fill the circle around the Madonna, and St. Stephen's Episcopal priest Father Markey would read from the Book of Common Prayer. Philip readily accepted my offer and took the next flight out of Cleveland for Evansville, the nearest airport to New Harmony. Late that evening, Annie Rawlings, Don Blair, Father Markey, and I led a travel-weary, emotionally drained architect into a coal-black space, toward a wreath of snow-white geraniums and candles that sputtered in the north wind.

If prayers for the soul of Homer Johnson brought comfort and closure to his son that cold winter's night, then the morning of May 1 of the same year brought excitement and hope to the architect, members of my family, several hundred townspeople, and many guests.

On that chilly May Day, Dr. Van Dusen—fortunately wearing his red woolen robe from the University of Edinburgh—led representatives from area churches, both Protestant and Roman Catholic, as well as two Evansville rabbis, one from the Washington Avenue Temple and the other from Temple Adath Israel, into the church. Leaders from Muslim, Buddhist, and Hindu faiths, as well as from Greek and Russian Orthodox churches, have since visited or led services in our enclosure, but in my regrettable ignorance of such leaders in 1960, they did not celebrate with us that May Day.

The *Evansville Courier* reported that about fifteen hundred people
attended the May 1 dedication of the Roofless Church.

Photograph by Bill Adkins, the Evansville Courier.
Courtesy Evansville Courier & Press Archive.

    Dr. Van Dusen will always be remembered gratefully for his role in the
worldwide ecumenical movement and for his writings on the Holy Spirit,
which for him was the undervalued member of the Trinity. At Mrs. Eliza-
beth Van Dusen's suggestion and through the generosity of Lawrence
Thurman—who was the curator of the Harmonist museum in Economy,
Pennsylvania—two Harmonist "night bugles" were borrowed from Old
Economy Village. With these, two competent trumpeters, Tom Lewis and
Jerry Muncie, from the Evansville Philharmonic Orchestra, announced

the opening of ceremonies. The horns sounded a clarion call, proclaiming the dawn of a new era for New Harmony and also for my country, for I remembered Tom Watson Sr.'s prophecy that whatever happens in middle America can be a centrifugal and radiating force, affecting for ill or for good every state in the Union. Representatives from France, M. Pierre Pelen, counselor of the French embassy, and Great Britain, Alexander G. Gilchrist, consul general in Chicago, joined our celebration.

Lunch for out-of-town dignitaries and guests was provided by local ladies under a large circular tent on the Poet's House lawn. The earthy vanilla canvas tent was edged with bands of strawberry and chocolate, like Neapolitan ice cream. The ladies, with my ten-year-old daughter Annie assisting, also made rounds of freshly baked Serbian peasant bread that were blessed by Dr. Van Dusen as our grace before the meal and distributed to all in fellowship and friendship.

That day of dedication will not be remembered solely for Dr. Van Dusen's stirring address, his outreach to different denominations, or home-cooked meals served under a carousel tent. I shall forever hear sounds coming from a calliope and see Alexander Gilchrist, Her British Majesty's exuberant envoy to our celebration, perched on top of the wagon at the keyboard of an ancient, still-functioning instrument.

Some months before, I had been the guest of honor at a small luncheon at the British embassy in Washington, D.C. The expressionless face and gigantic proportions of the butler who admitted me and the endless high stairways and corridors did not intimidate me for long. The immensely popular Ambassador Harold Caccia welcomed me warmly, as did Lady Anne Catherine Caccia. He expressed a genuine interest in New Harmony's Welsh, English, and Scottish forebears and gave an affirmative response to my request for a British envoy at the dedication ceremonies of May 1. Lord Caccia selected an ideal representative for our dedication day. Alexander Gilchrist was from old Lanark in Scotland, the town adjacent to Robert Owen's New Lanark. I had not, however, expected Gilchrist to conspire with my husband.

Aware of my plans for an interdenominational service and determined that the aura of sanctity emanating from North Street would not invade the whole of New Harmony, Kenneth Owen had located a nineteenth-century calliope and wanted its musician to circumnavigate the town. Upon learning of our Scottish guest's passion for music, either lowbrow or

highbrow, Kenneth turned the calliope over to Gilchrist. I am still squash-
ing rumors that I was infuriated by Kenneth's stunt and that it led us to
the verge of divorce. On the contrary, Kenneth's humor and penchant for
practical jokes balanced out the day.

The evening service of that memorable occasion belonged to Father
Tod Ewald, OSL, of Holy Innocents Episcopal Church and a chaplain at
San Quentin State Prison in the San Francisco Bay area. I had read of his
successful rehabilitation of inmates after their release from prison and re-
entry into the greater world. He and his wife, Mary, having no children of
their own, took into their home prisoners who were willing to learn about
the care and growth of vegetables and flowers. Through gardening and
under the watchful eye of the Ewalds, most of these former prisoners
learned how to kneel, first on the good earth and ultimately in church.
Most of them found self-supporting jobs.

I had invited Father Ewald to be a co-celebrant with Dr. Van Dusen, in
the hope that his healing ministry to prisoners would extend to those of
us who were not technically behind bars but, nonetheless, lived behind
the psychological walls that we build between others and ourselves. We
create our own prisons, more often than not. Carl Jung tells us that no
prison confines more than the one we don't know we are in.

I can still see Father Ewald standing before the arms of the Lipchitz
Madonna and wearing the bright blue cassock of the Order of St. Luke the
Physician. Only a few of those who had attended the morning celebration
came that evening for vespers and compline. Among them, however, were
Philip Johnson and Kenneth. Like Nicodemus of the New Testament (St.
John 3:2, 9), they had slipped in under cover of night, possibly seeking answers to difficult questions. If Nicodemus had failed to understand Jesus's
reference to a second birth and left asking, "How can these things be?"
then I had no reason to hope that either Kenneth or Philip would receive
answers from the apostle of St. Luke.

But they had bothered to come, each with a votive candle, and I was
immensely grateful for the presence of two indispensable supports—my
husband, ballast to my boat, and my architect, wind to my sails.

The Roofless Church continues its mission of being both an inclusive sacred space for religious services and a welcoming contemplative space for all peoples.

Photograph by Nancy Mangum McCaslin, 2014.

But history . . . is not a series of accidents; it has a special structure in each of its periods, and it has predominant trends and natural tendencies against which individual acts are of no avail. On this character of history all historical understanding and all adequate and meaningful historical action is based. Without such a structural necessity, history could not be interpreted at all, and no prophetic message would ever have been possible.

—Paul Tillich, "Storms of Our Times," in *The Protestant Era*

CHAPTER 20

Tillich Visits Houston

With the dedication of the Roof-less Church behind me and the dedication of Lipchitz's golden gate a year ahead of me, I could resume my efforts to engage Paul Tillich in the fortunes of New Harmony. Tillich, now at Harvard, had been unable to accept my invitation to preside at the dedication of the church because of his trip to Japan.[1]

I owe the launching of Paul Tillich's journey to New Harmony to my late father's close ties with Rice University. As a trustee of Rice Institute, which became Houston's first university, my father had befriended its president. Our family home on Sunset Boulevard was directly across from Rice. As a young child, I regarded the long, oak-shaded entrance avenue to the campus as a pathway for my doll carriage. As I grew older and bolder, it became a bridge to the biology building, for outside were chicken-wire cages filled to their ceilings with frogs destined for vivisection. None exist for public view on the campus today.

My father was a farsighted trustee of this now-renowned university. While his energies were primarily focused on helping direct oil revenues toward an endowment, he found time to consult with Tony Martino, Rice's head gardener. During Daddy's lifetime there were always hedges of Cape jasmine in the environs of Lovett Hall (architect Ralph Adam Cram's first non-Gothic public building), named for the university's first president, imported from Princeton: Edgar Odell Lovett. This distinguished gentleman and astronomer, wearing a bowler hat with ebony cane in hand, walked seven or more blocks between his office in Lovett Hall and his modest apartment at the Plaza Hotel. Declining my father's offer to provide him with a car and chauffeur, Dr. Lovett graciously replied, "Thank you very much, Lee, but walking is good and necessary exercise."

Family friendships with presidents of Rice continued long after Dr. Lovett's retirement, particularly with William Houston. Although for health reasons he was no longer an active president in 1961, Dr. Houston had nonetheless arranged for Paul Tillich to lecture at Rice the first week of April of that year for Religious Emphasis Week.[2]

News of this important event flashed green lights in my head. The *kairos,* or vertical dimension of time, had, for me, intersected with the horizontal lines of *chronos,* the here and now, actualizing the possible. Ever since reading passages of Tillich's writings that addressed the root causes of war and megalomania, I had wondered how to expose his wisdom to a wider-than-academic audience. The following words, for instance, should not burn only in a few educated hearts:

> He who tries to be without authority
> Tries to be like God who alone
> Is by Himself and like everyone
> Who tries to be like God
> He is thrown down to self-destruction
> Be it a single human being
> Be it a nation, be it a period
> of history like our own.[3]

I envisioned this statement carved deeply in granite and anchored in my beloved New Harmony, a town with a long history of peace. Suddenly, I knew that the time had come to unite aspiration and dream. I was, therefore, not surprised when Dr. Houston responded favorably to my telephoned invitation.

"Yes, Jane, I'll be happy to bring Dr. Tillich to tea at your house."[4]

Carol was at boarding school and Janie at college, but Kenneth would join us, including a few faculty members from Rice who accompanied Dr. Tillich and Dr. Houston. I had covered a round table with an antique embroidered cloth that had belonged to my mother and centered a bowl of fully opened yellow roses and a single candle upon it. Ten-year-old Annie's presence, together with the almond and citrus galette I had prepared that morning, placed us all in a blithesome mood and opened a way for me to reveal my idea.

Dr. Tillich listened attentively as I described my plan for a garden called Tillich Park that would contain quotations from his works. I watched anxiously for signs of approval, because he looked surprised at first. I did not wait long. Slowly a broad, boyish smile lightened his serious face. Downplaying the honor I wished to bestow, he exclaimed with unconcealed pleasure, "No one has ever named a park for me, Mrs. Owen!"

Two horrific wars and exile had not diminished his joie de vivre or his appetite for the new. My own spontaneous response was to take a rose from the tea table and give it to my guest. He accepted it, bowed his head in a wordless ritual of acceptance, and with laughter thrust it into the lapel of his gray raincoat. With body language more eloquent than his spoken words, he walked out the front door with Dr. Houston as though suspended by helium-filled balloons.

Ye fearful saints, fresh courage take,
The clouds ye so much dread
Are big with mercy, and shall break
In blessings on your head.

—William Cowper, *Olney Hymns,* "Light Shining Out of Darkness"

CHAPTER 21

MacLeod's Dedication of the Lipchitz Gate

On my arrival at the Stanhope in New York to visit Janie in mid-1958, Lipchitz telephoned with exciting news; he had completed the model for the gate.[1]

"When will you and Philip come to my studio?"

"Immediately, that is, when Philip is available and can drive me over."

By the late 1950s, Philip Johnson's architectural reputation had grown considerably, and his new offices on top of the Seagram Building teemed with activity. Philip rescheduled appointments, so he and I were soon en route to Hastings-on-Hudson like unleashed hounds on the scent of fresh game. Art lovers are an insatiable breed.

Lipchitz opened the door of his light-filled, high-ceilinged new studio, smiling more broadly than I had ever seen him do, grateful for the realization of his costly dream. Placing the small sculpture in our hands, he broke into French as a more immediate outlet for his enthusiasm: *"Voilà votre porte de cérémonie. Ça va?"* ("Here is your ceremonial gate. It's okay?")

The concept amazed Philip and me. Although roughly cast, the model was charged with genius. When closed, the vertical support of the gates' two leaves intersected with a horizontal beam to form a Latin cross. A pair of large circles occupied the lower arms; two taller ones rested on the upper arms. Above the gate, a larger circle framed the boldly sketched lamb.

I was deeply stirred by the strong beauty of Lipchitz's concept and the biblical insights they brought forth. The sacrificial lamb figures prominently in both the Old and New Testaments, but their individual purposes differ. In early Jewish rituals, a lamb is taken, bound and bleating, to be sacrificed, an unwilling offering to appease Yahweh. For Christians, Christ is the Lamb of God who goes knowingly, uncoerced, to his death. In my view, the Lipchitz lamb strides forward, head high, more like the lamb of the New Testament than that of the Old, which is a curious paradox coming from the hand of a devout Jewish sculptor.

At the time, I had no fixed notions about the two angels upholding the wreath for the Lamb of God, but later I wondered if they had flown in from Mecca. The Koran speaks of our need for angels. Ron Miller, in *The Gospel of Thomas: A Guidebook for Spiritual Practice*, tells a story attributed to Muhammad that could apply to these angels: "Every morning when people wake up, two angels descend from the heavens. One of them will say, 'Lord! Replace the wealth of a charitable spender.' And the other will say, 'Lord! Diminish the wealth of a stingy person who withholds his wealth from the needy.'"[2]

While Philip reacted with enthusiasm, he did not forget his obligation to right proportion. He explained that a forecourt would be required to sustain the impact of the monumental gate. Once again we three were of one mind. Philip indicated that architectural renderings with the added forecourt would soon be ready for contractual bids.

After my return to Houston, I found welcome news from both architect and sculptor. Philip wrote that the forecourt foundation would be laid and could receive the gates by early spring 1962. Lipchitz had begun a full-scale version of the model for the gate and assured me that it would be ready for casting in the bronze foundry before my hoped-for dedication date.

I began planning for weeklong May Day observances in 1962, which would culminate in a celebration for the Lipchitz gate. I asked George

MacLeod if he could leave his fabled island and his ministries throughout Scotland long enough to consecrate the golden gate on May 1. His positive response overwhelmed and humbled me, for his time was a precious and priceless gift. I was confident that a minister who could write about God, "He is Life: not religious life, nor church life, but the whole life that we now live in the flesh.... He is Reality: Love: Life . . . And God is the Life of life," would feel at home in a quadrangle open to sky, birds, flowering trees, and all human beings regardless of their race, color, religion, or lack of religion.[3] I also believe that Robert Owen would have felt more comfortable in a roofless, classless church than in a strictly Anglican church of the early 1800s.

Little wonder that my husband decided I was "getting goofy." Having heard more than enough of my preparations, he called a halt, wryly but firmly: "Would you and your playmate Helen Bullock stop inviting every dead Rappite and all my ancestors to your May Day parties!"

"No, Kenneth," I answered hotly. "I've only asked for their moral support, but I never sought Father Rapp's advice. You and I have never swallowed his dogmatic and millennial approach to religion. He was the prosperous televangelist of his day, reaping in the free labor of pious, obedient Germans who built three villages and appropriate mansions for him. I hope, however, that the Christian charity and work ethic of his followers rubs off on us today."

I paused for breath and continued more calmly. "As for your ancestors, you know how much I admire them, notwithstanding my opposition to Robert Owen's conviction that education alone would save the human race. But let's pray that his religious tolerance and compassion for all human beings, particularly factory workers, can touch the hearts of future visitors to New Harmony."

I planted my banner in Kenneth's ancestral turf, and he was letting it stand: perhaps a sign that he was relaxing his hold on the heritage that had inspired and sustained his goals. He had waited on tables and mowed lawns to earn money for his degree in geology from Cornell and to pursue a profession his great-uncle David and great-grandfather Richard had helped establish in America. After graduation, he put geology to good use in Texas. As previously noted, his oil revenues supported indigent Owens and restored the two houses where his ancestors had lived, worked, and procreated.

Of Kenneth's many labors, the least physically demanding and the most rewarding was the removal of letters, documents, and garments from nineteenth-century trunks we pulled from the Laboratory attic. Our excitement peaked when we opened a dog-eared art portfolio and discovered six pencil drawings by the painter, explorer, and naturalist Charles-Alexandre Lesueur. These unexpected windfalls were placed in professional hands: the manuscripts to Josephine Elliott and the garments to Harold F. Mailand, former textiles conservator at Indianapolis Museum of Art, now in private practice. A formal ivory satin gown had belonged to Rosamond Dale Owen, a granddaughter of Robert Owen, and been made for her in Le Havre after her marriage to the diplomat and travel writer Laurence Oliphant. Her book *My Perilous Life in Palestine,* published in 1924, should have been required reading for twenty-first-century Pentagon officials unaware of the cauldron of hatred for "infidels" into which they were pouring American soldiers. We also salvaged a gold-embroidered coat that had been worn by Rosamond's father, Robert Dale, when he presented his ministerial credentials to the Queen of the Two Sicilies in the early 1850s.

An ingrained modesty kept Kenneth from parading his heritage. The initiative to send these heirlooms to Mailand for conservation and eventual display in glass cases was mine alone. But the fact that Kenneth did not prevent me from exhibiting these garments suggested a softening of his view on privacy. He may have realized that the example of unselfish and creative people from the early Owen period could exert a positive influence on as yet uncommitted young people who lived outside Owen walls and who, like myself, did not possess a drop of Owen blood. Why hide these lights under a bushel basket?

Whatever Kenneth's reassessment of long-held attitudes, he brought me suddenly, buoyantly, to the here and now.

"Joe McCrudden has exciting news for us. Our prize heifer out of Domino is due to drop her calf. Let's go find the expectant mother and see how the birthing goes."

A cattleman's worst fear is a breech birth. I nodded consent, and through the car's open window Kenneth reached for his constant companion: one of many knobby canes that faithful Bob Moutray had carved for him from fallen cedar trees. Bob's perennial limp had never prevented him from crafting a cattle gate, the laying of brick walks around the Lab, or the transplanting of dogwoods from the farm's thick forests to inhabited gardens.

We parked the mud-splashed car not far from the 1860 Miller house that fronted South Main Street, a recent purchase because Kenneth needed to tie its wide and long apron of grass to the eastern flank of his Indian Mound Farm (37 on area map). Moreover, the rickrack of the front porch and the oriole window on the south wall appealed to him, conjuring the hope that, one distant day, a grandchild might restore the house, choose to live here, and engender an eighth generation of New Harmony Owens.[4] Kenneth, walking stick in hand, and I, with a tin pail for possibly ripe wine berries, climbed past Sled Hill into a field of unharvested hay, a fragrant mix of sweet timothy, fescue, and red top. Kenneth probed these grasses with Moutray's cedar cane, assuming that a provident cow might have chosen unstiffened straw for a manger bed.

We were drawing closer to the higher pastures of the mound, where I had received an unexpected summons seventeen years earlier. Since it remained for me a listening and truth-telling place, I was emboldened to submit a question I would never have asked in the pedestrian valley below, nor before Kenneth had shorn *la colline sacrée,* as Lipchitz called it, of its thorn trees. If the answer to my question would prove to be difficult for me, at least it would fall on soft, well-cushioned ground.

"I have a question for you, Kenneth."

"Make it a short one," he answered curtly.

"Did you find me a bit off-center when my brother introduced you to me in Houston?"

"Not in the least"—crisply but more gently.

I gave a cry of triumph. "That is to say, you would not have married the half-loony woman I've become in the mind-boggling town you brought me to? Please feel guilty."

Kenneth had, in fact, often chided me for wasting my time and resources here. He called it "overdoing," sometimes with humor, more often with dead seriousness. "The 'fruits' of your labors may never 'ripen,'" he had cautioned me, echoing my words, "and if ever they do, I don't see tourists 'consuming' them."

"The scientists and educators on 'The Boatload of Knowledge' did not find ready receivers either. Dividends on their investments came much later. Your ancestors were not bottom-line people, and I hope I'm not."

More adept than I in addressing the here and now, my husband interrupted my soliloquy. "Help me locate that pregnant heifer, and you'll regain your sanity."

Pointing his cedar staff southeast toward the cattle barn, he continued, "Our heifer may have wisely decided to calve close to McCrudden territory if there's a breech birthing. In that event, Joe would have to thrust bare hands into the cow's womb and reverse the abnormal feet-first entry."

Joe was both obstetrician and foster father to all Kenneth's cows. Luckily, his services were not required that day. On the lush meadow north of the barn, we discovered a complacent heifer, hooves firmly planted on curly-headed clover, her calf upright on gangly legs, tugging at a swollen udder like a piston pump. The mother cow was not looking with wonder at her newborn, but we stopped our advance before the miracle of birth. We retraced our path to the car parked by the 1860 house, my husband joyfully, I with "the thing with feathers," as Emily Dickinson calls hope, perched on my shoulder. Perhaps my not-for-profit dreams for New Harmony would have a safe birthing and my May Day tree would, in my lifetime, bear good fruit.

Feeling emboldened, I resumed plans for the formal dedication of *The Suzanne Glémet Memorial Gate* on May 1 (38 on town map).[5] Cultural and educational events would precede and complement the central celebration.[6] The evening before the dedication, a candlelight vesper service would welcome Lipchitz and his wife Yulla. Lipchitz read from the Psalms and Isaiah. The highly regarded soprano Adele Addison, a beautiful African American woman whose photograph appeared in a local paper, would bless us with her voice. Her contract with Sol Hurok, the best-known impresario of midcentury America, would not allow her to sing more than one complete song. She chose "Let Us Break Bread Together."[7] However brief our enjoyment of Addison's superlative voice, its impact upon those who had gathered at the south entrance of the Roofless Church, as they said, "to keep that . . . from singing," was immediate. The half dozen who had come in defiance heard her angelic voice beyond the wall. The magnificent sound must have dissipated their anger and prejudice, for we

Indian Mound Farm.
Blaffer-Owen family photograph.

never heard from racists again. If I needed proof that magnificent voices and powerful music are more effective weapons against real or perceived enemies than warplanes, I received it that evening in 1962.

Earlier proof had been provided in 1959 by the noted conductor Leonard Bernstein, when he took the New York Philharmonic to Moscow to play Shostakovich's Symphony no. 7, which had been composed during the siege of Leningrad. I believe the musical outreach of atonement for a nation's suffering touched more Russian hearts and minds in 1959, the chilliest year of the Cold War, than a sword rattling from Washington.

Another challenge came the next day. Dark storm clouds had been forming overhead and grew more ominous when George MacLeod took his place at the lectern in the Roofless Church. The spring sky, upon which I had relied for the unification of humanity with nature, thundered. The elements, however, had not counted on the staying power of our speaker. He was a descendant of pre-Calvinist Celts, and his strong and stirring voice rose above the clapping thunder. He finished the address, "The

Gateway Is Humility," that he had traveled a long way to deliver. Mac-Leod described Lipchitz's *Descent of the Holy Spirit* as "having the outline of an atomic bomb . . . . We stand, if we care to enter, on the edge of the most spiritual age the world has ever known." The clouds waited until he withdrew from the podium and led the recessional of participating clergy through the gates, as we sang "Lift up your heads, ye mighty gates; Behold the King of glory waits," before releasing their fury.

Driven like helpless leaves before a lashing wind and pelting rain, people sought shelter wherever there was cover or an open door, but not under the Neapolitan tent, for it had totally collapsed. But no one was lost or wounded in that gale, not even a dog or a cat.

I am still not sure what MacLeod's "God of All Life" had in mind that extraordinary day. It rained over the town and outside the golden gates, but not within the Roofless Church, which the Right Reverend George MacLeod called "a cathedral of earth and sky," until our dedication services ended. We witnessed, alternately, our Creator's destructive power and His mercy.

Above.

Standing together before the processional through
the golden gate: Philip Johnson, Jacques Lipchitz,
Jane Blaffer Owen, and Sir George MacLeod, 1962.

Photograph by James K. Mellow. Robert Lee Blaffer Trust Archive.
Courtesy of James K. Mellow and the Robert Lee Blaffer Foundation.

Facing.

Early in the day, Jacques and Yulla Lipchitz pose
with the Rappite (Harmonist) wagon, 1962.

Photograph by James K. Mellow. Robert Lee Blaffer Trust Archive.
Courtesy of James K. Mellow and the Robert Lee Blaffer Foundation.

But in the dazzled, high and unelectric air
Seized in the talons of the terrible Dove,
The huge, unwounding Spirit,
We suddenly escape the drag of earth
Fly from the dizzy paw of gravity
And swimming in the wind that lies beyond the track
Of thought and genius and of desire,

Trample the white, appalling stratosphere.

—Thomas Merton, "Song: Contemplation," in
The Collected Poems of Thomas Merton

CHAPTER 22

Estranged and Reunited

THE NEW BEING

After our buoyant Houston conversation in April 1961, when I told Tillich of my wish to create a park honoring him in my beloved New Harmony, further plans remained dormant until after the May Day 1962 dedication of the Lipchitz gate for the Roofless Church. I was then free to unite inspiration with resolution.

Paul Tillich came closer to New Harmony in 1962, his last year at Harvard and his first year at the University of Chicago, where his former student Jerald C. Brauer was dean of the Divinity School. It had been Dean Brauer's great pleasure to offer his beloved former professor the John Nuveen Chair of Theology and Tillich's great pleasure to accept. The Tillichs moved to Chicago in October 1962.

Despite the unavoidable inconveniences that go with the relocation of persons and baggage, Tillich was at the peak of his creative powers and influence. During his lecture tour of Japan, from May through mid-July 1960, he visited the renowned Buddhist scholars Daisetz T. Suzuki and Hoseki Shinichi Hisamatsu, whom he had known at Columbia and

Harvard, respectively. Tillich had been invited to Japan by the Committee for Intellectual Interchange.[1] Tillich's trip inspired the Bampton lecture series at Columbia in 1961, which were published in 1963 as *Christianity and the Encounter of the World Religions.* Tillich was completing the third and last volume of his *Systematic Theology.*

Henry Luce, the undisputed czar of midcentury American publications, wanted to mark the fortieth anniversary of the founding of *Time* magazine. In celebration of the occasion, Luce chose Tillich to be the principal speaker at a dinner on May 6, 1963, honoring the 284 persons whose faces had graced the covers of the magazine since its founding in 1923. (Tillich had been featured on the cover of its March 16, 1959, issue.) The title of the address Tillich gave in the Waldorf-Astoria ballroom that evening was "The Ambiguity of Perfection."

During or shortly after this star-studded event, Luce asked Tillich on what basis he would choose someone for a cover story. The latter suggested that the editorial board of *Time* should give more weight to wholeness and to character in choosing a candidate than to preeminence in a single area of competence. While I doubt that the editors of *Time* or *Life* took this advice seriously and began a search with a large magnifying glass for well-rounded individuals, I heard their editor in chief publicly acknowledge his great debt to the philosopher-king Tillich in the Roofless Church three years later.

My plans for a park to honor Paul Tillich in New Harmony began in earnest when Philip Johnson took me to Frederick Kiesler's New York studio in the summer of 1962 about the project. An early idea for a cave, which Philip and I considered but abandoned under the weight of other priorities, resurfaced as I began to envision Tillich Park (39 on town map). I sought a dwelling for the full-size figures of Jesus, Mary, and Joseph created by Frank and Elizabeth Haines. On behalf of the Robert Lee Blaffer Trust, my commission for the *Cave of the New Being* to house the Holy Family would emphasize the humble and modest origins of Our Lord and contrast with the royal grandeur directly across the street, as seen through Lipchitz's golden gate and into the Roofless Church from the vantage point of Tillich Park. I was intrigued when I met the visionary Austrian American sculptor and architect Frederick Kiesler. His seamless approach to building seemed to be an architectural reflection of Tillich's approach to education, namely, the interdependence of philosophy, theology, psychology, art, architecture, and religion.

I was unprepared for such a tribute to my efforts for reconciliation and was uncertain what Tillich meant by "justification," for theologians and laypeople understand the term differently. To my question about his meaning, he explained that justification does not refer to punishment or reward. Neither does it mean that the end justifies the means. To theologians, according to Tillich, justification rather means alignment of human will with God's will, a simple answer but a very difficult assignment.

Tillich's engaging suggestion prompted my next question: "If ever the day comes when our human wills connect with the divine will, shall all suffering and every division cease?"

Tillich's complete answer to my question would come the next day, Pentecost, with his words at the dedication. As we three retraced our steps in silence, I remembered other words that would suffice until morning: "Estranged and Reunited: The New Being," words intended for the entrance to his park. Tillich's words of promise had already been transferred from paper to stone. I hope that whoever stops to read them shall accept their challenge. Their author believed, as have all my wisdom teachers, that estrangement begins in the battlefield of the human heart, where the divinely planted real self is pitted against the fabricated, false self. Befuddled, war-weary humans should envy the acorn that knows it will grow into an oak tree and the kernel that, once planted, takes a direct, unhesitating route to fulfillment in an ear of succulent corn.

From the Roofless Church on the morning of Pentecost, Dr. Tillich explained the meaning of "Estranged and Reunited: The New Being" in his formal address:

> Now what is the estrangement which requires a new reunion, a new harmony? It is the estrangement of man from his true being in a threefold way: the estrangement from the ground of being, the estrangement from himself, and the estrangement from those with whom he lives. All religions, all social action, all healing attempts, and all forms of healing have tried to overcome these estrangements. Universal healing as envisaged in our great religions and personal healing have become so important. We have realized in our century, perhaps more than ever before, the estrangement of every person from himself and his true being. The healing of nations, social healing and political healing within the nation and between the nations, has become our deepest concern.
>
> ... By the act of dedication to which we shall proceed, we express the hope of a transformation of the old into a new being, here and everywhere in the universe. So may it be with our work as far as it can go, always in the power of the Spiritual Presence. Amen.[2]

Paul Tillich with Jane Blaffer Owen at the dedication of the
ground for Paul Tillich Park, Pentecost, 1963.

Robert Lee Blaffer Trust Archive.

I was overjoyed by the promise of hope implicit in these words.

We processed across the terminus of Main Street, where Tillich dedicated the ground of the park, unveiling the small stone that bears his name and words. Speaking informally on the lawn of Poet's House during a leisurely luncheon, the Tillichs felt here their strangeness being overcome with an almost miraculous experience of community. Paul Tillich also commented on "the heaviest package I have ever received": Kiesler's bronze model of *Cave of the New Being,* which "was immediately powerful in its symbolic character, even in the diminished form of a model." They looked forward with anticipation to returning to Tillich Park to see the finished work. I believe Hannah and Paulus left New Harmony that evening with happier hearts, eager for our next exchange.

The time and place for another meeting would depend upon how quickly Frederick Kiesler could complete his design for the *Cave of the New Being.* In August 1963, Kiesler sent a revision to the Tillichs at East Hampton, and William Crout, a former student assistant and an indispensable friend to his aging teacher, was present when it arrived. Over the course of the next year, however, Kiesler continued to produce increasingly ambitious and costly variations that ultimately compelled Philip Johnson, despite his respect for Kiesler's genius, to conclude that the design could no longer be translated into architecture. By early 1965, Philip advised me that it would have to remain "pure sculpture," and suggested that I ask Robert L. Zion, a landscape architect that he greatly admired, to submit plans for a grove of trees that would substitute for the *Cave of the New Being.*[3]

I went to Chicago on April 5, 1965, to ask for Paul and Hannah's blessing on my own suggestions for the park. Specifically, I wanted his approval to place in the park several passages from his published sermons that address prevailing maladies not only of the twentieth century but of all centuries. With some trepidation and a tote bag of drawings the Tillichs had not previously seen, I arrived at the apartment that the University of Chicago Divinity School had provided for its distinguished guests. I hoped that the change of plans for the park would not alter the foundations of our mutual trust, esteem, and friendship.[4]

As Hannah welcomed me, Dr. Tillich eyed the bag on my shoulder with curiosity. "What do you bring us?" he asked.

Reviewing the evolving plans and layout for *Cave of the New Being* are
Frederick Kiesler, Dr. Paul I. Rongved, structural engineer, and Len Pitkowsky, Kiesler's
studio assistant, at the site of Paul Tillich Park, October 14, 1964.

Photograph by John Doane. John Doane Collection.
Courtesy of Special Collections, University of Southern Indiana.

"Philip Johnson tells me Kiesler's cave is impossible to build and has recommended that Robert Zion, a very capable landscape architect, create a design for a grove of evergreen trees."

The decision obviously pleased them both, but especially Paul Tillich, who pillowed his massive head against the back of his thickly upholstered armchair, folded his hands, shut his eyes, and said with a smile, "I can already smell the needles."

"Have you any suggestions?"

Suddenly attentive, he answered, "Could there be a Cryptomeria tree in memory of my visit to Japan?" After a brief pause, he added, "And perhaps a chestnut tree? As a typical Prussian boy, I used to make soldiers with chestnuts. The small ones were foot soldiers, the big ones generals. Ach! Let's fight the next war with chestnuts! But what do you have here that you hold so tight in your hand?"

"Paper leaves for the healing of nations and people, wise words extracted from your sermons to be etched in stone."

Once again the professor, he adjusted his glasses and took the typed sheets from my hand. He read aloud to us the first of five quotations. "'Man and nature belong together in their created glory—in their tragedy and in their salvation.' Ah, that is very good, Jane. Did I write that?"

"Of course you did! I found it on one of the pages of your book *The Shaking of the Foundations*."[5]

Playfully, now no longer the professor, he admitted, "I would never pass an exam on Tillich."

Our visit ended with laughter, proof of the truth in Walter Kaufmann's remark that only the great philosophers laugh.

During the summer of 1965, I was not in touch with Paulus or Hannah. I knew their seclusion at their East Hampton house was important for them, for it provided a place for Tillich to refresh his thoughts in what he called his "backyard," the Atlantic Ocean. I had written to Hannah, however. By the time they had returned to Chicago for his fall lectures at the Divinity School, I had begun to feel a sense of urgency and could no longer contain my enthusiasm over the evolving park. I telephoned Dr. Tillich at his office in Swift Hall. My words rose like bubbles from an uncorked bottle of champagne.

"Your park will have earth mounds, or berms, to transform the flat terrain into a miniature Black Forest of Norwegian spruce. Hundreds of the conifers will rise from these tiny hills to shade visitors as they walk on mulched paths, discovering your wise words incised deeply on beautiful stones. No gray ladies of conformity that you have so often deplored. Lovely, striated granite, as if watching dawn or sunset."

I shall never regret my impulsive call or forget his response.

"Thank you for telling me this, Jane," he said. "You have made me very happy."

We never spoke again, for on October 22, 1965, not long after my call, his own effulgent sun slipped below this world's rim.

I was surprised to receive a telegram later, which read: "Would there be a place in the park for Paulus's ashes? Love, Hannah." This unexpected message stunned me for two reasons. First, Tillich's ashes had been interred in an East Hampton cemetery; second, the New Harmony park had never been conceived as a gravesite. My motive had been to honor a man deserving of honor and to expose portions of his wisdom to the general public.

Regaining my power of speech, I telephoned my assent to Hannah but questioned her reason for changing the setting of her husband's ashes. She replied without hesitation that the East Hampton cemetery, with its rows of gray stones, seemed like an impersonal real estate development and that New Harmony would be more congenial to Paulus's spirit.[6] I could not disagree but hoped that the interment could be deferred to Pentecost of 1966. The park would not be ready for six months. Also, she and I would need all of that time to organize a service worthy of one of the most encyclopedic minds of the twentieth century and one of the most charismatic and beloved of men.

I was still too bewildered by Hannah's largesse to proceed immediately with plans for the ceremony. On her behalf, however, I did instruct the chairman of the Robert Lee Blaffer Trust Whitfield "Pat" Marshall to write to the East Hampton cemetery regarding Hannah's request.[7] With that obligation fulfilled, my thoughts needed to stand still. They needed refreshment from the rich and ancient soil of New Harmony's past before they could turn to the future and its demands.

Mature Norwegian spruce trees dwarf the Rosati bust
Head of Tillich in Paul Tillich Park.

Photograph by Darryl D. Jones, 2014.

Where are the souls that quickened us
and brought us here—pilgrims
seeking more than an arrangement of bones?
Yet the air
does sing with their signature
Sometimes everywhere.

—Murray Bodo, OFM, "Holy Relics," in *Wounded Angels*

CHAPTER 23

The Undying Dead

P aul Tillich would not be the first intellectual of great stature to be laid to rest in New Harmony.

Thomas Say's tomb stands under a grove of dogwood trees behind the Rapp-Maclure-Owen House (40 on town map). He was not only this country's first published entomologist and conchologist but also an intrepid explorer and surveyor, having helped define our northwest boundary with Canada. Recent proof of his immortality was demonstrated in the March 2006 issue of *Smithsonian* magazine. The writer's essay on coyotes gives credit to Say for conferring the Latin name *Canis latrans* (barking dog), upon that otherwise colorless animal.

Thomas Say's pink conch shell—still in the Laboratory when the artist-architect Frederick Kiesler discovered it during his New Harmony visit in October 1962—was an impetus for the original design of the unrealized *Cave of the New Being* for Tillich Park, which Kiesler preferred to call the *Grotto for Meditation*. Philip Johnson had declared it "unbuildable" in the mid-1960s as architecture, even as he acknowledged

Thomas Say tomb and monument across Main Street from the Kilbinger House
(*left*) and Harmonist Community House No. 2 (*right*), in 1906.

Photograph by Homer Fauntleroy. Don Blair Collection.
Courtesy of Special Collections, University of Southern Indiana.

the talent of the visionary Kiesler. Time and technology, however, would make the impossible possible through the efforts of students and faculty associated with the Grotto Project—Ben Nicholson, Joe Meppelink, and Andrew Vrana—at the Gerald D. Hines College of Architecture, University of Houston. On January 26, 2010, a digitally fabricated interpretation, *New Harmony Grotto,* was unveiled. I was both astounded and thrilled, my spine tingling, as I walked through what had once been considered only fantasy. It took nearly fifty years before we caught up with Kiesler's genius. I am pleased that the peace of New Harmony will extend into Houston, offering weary students on campus a place of spiritual renewal not far from the Blaffer Gallery, which honors my mother.

I can't resist adding yet another instance of Thomas Say's enduring presence in New Harmony, which was brought to my attention by an attractive young entomologist on a hot summer's day in 1987. While I watered the waxen white August lilies that enliven the Rawlings House picket fence, she hailed me from the sidewalk.

"Are you Mrs. Owen?"

"So I am told. What can I do for you?"

"I am Dr. Catherine Thompson from Florida. I've come to search for a red ant that Thomas Say discovered when he lived in the Maclure house, across the street. He records it as invading meat and his seed collection. That's why he named it *Myrmica molesta;* it molests. I understand that this house now belongs to your husband and that I would need his permission to set my traps on his property. Would he mind?"

Kenneth was at his Pennsylvania horse-breeding farm. As he was a man of science and scientific curiosity, I was certain he would applaud Dr. Thompson's mission, so I readily gave her permission to plant her specially designed vials on the grounds of the Rapp-Maclure-Owen House and around the grass mound of Say's tomb.

The next morning rapid knocking on my front door came from an excited, victory-flushed entomologist.

"Of the twenty-four traps I placed near the house, two are filled with specimens of *molesta*! They liked my tuna fish oil bait, and I am thrilled. Please thank your husband."

I am indebted to Lois Mittino Gray's fine article in the *Posey County News* for aiding my memory with details of Dr. Catherine R. Thompson's rediscovery. Ms. Gray teaches biology in New Harmony's high school. In 2008, she was presented with the National Rural Teacher of the Year award at the one hundredth National Rural Educators Association convention in San Antonio. In New Harmony, we may no longer have Pestalozzi educators Marie Duclos Fretageot, William S. Phiquepal (who both arrived on "The Boatload of Knowledge"), or Joseph Neef, but we still have the finest educators.

Maple Hill Cemetery, south of town where the gentle hills begin, is the resting place of many notable New Harmony residents. Constance Owen Fauntleroy established the first women's club in America, the Minerva

Society, in 1859, in the parlor of the Fauntleroy House (41 on town map).
Two of Robert Owen's remarkable sons, Richard and David Dale, and one
of his granddaughters, Rosamond Dale Owen Oliphant Templeton, who
wrote *My Perilous Life in Palestine,* are interred in Maple Hill, where the
trees are more impressive than the monuments. Beloved members of
Kenneth's own Owen family are there, as is our precious daughter Carol
Owen Coleman.

Not all of New Harmony's patriarchs and matriarchs lie under its maple and dogwood trees. Indeed, several of them continue to make contemporary news. For instance, Charles-Alexandre Lesueur, French artist
and ichthyologist, sketched and gathered fossils and fish in the Wabash
Valley for more than a decade after his well-documented voyage to Aus-
tralia and Tasmania and before his return to his native Le Havre. A
three-volume biography of his life is nearing completion.[1] Its author, Ritsert Rinsma, tells me that a graphic novel based on Lesueur's adventures
in the South Pacific has also been published.[2] Interestingly enough,
Lesueur's sea voyage itself has made fashion news. Hermès, the celebrated
French designer and distributor of silk scarves and leather goods, has recently offered the public a chance to own a scarf imprinted with the faces
of Lesueur and three of his fellow explorers. Their sailing ship, *Le Géogra-
phe,* is at the center of the design.

Lucy Sistare, an educator and artist, studied drawing and painting at
Madame Fretageot's school in Philadelphia with Lesueur and John James
Audubon. She met Thomas Say on "The Boatload of Knowledge," and they
married. She illustrated and hand-colored his textbook *American Conchol-
ogy.* Lucy Sistare Say was the first woman elected a member of the Academy
of Natural Sciences of Philadelphia.

Frances "Fanny" Wright, feminist and abolitionist, delivered New
Harmony's Independence Day speech in 1828, and the tradition lives on.
President Linda L. M. Bennett of the University of Southern Indiana
spoke thoughtfully about "New Harmony, Education, and the Common
Good," at our July 4, 2009 celebration.

We revere and honour the past, but we do not see these as dead and fossilized stones—they are living stones carrying the past into the future, responding to the new demands and expectations of succeeding centuries.

—Esther de Waal, *Seeking Life: The Baptismal Invitation of the Rule of St. Benedict*

CHAPTER 24

Paul Tillich Park

I needed stones large enough for Tillich's healing messages. My geologist husband once again held a lamp to guide my feet.

"Great-grandfather Richard was the first professor of geology at Indiana University, and its first building bears his name, Owen Hall. I've contributed to a room in his memory. I know a young teacher who may be able to locate a few sizable native Indiana rocks for in between your evergreens."

Kenneth's call to Dean Pennington in December 1965 brought immediate results. The alert geologist knew that a highway was under construction outside Indianapolis, and he headed there on the chance that road equipment would turn up long-buried boulders. I'll never forget the excitement in Pennington's voice when he telephoned Kenneth, for I was listening in.

"Tell Mrs. Owen that a glacier has deposited some solid granite stones suitable for inscriptions. Their coloration is unusual. They'll do for her 'Christmas trees'!"

Kenneth thanked him heartily and offered compensation.

"Don't pay me a penny," Pennington replied, "for having had the time of my life, Mr. Owen. Just pay the truckers who'll haul them to New Harmony."[1]

Although I was not in town for the unloading of my prehistoric windfall, I returned in late spring to welcome Ralph Beyer, the eminent London-based letterer of Coventry Cathedral. His uneven, forceful, chiseled letters—like those found on early Greek tablets—were often gilded by his charming wife, Hilary.[2] He had been trained by England's well-known sculptor and typeface designer Eric Gill and had also studied under the German classicist Rudolf Koch. I learned from Ralph that his father, Oskar Beyer, the art historian, had been a good friend and colleague of Tillich's at the University of Dresden prior to World War II, and their families were close. Ralph described cutting Tillich's words into the boulders as "work which is very near my heart."[3] Many of my endeavors for New Harmony seemed to be guided by a will greater than mine.

Close by the aborning park stood a few homes. One belonged to Walter "Luke" and Kathleen Mathews, staunch allies of mine. Kathleen grew the only pink lily of the valley in town and gave me as many as my garden would hold, plus a bushel basket of coral bells. Luke's livelihood came from his insect-spray service and the sale of dew worms for fishermen. His principal client was Harry "Catty" Brand. But their main occupation in the spring of 1966 was watching Ralph Beyer incise letters into stones. Luke finally voiced their misgivings, which were heard throughout town: "Poor Miss Jane imported this 'bloke' all the way from England, and he can't print straight." Local disappointment notwithstanding, Ralph transferred Tillich's quotations into stone. However, one of my original selections—which I had shared with the Tillichs in their Chicago apartment during our joyous exchange—would have to be left out: "Religion is the substance of culture, culture is the form of religion."[4]

I was particularly partial to the tallest among the silent stones, its beauty independent of the hand of man. This stone would become a tombstone, inscribed with alpha and omega dates and an epitaph. Whenever it rains, lines of pink and patches of lavender appear.

TODAY WE KNOW
WHAT THE NEW TESTAMENT
ALWAYS KNEW· THAT MIRACLES
ARE SIGNS POINTING TO THE
PRESENCE OF A DIVINE POWER
IN NATURE AND HISTORY AND
THAT THEY ARE IN NO WAY
NEGATIONS OF NATURAL LAWS

Ralph Beyer with a lettered stone in
Paul Tillich Park, 1966.

*Paul Tillich Archive. Courtesy of the
Robert Lee Blaffer Foundation.*

Fortunately, I had known that a portrait bust of Tillich would be essential for the park and had arranged for him to meet the very fine sculptor James Rosati, whom Tillich and I both admired. The appointment for a sitting was mediated by telephone, and happily a harmonious working relationship developed between subject and sculptor. While the sitting was under way in Jim Rosati's New York studio, earthmoving machines were preparing the ground of Tillich Park. Paul Tillich did not live to see the completion of either. The portrait bust was not ready for the commemorative service that Hannah and I were busily planning.[5]

Sculptor James Rosati with the portrait bust of Paul Tillich at its unveiling, 1967. *Head of Tillich* © 1967 James Rosati.

Photograph by James K. Mellow. Paul Tillich Archive. Courtesy of the Robert Lee Blaffer Foundation, James K. Mellow, and the Estate of James Rosati, jamesrosati.org.

As Pentecost quickly approached, I remembered with sadness that Paul and Hannah had spoken of revisiting the Poet's House in the month of May, when our peony fields would be in full bloom.[6] He had once explained to me that the German word for "peony" is *Pfingstrose,* "rose of the Spirit," for it bloomed at Pentecost. He had added, "It is not sacrilegious to worship them."

Although hardly complete, Paul Tillich Park would be ready in a few short weeks to receive his mortal remains and become a sacred place. As I surveyed the transformation, my thoughts traveled back to Pentecost 1963, when Paul and Hannah were last here. New Harmony and the landscape surrounding it had reminded both of the Tillichs of childhoods in Germany. On the Poet's House lawn that afternoon, Tillich had also said, "In any case, my impression of this place is an impression of something astonishing, surprising, great in itself, in its past, and in its present. And my wish is that it may remain great also in its future."[7]

Paul Tillich will be pointing the way.

—Henry Luce

CHAPTER 25

Paul Tillich
Commemorative Service

Now, to my amazement, our enlarged portal was to receive the ashes of Paul Tillich. My first assignment from Hannah Tillich had been to write an announcement letter to his colleagues and friends, informing them of her decision.[1] The list she gave me included not only presidents of divinity schools and universities but also the names of artists, poets, musicians, and museum directors. Tillich was the only theologian ever invited to address members of New York City's Museum of Modern Art.[2] An even more unorthodox departure for a theologian was Tillich's enthusiastic support of Joan Baez in her early years. No sphere of knowledge or art was beneath his attention, nor was any form of religion.

Many of those to whom I had written arrived for the services: some former students by motorcycle, dignitaries such as Henry Luce by private jet, many others by car. I was too intimidated by Luce, a person of great wealth and power, to accept the honor of knocking at his door to awaken him before the interment at dawn on Sunday, May 29, 1966. I was more comfortable with Jerald C. Brauer, dean of the University of Chicago Divinity School, and turned to him. Jerry's penetrating blue eyes, crew cut, and contagious smile belied my preconceived idea of a divinity dean. "You're just the one, Jerry, to awaken the great Henry for the services tomorrow," I told him on Saturday at a reception for Hannah Tillich in the courtyard of the Red Geranium Restaurant (43 on town map). He consented, with reservations.

Before leaving Houston, I had asked Preston Frazier, founder of an innovative candle shop, to create a thousand white candles shaped like doves. Annie Rawlings helped me unpack and place them on tables outside the Lipchitz gates for our out-of-town guests and for anyone who wished to join our evening procession on the eve of the interment, which would follow a concert by the Evansville String Trio in the Roofless Church honoring Hannah. I lit a candle and handed it to my husband. Confident that no one would observe him in the dark, Kenneth accepted my gift and joined Jerry Brauer and me as we crossed the narrow lane that separates the Roofless Church from the park.

We entered a seeming forest fire. More than a hundred candle bearers had preceded us and planted their wax doves in the earth beside the lettered stones or directly under the still-moist Norwegian spruce. The young saplings only appeared to burn, because there was no smoke, only a delicious aroma arising from the contact of heat on evergreen needles. Moved and astonished, I cried out, "Come, Kenneth; come, Jerry, Philip, Rollo; come inhale nature's incense!"

My husband may not have read chapter 3 of Exodus—"the bush burned with fire and the bush was not consumed"—but he behaved as though he had seen the very bush that had startled Moses on Mt. Sinai. Breathless, hands extended, he called out, "Forget the incense, Jane. Just look around you! There's never been such a sight in New Harmony. Run, run! Bring the whole town!"

Apostle of community and inclusiveness, I had placed an open invitation via the *Posey County Times* and *New Harmony News* to anyone who wished to plant a candle in the park. I had failed, however, to follow through with personal invitations to churches and civic groups. Not for the first time had Kenneth's unexpected exuberance bested my preconceived trump card.

The poet Stanley Kunitz's description of himself described my husband well: "What's best in me lives underground, / rooting and digging, itching for wings."[3] Kenneth had found his wings, and they had outflown mine.

Later that night, Jerry Brauer was neither flying nor exuberant. He addressed me with a doleful countenance: "Jane, I've only brought one pair of trousers, and they are completely covered with wax. I can't wake up Henry Luce looking like a melted candle."

As the daughter of a mother who preferred candles to lightbulbs and whose childhood home had been described by an Englishman as "situated so far in the country that electricity had not yet reached it," I knew how to solve Jerry's problem.

About two hundred friends and colleagues of Dr. Paul Tillich attended the reception for Hannah and family before relocating inside the Red Geranium Restaurant for the banquet. Saturday, May 28, 1966.

Photograph by James K. Mellow. Paul Tillich Archive. Courtesy of James K. Mellow and the Robert Lee Blaffer Foundation.

The tall stone that bears Paul Tillich's name,
alpha-omega dates, and epitaph, 1966.

Photograph by James K. Mellow. Paul Tillich Archive.
Courtesy of James K. Mellow and the Robert Lee Blaffer Foundation.

"Never mind the wax, Jerry. Just stop by my kitchen tomorrow on your
way to awaken Henry Luce. You'll have to take off your pants, so I can remove every bit of wax with blotting paper and a hot iron."

Next morning was Pentecost. It brought us no tongues of fire or the
sound of rushing wind, only enough early light from my kitchen window
for me to place a pair of wax-laden trousers on my ironing board. The
dean's laughter and mine would have delighted Paul Tillich, a theologian
and philosopher who knew how to laugh.

The step from the ridiculous to the sublime was a very short one for
Jerry and me as we escorted the somber and silent publisher of *Time* and
Life toward the gravestone, which would turn a deep rose when moist
from dew or a rainfall:

PAUL JOHANNES TILLICH
1886–1965
AND HE SHALL BE LIKE A TREE
PLANTED BY THE RIVERS OF WATER
THAT BRINGETH FORTH HIS FRUIT
FOR HIS SEASON HIS LEAF
ALSO SHALL NOT WITHER
AND WHATSOEVER HE DOETH
SHALL PROSPER

There were just twelve of us at the gravesite. The minister of St. Stephen's Episcopal, the Reverend Arthur Hadley, helped Mrs. Tillich by burying the ashes behind the stone on a mound of soft earth and spoke a few words. Standing close by were the Tillichs' children: son René and daughter Mutie Tillich Farris, who was joined by her husband and their children, Ted and Madeline, forming an intimate family group. Rollo May, Henry Luce, John Nuveen, Jerry Brauer, and I stood at a distance, heads bowed, our hearts full. Following the private interment, Rev. Hadley presided at the eight o'clock communion service in the Roofless Church that morning. Henry Luce delivered the first words honoring Tillich from a lectern before the frontal arch of the canopy. He spoke briefly but with feeling and a question mark on his face that seemed to ask, "How does one go into the unknown?" Dean Jerry Brauer remembered his mentor and friend.

In the late afternoon, a resplendent sun and the sound of trumpets charged the day with energy and restored our spirits for the formal, public service. The ceremonial gates were opened wide to admit the eighty-voice combined choir, including the Indiana University Chamber Singers, that performed three of Dr. Tillich's favorite hymns.[4] Michael Angelo, a tall African American cross-bearer, led the procession. Ministers of several denominations and Tillich's family and friends followed. The Rt. Rev. John P. Craine, bishop of the Episcopal Diocese of Indianapolis, gave the homily. Rollo May offered the final tribute. His words were eloquent and deeply moving. But as moving as the speaker's words were, we were all the more moved by the words of Paul Tillich with which Rollo May brought the eulogy to a close on that day of drama, beauty, and triumph:

> We are given existence in time. The meaning of it is, that we shall give meaning to these transitory hours in creation, joy, love, power. All this has an eternal dimension and a transitory character together. It is transitory, but it is not only transitory, and therefore it is worthy to be lived—in spite of [its transitoriness].[5]

Above.

Dean Jerald Brauer at the podium in the Roofless Church.

Photo by James K. Mellow. Paul Tillich Archive. Courtesy of
James K. Mellow and the Robert Lee Blaffer Foundation.

Facing.

Henry Luce with Jane Blaffer Owen after the morning service.

Photograph by James K. Mellow. Paul Tillich Archive. Courtesy of
James K. Mellow and the Robert Lee Blaffer Foundation.

Paul Tillich Park possesses the duality, like the man himself, of having a public aspect, honoring one of the greatest men of the twentieth century, and a private aspect, for his family. The familial dimension of the park was renewed some thirty years later, following the death of Mutie's daughter, Madeline; a plaque adjacent to its entrance bears witness to the loss of a friend who lived and worked for a time in New Harmony:

MADELINE LAURA FARRIS
1956–1999
BRIGHT AS A SUNBEAM,
QUICK TO LAUGH, THOUGHTFUL,
HONEST, LOVING AND STRONG,
HER CLEAR VISION, HER COURAGE
STIRRED ALL WHOSE LIVES SHE TOUCHED.
GRANDDAUGHTER OF PAUL TILLICH

wise and large-hearted people would have to help me raise them. My experience on Indian Mound, real or imagined, taught me that my efforts alone would only rattle the sash of closed windows. Our windows, once open, would need to be wide enough for people—wise or not, courageous or fearful—not only to peer inside but also to be welcomed within.

I have already expressed gratitude to New Harmony residents who shared their ideas and talents with me, but I've not adequately thanked allies beyond our borders.

John Craine, bishop of the Diocese of Indianapolis, was the first outsider to give our window an upward shove. He directed able parish priests of our St. Stephen's Episcopal Church: Rufus Simons, Ernest Tilley, Ralph Markey, Arthur "Art" Hadley, Gene Harshman, Robert Webb, and the Glovers, the last with the plural *-s* because Mortimer W. "Mort" Glover III brought his wife, Eugenia "Genie," to the parish (44 on town map). New Harmony owes the revival of its long-dormant tradition of great music festivals to this talented and tireless patroness of music who established the New Harmony Festival of Music.

Other benefactors from the state capital came: Harry and Jane Wade and the Herringtons. Governor Roger Branigin not only generously provided funds to our library for the addition of a repository for rare books and manuscripts but also conspired with Bishop Craine to keep my young restaurant, the Red Geranium, alive (43 on town map). An alien Texan might not have obtained an Indiana liquor license without the combined efforts of church and state.[2] Gary and Mary Ellen Gerard came in 1966 to guide the Red Geranium.

Strong arms from overseas have opened a wider and taller window. Anyone who looks through this enlarged opening can see as far as St. Columba's holy island and Thomas à Becket's Canterbury Cathedral. Previous chapters have highlighted New Harmony's debt to George Mac-Leod, the founder of the Iona Community; but none have yet acknowledged our gratitude to Rev. Canon Herbert Montague Waddams and to Esther de Waal, the founders of Benedictine Spirituality programs at Canterbury and later the leaders of New Harmony's first Benedictine ritual in 1983. Esther, an Anglican, introduced a new generation of laity from many denominations to the rule of St. Benedict through her 1984 book, *Seeking God: The Way of St. Benedict.* She is a prolific writer and scholar on Celtic, Benedictine, and Cistercian spirituality, and her journey through the contemplative writings and photography of Thomas Merton becomes an inward retreat-in-a-book for those of us who admire the humble Trappist monk's works and life.[3]

Herbert Waddams was a uniquely gifted and greatly loved canon of Canterbury at a perilous time in the fortunes of New Harmony's St. Stephen's Episcopal Church. The cause of a dispute has evaporated from my mind, but, however insubstantial, a controversy had divided the parish into two hostile camps. Earth tremors traveled as far as Houston to disturb my sleep, prompting me to place a long-distance call to my friend in Canterbury, asking Canon Waddams's help in settling a local tempest.

"Yes, Jane, I'll come if I am permitted."

Twenty-four anxious hours later, I learned that Herbert's boss, Archbishop Ramsey, had given him a month's leave to help extinguish St. Stephen's fires. This able diplomat did precisely that, beginning with individuals in private discussions and ending with a group gathering where everyone was pronounced guilty. Peace in its entirety would not have returned had this "man of God and of sod and sky" not only scolded but also regaled us with stories that brought tears to our eyes.

My gratitude and affection for Herbert Waddams found expression in the small circular chapel of the New Harmony Inn Entry House that bears his name and was dedicated in May 1974 (45, 46, and 47 on town map). Ralph Beyer, who had lettered the precious stones in Tillich Park, carved the Ten Commandants tablets that encircle the exterior of Waddams Chapel. While many visitors worship or meditate in this intimate space, none have been more constant than participants of the actors' and writers' workshops that have taken place in New Harmony for more than two decades. Actors, playwrights, directors, filmmakers, and students of the New Harmony Project begin their demanding days with an early service in their "Rocket Chapel," from which their prayers are "launched" through a peaked glass ceiling. Long before space capsules blasted off, the prayers of Roma Gypsies were called *saetas* or "arrows," for their intent was like that of a rocket, a direct, swift passage to the throne of the Almighty. Suffice to say that the windows of New Harmony have widened to form a spacious portal.

Waddams Chapel interior.

Photograph by Darryl D. Jones, 2009.

Waddams Chapel exterior of the Evans Woollen designed
Entry House and New Harmony Inn (*left*).

Photograph by Nancy Mangum McCaslin, 2013.

His purposes will ripen fast,
Unfolding every hour;
The bud may have a bitter taste,
But sweet will be the flower.

—William Cowper, *Olney Hymns,* "Light Shining Out of Darkness"

CHAPTER 27

Tumbling Walls

The story of "Our Lady of Several Names" and of her three sacred sites and her entry into my life has not been an easy one to place on paper. Reciting my story has left me feeling, at times, uncomfortably exposed and vulnerable. But writing that story has not been as difficult or painful as remembering the experience of watching Our Lady's enclosure in New Harmony dissolve. I wish this chapter could be omitted in its entirety. Yet her four walls contained for me a precious fluid, and from 1961 onward it began seeping out of what would become within a decade a severely cracked vessel.

The Third Canticle of Isaiah (60:18) expresses the purpose of a consecrated container better than any words of mine:

> Violence will no more be heard in your land,
> ruin or destruction within your borders.
> You will call your walls *Salvation*,
> and your gates *Praise*.

That grand old prophet would have likened the shattered walls of any temple to a bleeding wound, the spilling of life-sustaining praise and prayers.

Human tragedies and natural disasters give us sufficient cause to weep; so why should I, or anyone, shed tears over the demise of four brick walls? A tragic event in World War II, the war of my generation, provided an impetus for rebuilding the crumbling walls of the Roofless Church.

Of all its heinous crimes against structures, the Nazi air raid that destroyed Coventry's cathedral was, for me, the hardest to forget or forgive. While in London on our way to Iona in the summer of 1955, I wanted my daughters to experience the horrors of war and, simultaneously, the resilience of the human spirit. So it was that the English driver, our nurse Emma, Janie, Carol, and I all stood solemnly before a giant, blackened cross assembled from roof beams salvaged from the burnt cathedral. It rose majestically from the center of its shattered perimeter. Two words were carved into its horizontal arms: "Father Forgive."

If citizens of a devastated city could rise to such Christlike heights, how could Americans, old and young, remain untouched by Coventry's example? If all warring factions could grasp the full meaning of Coventry's cross, Sister Carita's prophetic banner words would come true: "Someday, someone shall give a war and no one shall come."[1]

But the tumbling walls of our Roofless Church, unlike Coventry's charred remains, did not send a New Testament command to the world. Our new, clean bricks fell as the result of human miscalculation, not because of Nazi bombs. Philip Johnson was not, to be sure, a heartless air raider intent on the destruction of a church that had brought him his first award from the American Institute of Architects. He had, however, kept me waiting nine troubled years for effective remedies.

In the early spring of 1961, scarcely a year after its baptism, the Roofless Church had given me cause for alarm. White, powdery streaks were staining large portions of the north wall. I had called the architect for an explanation. (Photographs of the Roofless Church in earlier chapters clearly show the phenomenon.)

"Just a little efflorescence," Philip Johnson had answered blithely. "A minor matter that a coating of polyurethane will quickly remedy."

Thereby assured that the bricks were suffering from a temporary illness, I had relayed Philip's prescription for their recovery with unquestioned faith to our New Harmony maintenance men, and polyurethane was applied.

Had I consulted my dictionary at the time and read that efflorescence is "a substance due to the emergence of moisture which turns to a fine powder on exposure to air," I would have realized that water was actually seeping into the walls and would have sought advice from engineers unconnected with the Johnson office. But, susceptible to Philip's charm and erudition, I did not question his facile remedy for a fatal disease. Unaware of a serious problem with the bricks, I had asked Lipchitz to proceed with the model for a large ceremonial gate, which Philip had approved.

Seeing the external walls of the Roofless Church collapsing before my very eyes, I struggled to know what action to take. The Roofless Church was not my personal oratory but a public place maintained by the Robert Lee Blaffer Trust and under the spiritual supervision of the Episcopal Diocese of Indianapolis because of my affiliation. My bishop and friend John Craine often came to us, entering and closing the south gate behind him for private prayers. The Roofless Church became a balm for him in times of sorrow and a place of celebration in times of thanksgiving. He shared my pain over the plight of the crumbling walls and encouraged me to repair them, advising, "This is as much my church as it is New Harmony's. However, I haven't the time or resources to fight for it. You'll have to, Jane."

John Craine came close to fitting the classic description of a saint: a person with a heart of fire toward God, a heart of flesh toward others, and a heart of steel toward himself. He was a churchman with the face of a Celtic warrior. I am proud that his portrait photograph hangs in the John Craine Room of the New Harmony Inn.

My worldlier friend Walter Muir Whitehill of Boston's Athenaeum offered a practical solution, his blue eyes flashing. "Don't listen to any more of Philip's gobbledygook. I think you should consult an engineering firm in Cambridge, called Stanley Newman. Their warning to architects who want to build sculptural fantasies is seldom heeded. A year after completion a roof leaks, a wall collapses, and the architect—more often than the client—comes crying for help. I suggest you invite someone from Stanley Newman to diagnose Philip's toppling walls."

When a person of Walter Whitehill's erudition and integrity speaks, it is wise to listen. Queen Elizabeth II had listened with undisguised delight when Whitehill, escorting her to the Old State House during her 1976 bi-centennial visit to Boston, said, "It is my pleasure, Your Majesty, to intro-duce you from the balcony, the place from where your ancestor was once denounced."

Regrettably, Philip Johnson did not take kindly to my decision to act upon the Sage of Boston's advice.

"When a patient is as sick as your walls, Philip," I ventured, "and the family doctor's remedies aren't working, isn't it time to call in a consultant?"

The fine line between Philip's eyebrows deepened. "What and who are you talking about, Jane?"

"Walter Whitehill has suggested that an engineer from Stanley New-man be engaged to inspect what remains of the walls of your almost wall-less church."

The architect whose palliative remedies I had accepted for nine years suddenly shut his eyes, blinded perhaps by the light of truth that he had chosen to ignore. But a realistic, thorough analysis of the several causes for the deterioration of the walls did come from the Stanley Newman engineers, along with an estimate for rebuilding and repaving the entire *temenos*.

Some of the trustees in whose hands I had placed the assets of my mod-est trust had lost patience with Johnson. They had footed the bills for ill-advised, short-term solutions for nine years. They balked before the sizable sum that would be needed to rebuild the walls from scratch and finally took their grievance to court. I shared their sense of betrayal, but not without intense sadness, for the decision would cost me a valued friend. The rupture of my friendship with Philip would be like the cutting down of a living tree that had given me many delicious fruits. But, with deep regret, I came to realize that this tree of friendship had grown too close to my walls and its roots were undermining the foundation. Either the tree or the walls would have to go.

My trustees felt compelled to bring a damage suit against Philip John-son's firm, which was filed on April 30, 1971.[2] Articles appeared in local papers.[3] The process, with depositions and filings, took years to wend its way through the legal system. In 1976, jurors from Evansville were per-mitted to visit the scene of the crime, an uninhabited plaza defined by stacks of fallen, water-soaked bricks. The walls of the Johnson-designed

This photograph, an exhibit from the 1975 legal proceedings, has deteriorated over time and through inadequate storage but shows damage to the walls.

Robert Lee Blaffer Trust Archive. Courtesy of the Robert Lee Blaffer Foundation.

A moldy exhibit with photographs showing the damaged walls of the MoMA sculpture garden taken on November 14, 1974, by William Hanna and Don Blair.

Robert Lee Blaffer Trust Archive. Courtesy of the Robert Lee Blaffer Foundation.

sculpture court of New York's Museum of Modern Art had also suffered from a flawed design.[4] There was no doubt in anyone's mind where the responsibility lay, and justice was quickly rendered. An estimated sum for rebuilding a wall-less church was billed to Johnson Associates.

Engineers from Stanley Newman were engaged and their recommendations implemented. Their designs called for expansion joints, weep holes, and limestone caps to extend beyond the brick walls, all measures intended to prevent the intake and retention of moisture between the inner and outer masonry. Johnson's original design had not specified weep holes or expansion joints. He had insisted that the limestone coping on the top of the walls not extend over the bricks and that the flashing in between brick and limestone remain invisible. Time and weather proved the design useless. (I had not as yet heard of the satin bowerbird, which constructs his bower solely for aesthetic reasons.) In short, the prerequisites for sound construction had all been omitted.

Nor, I remembered, had Johnson thought of guttering to catch rainfall from the shingled canopy until Don Blair, overseer for construction, brought up the subject. Don asked a question apparent to him but hidden to the renowned architect: "Where will water go from the roof?" Openings were subsequently provided in the pavement to carry off rainwater. Unfortunately, no one in or outside Philip's New York office questioned his competence in the building of a wall. Many superstar architects do not heed warnings from engineers, who, under their captain's orders, must obey or quit.

It should interest modern-day builders that the Egyptian word for architecture translates as "firm things." Not surprisingly, the pyramids of Egypt have survived plunder, sandstorms, and the assault of centuries. Contemporary builders might also remember that the celebrated first-century Roman architect Vitruvius asserted that a structure must exhibit the three qualities of *firmitas, utilitas,* and *venustas*—that is, it should be durable and useful, and it should delight.

The original limestone floor of the Roofless Church, unshielded from the intense heat of Indiana summers, had buckled and cracked and was replaced with grass. Flowerbeds on either side of the canopy were also removed and replaced with sturdy turf. Undamaged limestone pavers were salvaged to create a wide walk from the ceremonial gates to the canopy and a narrow path leading from the south entrance.

Sitting with Philip Johnson in the balcony of the Roofless Church.
Photograph by James K. Mellow. Courtesy of James K. Mellow.

Over the years, I have purchased another farm and wooded land beyond the Roofless Church to safeguard the view from the balcony as seen from its inception. The fields directly north were planted each year in corn or soybeans by Kenneth's Indian Mound crew, but not before spring floods had brought their rich deposits of alluvial mud. Likewise, but on a much larger scale and over many millennia, has the Nile overflowed its banks, enriching Egyptian farms. When our Wabash recedes and the fields are dry enough to plough and seed, I often sit on the balcony to watch green shoots of young corn or soybeans break through the soil in even rows that translate for me under starlight not only into the American flag but also into an earth flag of all people who plant in even rows.

The potential for worldwide or personal reconciliation is never easy, but Professor Tillich's words at the entrance to his park, "Estranged and Reunited: The New Being," offer hope.

When I consider everything that grows
Holds in perfection but a little moment

—Shakespeare, Sonnet XV

CHAPTER 28

Glass House

L ooking back in my ninety-fifth year, with all passion spent, I can still taste the pleasures I forfeited with the removal of that fruited tree of friendship. Philip Johnson's lunch table at the Seagram Building's Four Seasons Restaurant had been the hub of New York's political, art, and architectural life. Charismatic, handsome Mayor John Lindsay would sometimes join us for coffee, as would Patrick Moynihan, New York's justly beloved senator, his lips two ripe cherries bouncing with mirth, or Andy Warhol, his boyish face and hair having seemingly emerged from a flour barrel.

This glamorous world was a far cry from my husband's horse farm in Pennsylvania and my daughter's tutors at the Stanhope Hotel. Albeit on the periphery of Johnson's urbane world, I reveled in my borrowed feathers. Sometimes Philip teased me about my faith but also wished he had it. (Philip once admitted that he had sheltered me from the more flamboyant and decadent aspects of the New York lifestyle, out of respect for my religious sensibilities.) "Fine," I had said about his interest in my faith,

"I'll introduce you," and had looked for opportunities to expose an atheist architect to a priestly inhabitant of my church world.

Canon Herbert Waddams's arrival in New York in the winter of 1965 to give a series of lectures at the General Theological Seminary of the Episcopal Church provided an opening. I was already there, having returned with Janie after Christmas, and made haste to bring Herbert to Philip's "table for all seasons" but not all people. Not surprisingly, their congeniality was instant. Herbert was as well schooled in architecture as he was in theology, and his keen wit was equal to Philip's. Eager to continue their spirited conversation, Philip asked Canon Waddams to accompany him to Connecticut for the weekend, an invitation that included lucky me.

A light snow, which had only dusted our train as it pulled out of Grand Central Station, was falling energetically as we neared New Canaan. Philip expressed relief to find his driver waiting for the three of us at the station. We were warned, however, that a major blizzard was approaching. We could either return to New York on the next train or risk exile in the country for an indefinite number of days. Herbert's lectures at General Theological Seminary were not to begin until Tuesday of the following week and Janie was in Emma's capable hands. We opted for an expedition into a no-man's-land of unlimited snow to a house without walls. And why not? I was fond of a roofless church.

Our hour-long drive on a barely navigable road brought us to the low stone wall that defined Philip's domain. Headlights revealed a modest opening, slightly wider than our car, which evoked for me the wardrobe door through which Lucy, Edmund, Peter, and Susan entered Narnia's frozen kingdom.

Suddenly a rectangle of pure ice floated on a white sea of snow: a house of cold glass segments divided by vertical bars of steel. The solitary concession to substance, a brick tower with ascending smoke, pierced the flat roof proudly, as though to say, "I'll be standing here long after these ice blocks have melted."

We trudged through snow as soft as swan's down to the warmth of a bright fire in a semicircular hearth. Not allowed leisure to look or linger, we were quickly dispersed to our respective guest quarters—Herbert to the New England clapboard house near the road and me to a small bunker on level ground, an opaque counterpoint to its transparent neighbor.

I entered a room unlike any I had ever seen or imagined. Pale pink Venetian Fortuny cotton damask curtained the walls from ceiling to floor, concealing windows, doors, and private areas. Soft light from hidden sources illumined a canopied ceiling—a concept that Philip had taken from the London townhouse of the "accidental romantic" Sir John Soane, the early nineteenth-century British architect.

Two other features of this un-Miesian fantasy tempted me to sever my ties to planet Earth: rheostat lighting and a sculpture. Ibram Lassaw's rectangular sculpture of lightly gilded metal and wire, aptly named *Clouds of Magellan,* hovered above an unframed mattress covered with the fabric of the curtained walls. Had a voice whispered in my ear that I had only to turn the dial of a remote control to explore outer space, I would have believed it. I resisted the temptation, confident that good company and a delicious dinner awaited me a few yards distant from the solid door of the guesthouse. But before crossing over, I would exchange my pedestrian uniform consisting of a skirt, blouse, and pullover for a garment with an exotic history.

Several years before my marriage, I was introduced to Valentina Schlee, a Russian-born émigré dancer turned dressmaker.[1] Valentina had slowly but surely mastered the art of dress design, and she clothed some of New York's best-known actresses: Lynn Fontanne and Katharine Cornell in the 1920s and '30s as well as Greta Garbo and Katharine Hepburn in the 1940s and '50s. Occasionally, and only after an interview, she would design for the wife of a prominent businessman or diplomat. Valentina was notorious for refusing to dress any woman, however highly placed, whose face did not interest her.

I was neither an actress nor married to an important New Yorker, but I had the good fortune to be a friend of the Watson family and to be visiting them when their always surprising patriarch, Thomas J., decided to take his "kept women," daughters Jane and Helen, and their incomparably beautiful and gracious mother, Jeanette, to meet one of his discoveries—in this case, the dressmaker Valentina. Uncle Tom had heard that she had dared to create wool evening dresses for ladies who summered in Maine, as the Watson ladies did.

I'll never regret that I tagged along for Aunt Jeanette's fitting of a long sapphire-blue dinner gown made of hand-loomed wool. My memory of

Valentina remains vivid and intact. I can hear her deep, unhurried voice and see the silk jersey snood under her pillbox hat and the ivory cigarette holder she wielded like a conductor's baton to command or reprimand a cowering seamstress. Below her theatrical veneer, however, lay the hardwood of a thorough knowledge of the history of clothing. Her hooded evening cloaks, for instance, were lifted from a medieval tapestry; her close-fitting caps were taken from the head of a Botticelli pageboy; her double skirts, the outer one slashed down the center to expose one of another color, had in less democratic centuries belonged only in the wardrobes of queens. As I learned more about Valentina's creative "borrowings," I found the rumor entirely credible that Andrew Mellon, the donor of Washington's National Gallery of Art, had been one of her early backers.

After that first introduction and during one of my weekend-from-college visits with the Watson family, I gathered the courage to present Valentina with a page from a Christie's art catalogue of a twelfth-century pen-and-ink drawing of an unidentified woman, possibly a servant. Having learned from my mother that style was more lasting than fashion, I had been attracted by the beauty and simplicity of this ordinary woman's dress and its hand-woven, almost tactile texture on the printed page.

Valentina handed her cigarette-holder scepter to an attendant and cradled the page tenderly. "See how precisely the long sleeves fit into the armholes of the bodice? Why hide well-cut seams! They are like the posts and beams that keep a house from falling. Yes, my dear, a well-designed dress or coat is, in my philosophy, simply good architecture and therefore livable. One should be able to sleep in one's dress on a chair as comfortably as in a bedroom, and your garments should last your lifetime."

A look of genuine pain shot across her face. "Designers today have forgotten that dresses should be built, rather than decorated. Having no idea of architecture, they rely on baubles and on buttons that don't function as buttons."

The founders of the Bauhaus school of architecture would have applauded her philosophy of dress. They had after World War I cleared out the Augean stable of frivolous architecture, warning us that an earthquake would have shaken the architecture off New York's Empire State Building.

Tillich too would have shared Valentina's disdain for imitation and her genius for extracting from the past whatever was timeless and useful.

A quotation from his article "The Lost Dimension of Religion" under-scores his agreement with an architect or designer who "removes the trimmings taken over from past styles because they cannot be an honest expression of our own period. He [or she] prefers the seeming poverty of a purpose-determined style to the deceptive richness of imitated styles of the past."[2]

Valentina's equanimity returned. "Yes, I'll adapt this drawing into a winter evening dress for you but not copy it. I'll look for thin wool in pale lavender for the body. The long sleeves could be made of a no-color silk jersey. There will be an unattached wimple for your head in the same beige as the sleeves. These soft materials should fall gracefully when you walk, yet, if we succeed, they would bring to mind a carved figure of weathered stone when you stand still."

Canon Waddams's knock at the door returned me to the present mo-ment, and together we walked the short distance to the Glass House. It was now well past nine o'clock, and Philip seated us at once at his dinner table, amid shadows formed by tall candles and the glow from a fire in the brick hearth. Faint exterior lighting hidden under the eaves of the flat roof illu-minated the mounting snow.

An observer, looking in, would have wondered whether we were actors or audience in the drama unfolding within four transparent walls. Philip had donned a quilted white Japanese boxer's jacket, my host gift. Canon Waddams wore a dark suit and his cleric's collar. I was clothed in Valenti-na's semi-medieval gown.

Later, we exchanged our dinner chairs for leather and steel Miesian Barcelona chairs to watch, spellbound, the silent snow that was falling consistently but not overwhelmingly, else we would have missed the drama of the singular scene. Piled snow defied gravity and rose up in re-sponse to fresh falling snow. It may not be unusual for snow to behave this way, but without Philip's subtle lighting, its "levitation" would have passed by unmarveled.

We sat transfixed. Philip leaned back in his chair, hands folded, his face in the half-light resembling the poet Baudelaire's face as Rodin had im-mortalized him. I too had become sculpture, but not of bronze, because my dressmaker's medium was hand-woven wool. Herbert stood between us, a black silhouette.

Remembering that Herbert trained with a Gregorian choir as a young priest, I asked him to sing. Gregorian chant is modal, its soft peaks rounded—indeed, like snow. While we watched tidal waves of rising and falling snow and listened to Herbert's glorious voice, an attenuated, flesh-less Giacometti sculpture looked down on us from a contemporary ward-robe that separated sleeping from living space.

As already fallen snowflakes spiraled upward at the touch of oncoming snow, I wondered, "How long will our halfway-to-heaven journey last?" No longer, perhaps, than a fully open and near-perfect rose can retain its petals when a strong wind blows. That enchanted evening was not halted by a sudden gust. Its petals were shattered by a shrill ring of the telephone.

Philip jumped from his chair to silence the phone, as if responding to a pistol shot. His "No" to the caller was decisive before he said more softly, "You are not in a state to drive here or anywhere. Stay home with your wife." He concluded in a near-whisper, "And I have two guests to care for."

He turned toward us sadly. "Please help me forgive an old friend, a bril-liant man and great impresario, but tonight he's extremely drunk." The caller was Lincoln Kirstein.

The enchantment broken, the evening late, Herbert and I thanked our embarrassed host and left for our designated quarters.[3]

The Glass House in winter, 2011.

Photograph by Stephanie Lin.

In Christ there is no east or west,
in Him no south or north;
but one great fellowship of love
throughout the whole wide earth.

—Music from an African American spiritual, text from Oxenham

CHAPTER 29

Orchard House

W here would I look for the healing memories that had been uppermost in my brother's mind during the dedication of the cornerstone of the Roofless Church in 1959? An unexpected opportunity came my way twelve years later in 1971: a two-story house on North Street in New Harmony was for sale between a corner lot that stored heavy equipment and a small structure that was more shed than house, an uninhabited shell (48 on town map). Heavy equipment was removed from the corner lot, and the shed on the west side was demolished, once again demonstrating that preservation is as much about subtraction as restoration. Although I had to buy three properties, arguments in favor of restoring the 1860 house to its former elegance were not lacking.

First of all, it resembled on a smaller scale Lincoln Home National Historic Site in Springfield, Illinois. Second, the faded corncob yellow of its exterior walls was a reminder of the original owner's status as a "corn king" in town. His name was Levi Lafayette Lichtenberger, ecumenically

257

correct and in sync with my respect for Jewish, Catholic, and Protestant faiths. The antebellum house would be an ideal repository for objects I had collected over the years because of their bearing on the paramount issues of all centuries—those of war, estrangement, and reunion.

One of the acquisitions was a Picasso reproduction that, unlike his famous *Guernica* from the Spanish Civil War, has received little attention. From my perspective as a southerner, the work poignantly combines his memories of the recently ended World War II and our own War between the States. In the print, against the background of a blue flag with red bars and white stars, similar to that of the Confederacy, we see a distorted, lean white ewer or pitcher, standard chinaware for Americans in the mid-nineteenth century. Further down, upon a narrow, lead-gray border, Picasso buried several horizontal white daisies, petals intact, a reminder of the countless young men killed in the flower of their youth during wars. This print by the greatest artist of the twentieth century is for me more heartbreaking than a painted or photographic rendering of an actual battle.

Other acquisitions would contribute to my theme for the house, including a northern wardrobe and a Confederate officer's map. Biographies of Lincoln and Lee would lie on a table desk, and my Picasso print would adorn the entrance wall to the Lincoln and Lee Room upstairs.

I had another object for a house of reconciliation—a post-Civil War cast-iron hat rack. Our reunited states are represented by the stars in a shield at the center below a small mirror. A pair of cast-iron rifles point toward the shield; a sculptured green olive branch laces them together. From hooks on either side of the garland hang soldiers' caps, one Confederate gray, the other a deep Union blue.

Facing top. The framed print of an ewer against a starry background by Picasso hangs in the hallway.

Photograph by Darryl D. Jones, 2013. The original work is at the Musée Picasso, Antibes: Pablo Picasso, L'Aiguière au fond étoilé, 15 septembre 1946. Huile, gouache et crayon sur papier doublé marouflé à la cire sur toile, montée sur support rigide. 65.5 × 50.5 cm. MPA 1946.2.8 © Musée Picasso, Antibes. © 2014 Estate of Pablo Picasso / Artists Rights Society (ARS), New York.

Facing bottom. The Lincoln and Lee Room.

Photograph by Darryl D. Jones, 2013.

Living room with the post-Civil War cast-iron hat rack.

Photograph by Darryl D. Jones, 2013.

A few possessions that reflect my antipathy to war and my hope that the forces of life would one day outlast the wings of war, however, do not furnish a house. Other than Picasso's subtle, anguished reference to uncivil, fraternal wars and my cast-iron hat rack, the wardrobe, and the map table, the house that I had purchased and named for the Harmonist orchard it had replaced remained empty.

My daughter Janie, who by this time was married and living in New York City, sensed that the Orchard House deserved professional oversight and introduced me to Mark Hampton, a young decorator who had helped her and her husband with their New York apartment. With her customary thoroughness, Janie had researched Mark's background and shared her findings with me. During his junior year abroad at the London School of Economics, Mark worked for several months as a draftsman and apprentice to the celebrated London designer David Hicks. On returning to New York, he worked for a summer for Sister Parish and then for six years for Eleanor McMillen Brown at the decorating firm she founded, the prestigious McMillen Inc. Mark's most impressive credential, however, was his profound grasp of the history of art and architecture, which is a grounding rarely found among his colleagues. In fact, one could fairly say that this young Hoosier-born decorator's informed and refined taste had brought the art of interior design to new levels.[1] He was also a gifted painter who could illustrate his proposals to a client with seductive watercolors.

Garden Gallery.

Photograph by Darryl D. Jones, 2013.

I didn't give Mark time to submit a formal layout of the Orchard House rooms, for I needed his unique talents as soon as he could take time away from his own clients at McMillen. He was as eager to begin his first commission in his home state as I was to learn from him.

Our initial meeting, however, was not in Indiana but in New York City. His hand at my elbow, his feet two steps ahead of mine, Mark led his wide-eyed client through an as yet ungentrified area of Manhattan, unfamiliar streets filled with warehouses and workshops, near the river on the Upper East Side in the nineties, to the office and workplace of Guido Di Angelis, not to an immaculate showroom where licensed decorators exposed their clients to ready-made furniture. We slipped into a warehouse-size dusty back room alive with skilled craftsmen and upholsterers. A senior Di Angelis, a silver-haired handsome Italian American, left his desk to ask Mark to clarify his instructions for the Orchard House's sofa and armchairs. Briefly, they agreed not to reproduce uncomfortable,

The Sarah Campbell Blaffer bedroom downstairs features the
canopy bed belonging to Jane Blaffer Owen's mother.

Photograph by Darryl D. Jones, 2013.

stiff-backed Victorian furniture. While respectful of the contours that defined sofas and chairs of that period, they chose soft down for backs and
arms, not tightly packed horsehair. Taking Mark's philosophy of adaptation
still further, I relate it to one of C. S. Lewis's metaphors of the hereafter:
"My form remains one, though the matter in it changes continually, I am,
in that respect, like the curve in a waterfall."[2]

Whether our decision to furnish the Orchard House in the spirit and not
the letter of mid-nineteenth-century America was right or heretical, many
guests, invited friends, and family members have found comfort in its upholstered chairs and sofa within the living room walls of Hampton red.
From a witches' brew of five shades of red and a touch of lamp black, Mark
had extracted an antique red closer in color to the worn leather binding of
an old book than to a painted red. It is a perfect foil for Di Angelis's forest-
green sofa, Mark's Roman shades at the four windows, and the pocket doors
that open into the corn-husk-yellow garden gallery. White trim on the window shades, doorways, and baseboards, as well as contemporary paintings, snap this dreamy room out of a previous century and into a new one.

Oddly enough, in the fall of 1976 during the Carter-Mondale campaign, Joan Mondale decided to stop in New Harmony. An art historian,
she may have come more to enjoy our architecture than to gain support
for her husband's ticket, for Democrats and Republicans alike have tradi-
tionally bypassed southern Indiana as "a place with more cows and pigs
than voters." I was not in town to welcome Mrs. Mondale, but she was
sufficiently impressed by the Orchard House to inquire about its decorator and subsequently to invite him to decorate the first Carter-Mondale
Christmas tree in the White House.

Four years later, the Reagans asked him to paint as a watercolor the
green room in the White House festooned in Christmas décor; the image
became their official Christmas card. Though Mark had decorated Blair
House, the president's guest house, for the Reagans, Mark's most important Washington commissions came from George and Barbara Bush.[3]
During the Reagan administration, Mark worked for them redecorat-
ing the Admiral's House, which is the vice president's residence. When
George H. W. Bush was elected president and the Bushes moved into the
White House, Mark decorated the private family rooms and the Oval Office. Mark also decorated their "summer White House" in Maine and
their retirement home in Houston. New Harmony had been and continues to be an incubator and a hatchery.

The village of New Harmony was peculiar in that it was not founded for livelihood nor gain, but for and upon an Ideal. An Ideal society was to be instituted here, a generous way of life never known before. New Harmony was founded for no other reason than that a Certain Dream might become visible in the world.

—Caroline Dale Snedeker, *The Town of the Fearless*

CHAPTER 30

Rapp-Maclure-Owen House Restoration

After Kenneth Owen sold his Pennsylvania horse farm, he turned his attention to New Harmony. Forty years had passed since he had purchased the Granary and Corbin home from Miss Laura's heirs.[1] In 1989, he finally began restoration of the Rapp-Maclure-Owen House. Kenneth was actively involved in the process and oversaw all the workmen, particularly those who were removing paint from the well-crafted poplar moldings and baseboards.

Together we asked Loren Dunlap, a native Indiana artist, to create the murals for the front entrance hall. Loren met this formidable challenge with sensitivity and skill. There was no instant, digital mural. He devoted a month to research in the archives of the Working Men's Institute, photographing trees, and making small-scale models. Two months were needed for the hard labor of applying his concept to four separate fourteen-foot-high walls. Brilliantly, he linked them with the rippling shores of the Wabash River, bordered with native flora and fauna.

Loren Dunlap's murals (1990) show the Wabash to the left
and the town as it appeared to Bodmer to the right.

Photograph by Darryl D. Jones, 2013.

The scene on the north wall was inspired by the watercolor painted in 1832 by the Swiss artist Karl Bodmer of the overview of Father Rapp's town as it appeared from Indian Mound, or someplace close to it. Loren did not, however, replicate Bodmer's somber colors. Kenneth and I were so pleased with Loren's color sense that we gave him full rein to choose and mix the paints for the music and dining rooms and to purchase William Morris and Colefax and Fowler wallpapers for the library and master bedroom.

Kenneth's ultimate delight was in placing the furniture, paintings, and artifacts where, to his discerning eye, they belonged and where he devoutly wished they would always remain. Most furnishings were from his own collection, but some, luckily for posterity, were gifts from descendants of the original Owen/Maclure colony. Rapp-Maclure-Owen House will serve as a center for research and a repository for Owen family materials, including early New Harmony artifacts, under the auspices of the Owen/Maclure Foundation. We in New Harmony today simply refer to the restored house as "the Maclure mansion," emphasizing Maclure's lasting legacy in our town.

Although Albert Arthur Hodge left New Harmony after high school to teach in the northern part of the state, evidence of his generosity remains. As the only descendant of Madame Marie Duclos Fretageot, Albert inherited her 1821 square piano, her eighteenth-century clock, and the school bell with which she awakened her pupils on the third floor of what had been Father Rapp's mansion. Albert gave his heirlooms to Kenneth when the restoration of the Rapp-Maclure-Owen House began.

Objects loaned to or purchased by Kenneth were also placed in the house. Historic New Harmony has loaned us a cane-back Scottish canapé sofa for the music room. David Tanner and his father, Ben, descendants of Robert Dale, contributed period pieces.

Ben Storey and his sister Constance Wheeler, direct descendants of Jane Dale Owen Fauntleroy, gave unselfishly of their inherited Owen memorabilia: a Robert Owen armchair, a miniature of a Dale ancestress, silver dinner knives, and a doll chest brought from her native Scotland by Jane Dale Owen, the only one of three Owen daughters to join her brothers in the New World. Ben Storey, an Episcopal minister and invaluable family friend, enabled Kenneth to acquire the portrait of Anne Caroline Dale Owen, Robert Owen's wife, which now can be seen in the Laboratory alongside portraits of her sons Richard and Robert Dale.

Treasures in the music room include Madame Fretageot's 1821 piano and
her eighteenth-century clock (on the table beneath the mirror).

Photograph by Darryl D. Jones, 2013.

Alexander Maclure, brother of William, had purchased furniture in
Philadelphia after the 1844 fire, including a double bed, a dresser, a wash-
stand, and a small table replete with chamber pot. These pieces were
hand-painted with the flowers and fruits characteristic of Victoriana;
although ornate for Kenneth's taste, they now reside in the master bedroom. Since the unmarried Maclures left no heirs, these pieces found
their way first to Bay St. Louis, Mississippi, on the Gulf Coast, and then
back to the Maclure house, thanks to two remarkable Owen descendants,
the grandchildren of David Dale Owen.

One of these descendants was the writer Caroline Dale Parke
Snedeker, whose books have withstood the test of time and been recently

Jane Blaffer Owen admires the portrait of
Anne Caroline Dale Owen
in the David Dale Owen Laboratory.

Photograph by Darryl D. Jones, October 2007.

Master bedroom with Alexander Maclure's Victorian furnishings.
Photograph by Darryl D. Jones, 2013.

Above left, *The Shepherd* and *right*, *The Prophet*, © 1968 Herold Witherspoon.

Photograph by Darryl D. Jones, 2013. Courtesy of Herold Witherspoon.

Below. The wall of windows in the Tillich Dining Room
provides a view of Paul Tillich Park.

Photograph by Darryl D. Jones, 2013.

True art breaks through smooth surfaces and deepens our understanding. Rodin's works did that for me, and I've commissioned sculptures for New Harmony that engage our minds and reflect the period of history in which we live.

No one has thrown vegetables or eggs at the statues I have placed outdoors in New Harmony. For the most part they have been ignored, perhaps for the same reason that Israelites plugged their ears to Jeremiah's exhortations. For instance, to look carefully at Stephen De Staebler's sculpture *Angel of the Annunciation,* planted among the crabapple trees on North Street, is to sense a stern warning from a heavenly messenger (50 on town map). Variously called Gabriel or Gabriela, the hermaphrodite angel extends a long arm, like a sword about to fall, as if to say, "Shape up or else!" The legs, one male and the other female, are broken and bruised by the world it has entered, not the one it has left.

A second De Staebler figure stands beside the Lipchitz gate in the northern half of the forecourt of the Roofless Church. His *Pietà* conjoins the death and resurrection of Jesus within the single body of his Mother, events that artists more often view separately (51 on town map).

Douglas G. "Doug" Adams, a renowned professor of religion and art at the Pacific School of Religion in Berkeley (until his recent and untimely death) has written with passion and precision about De Staebler's unusual interpretation of the crucifixion.[4] Adams has called this *Pietà* in the Roofless Church the successor of Michelangelo's *Pietà Rondanini* in Milan's Castello Sforzesco. I've made no such claims in my own description of it, available at the Entry House of the New Harmony Inn, but I have witnessed the healing power of this extraordinary work of art.

A tall hedge of clipped yews screens the forecourt from the central *temenos.* They grow from soil placed in long limestone planters on either side of the west entry of this garden court. The planters also accommodate visitors who require more than a passing look at the *Pietà* and who choose to sit facing the statue. While I was sitting there quietly one

Facing top. Angel of the Annunciation, © 1999 Stephen De Staebler.
Photograph by Darryl D. Jones, 2009. Courtesy of Stephen De Staebler Estate.

Facing bottom. Pietà, © 1988 Stephen De Staebler.
Photograph by Nancy Mangum McCaslin, 2013. Courtesy of Stephen De Staebler Estate.

moonless night, a sudden stirring in the hedges suggested I was not alone. Parting the branches, I discovered a previously hidden neighbor, a woman unknown to me. I must have startled her, for she rose to leave. In broad daylight I might have watched her move on without a word. But under cover of night, we were related, two anonymous filings drawn forcefully to the same magnet.

"Please don't leave. There is room for both of us here."

Softly, unhurriedly, she replied, "I've sat here long enough. It is time to go."

Her name and port of origin did not matter to me, only why she had chosen to come and to linger beside De Staebler's *Pietà,* and I asked her. She stood close enough to the light pole illuminating the statue for me to observe her serene and beautiful face. She was a woman about my age, her salt-and-pepper brown hair drawn back from a broad brow and widely separated, soft brown eyes.

"I came here because I have recently lost my only son. Whenever I look at this image of the Mother of Christ standing tall and moving forward in spite of her great loss and grief, I know I must do the same."

In the shadow of solemn yews, two strangers clasped hands for a few seconds. Though we have not met again, I am confident that this other mother received healing from her encounter with De Staebler's *Pietà* as I did, and continue to. A genuine work of art and of literature does not ignore human suffering or injustices but, to draw upon the title of one of Reinhold Niebuhr's most important books, can take us "beyond tragedy."

I have thrust this story upon a patient reader in the hope that he or she can tell mothers and fathers who have lost sons or daughters that there is a healing balm for them in the Roofless Church and also in Carol's Garden, close by.

In the mid-1960s, the young Indiana artist Loren Dunlap, whom I greatly admired, completed his murals for the ceiling and walls of a private dining room in the Red Geranium Restaurant. Loren was working primarily in New York City at that time. During one of my visits to Janie, he introduced me to Edward Gilbert, a talented English artist and designer of gardens and spectacular balls. Mrs. Paul "Bunny" Mellon had chosen him from a long list of hopeful candidates to create a setting for her daughter's outdoor wedding at Oak Spring near Upperville, Virginia. This important commission for May 15, 1968, however, was never fully re-

Loren Dunlap's 1965 mural depicting paradise along the Wabash River
in the Grapevine Bar at the Red Geranium.

Photograph by Darryl D. Jones, 2013.

alized. For no known reason, some thugs knocked Edward down on Park
Avenue in New York City. Loren brought his bandaged friend to me and
asked if I could take Edward to New Harmony to regain his strength.

I was impressed by Edward's inability to feel sorry for his plight or anger at his attackers. "Just think, Mrs. Owen," he had said, "they spared my
eyes and my hands."[5] The wounded artist came to my favorite town, where
I installed him in the Poet's House. He spent his days sketching proposals
for my backyard, and I selected one for immediate realization, a checkerboard of brick-bordered squares filled with flowers and herbs. Another
drawing was also implemented, the addition of a screened porch (the
Pleasure Boat) to the back of Rawlings House.[6]

The translation of his drawings into brick and mortar, combined
with Bertha Smith's culinary skills and our community's custom of greeting visitors with warmth and welcome, helped Edward to achieve a complete recovery.

Checkerboard garden and the Pleasure Boat at Rawlings House.

Photograph by Darryl D. Jones, 2013.

There was yet another challenge to Gilbert's inventive mind, an empty lot fronting North Street, from which I had recently removed a cottage that was too small for its six inhabitants. The mother and four daughters were exceptionally beautiful, and the youngest was a close friend of my daughter Annie. Their father readily accepted my offer of a bigger and better house on Granary Street in exchange for their property, a trade-off that benefited everyone. I had no idea, however, what to do with the yawning gap this transaction left between the 1840 Garden House and the Owen Community House (which now houses the Artists' Guild) (53 and 54 on town map).

Edward Gilbert, however, knew precisely how to fill that vacancy and handed me his concept: a grid of equidistant Bradford pear trees. We planted them that spring. Their eventual snowfalls of white blossoms in early April and scarlet leaves in late October gladden the eyes of anyone who walks along North Street, reason enough for their existence.

A decade later, in 1979, Gilbert's orchard assumed a larger, more personal purpose and a name, Carol's Garden, in memory of the beloved daughter who died that year at only thirty-five (55 on town map). One day, I brought an aching heart there, along with my two hands and a drawing pad. My pencil erased four trees at the center and replaced them with a circular fountain from which four paths led to an embracing outer pathway. I had inadvertently drawn a mandala, a

The welcoming entrance to the screened Pleasure Boat.

Photograph by Darryl D. Jones, 2013.

configuration that symbolizes wholeness and is found in the sacred texts and art of Buddhists, Hebrews, and Celtic Christians. For Carl Jung, the mandala symbolizes "a safe refuge of inner reconciliation and wholeness . . . a synthesis of distinctive elements in a unified scheme representing the basic nature of existence."[7]

The ally needed for Carol's Garden was not far away. An Indiana art magazine arrived unsolicited that November. An article introduced me to the work of David Rodgers, a sculptor living in Bloomington.[8] Our collaboration began shortly after his first visit to New Harmony. Carol's *Fountain of Life,* designed by David for Carol's Garden, emits a single, forceful upward shaft of water (56 on town map). Underwater lights illumine the surrounding pool and the Bradford pear branches and leaves that arch above. David also carved two limestone benches, placed east and west of the fountain, half hidden by oak-leaf hydrangeas.

Our plans moved swiftly to fruition, propelled, I believe, by Carol's ever-present spirit and the blessing of Bob Lax, Thomas Merton's lifelong friend. I had met this remarkable and saintly poet while we were both at the Abbey of Gethsemani, Merton's Trappist monastic community in Kentucky. Robert Lax was there to lecture, I to listen. I have since read his book *The Circus of the Sun,* where I found a fitting introduction to Carol's Garden, which serves as the epigraph to this chapter. Now that I have described the plan and spirit of the garden, Lax's words bear repeating here:

> And in the beginning was love. Love made a sphere:
> all things grew within it; the sphere then encompassed
> beginnings and endings, beginning and end. Love
> had a compass whose whirling dance traced out a
> sphere of love in the void: in the center thereof
> rose a fountain.[9]

The good man who gave us these beautiful words spent his last days on Patmos—the Greek island where John wrote the book of Revelation—caring for his many cats and enriching the lives of everyone who came his way.

Carroll Harris Simms created a mother-daughter bench, placed at the southwest corner of Carol's Garden, which the artist explains has forms and symbols showing "the belief in the return of the seasons: the resurrection, continuity and the rebirth of life" (57 on town map).[10]

Carol's Garden and *Fountain of Life.*
Photograph by Kent Schuette, 1996.

I have garnered other blessings over the years for my daughter's garden, most memorably that of J. Pittman McGehee, who was at the time dean of Houston's Christ Church Cathedral. Pittman had accepted my invitation to lead our Benedictine retreat one year in the mid-1980s. One afternoon between lectures and prayer times, he visited Carol's Garden with me.

We entered from North Street and made our way past the tall ferns and blue-green *Hosta sieboldiana* that lined the path toward the central fountain. Suddenly, out of a sea of foliage, arose the tiny, blue-clad figure of Pee Wee York, New Harmony's cheerful weeder and my co-creator, for I could not have begun the garden without Pee Wee. He was always ready to hold one end of my measuring tape or to take my hand when I needed to hear, "You done good, Mrs. Jane." I can still see his head tilted back to receive Pittman's offered hand, his wide grin and his pale eyes twin pools of clear blue water. Two months following his New Harmony visit, Pitt-man sent me a poem featuring our garden genie.

I called Pee Wee from his weeding to the Pleasure Boat, my spring and summer screened office at Rawlings House, and told him, "Here is a lovely poem, Pee Wee, which you inspired the dean of Christ Church to write. He has sent a copy to me and one for you." Suddenly solemn, his pale eyes moist, the garden genie asked permission to return to his boardinghouse. Believing him overcome with emotion, I asked, "Do you need to lie down?"

"I'm okay, Mrs. Jane. I just need to put this here poem in my icebox."

An unknown young man provided me with a powerful memory of Carol's Garden. Small weddings have often taken place in the pea-gravel circle around the fountain. Children bring their dogs for a drink of water, and visitors walk its paths silently. But no one had ever sung there—not until late one summer's afternoon when the words of "Amazing Grace," carried by a rich tenor voice, reached me in my own garden many yards away. I hurried through the south gate to follow the voice to its source and discovered that it belonged to a young man scarcely older than twenty.

He stopped his song and asked apologetically, "Perhaps I shouldn't sing here?"

"Please go on," I entreated. "I've come only to hear you better and to ask, if you don't mind, why you have brought your beautiful voice to this garden."

"Thank you for not minding, ma'am. I lost my mother a few weeks ago, and it helps me to sing here."

E. Garrett Garage.
*Don Blair Collection. Courtesy of Special Collections,
University of Southern Indiana.*

Encouraged by the state's new interest and generosity, Harmonie Associates gathered momentum, gained members, and offered excellent
programs. It lacked, however, the infrastructure that only a more experienced organizer could provide. My cross-country lifestyle kept me from
an active and consistent role in community enterprises. But I wanted
Harmonie Associates to succeed and to bring my tithe to their storehouse.
I did so in the person of Ralph G. Schwarz, a former colleague of Helen
Duprey Bullock at the National Trust for Historic Preservation. Highly
recommended and with impressive credentials, Ralph had been director
of building planning, construction, and operations for the new Ford
Foundation building in New York. Architect Kevin Roche's handsome
building was now complete, and Ralph, having taken on some interim re-
sponsibilities for the National Trust, was free to accept my invitation to
New Harmony in the fall of 1972.

Ralph Schwarz was given two assignments: the creation of a bookstore and the formation of what came to be Historic New Harmony, Inc. (65 on town map). He fathered both entities with precision and a sure grasp of history. He created large poster boards with photos of the people and places that had shaped our little history and hung them from the ceiling of the Red Geranium Bookstore, which prospered from the maternal guidance of Donna Creek.[3] I eventually closed it when another bookstore opened on Main Street, and leased the empty space to Annette Buckland for her Antique Showrooms in the Mews; Ralph's informative posters still hang from the ceiling of its entry (59 on town map). Ralph also assisted me with the addition of Waddams Chapel and a swimming pool for the New Harmony Inn in his role as trustee for the Robert Lee Blaffer Trust (60 on town map).

Ralph had even more ambitious plans that went beyond these projects and far beyond the resources at my disposal. We decided the time had come to elicit the help of Indiana's largest foundation, the prestigious Lilly Endowment. Luckily my Evansville friend Bob Orr was lieutenant governor in 1973, and he arranged for Ralph to meet with members of the Lilly board at their Indianapolis headquarters. Ralph's previous experience with the National Trust and the Ford Foundation, combined with his disarming personality, made him an ideal envoy or, more accurately, a bridge builder—for had not the Catholic Church derived the title of its supreme authority from the Latin term for the man who could engineer the best bridge, the *pontifex maximus*, hence pontiff? Ralph's ascending role in the fortunes of New Harmony bore traces of Vatican authority. I was not surprised to learn that the members of the Lilly board had granted the requests of a man aglow with the aura of papal infallibility. I dared to believe we stood on the threshold of a golden age for New Harmony.

The goals that Ralph and I shared swiftly leapt into reality. Ralph acquired offices for himself and his growing staff on the second floor of the J. Breith Building on Main Street (61 on town map). No time was lost in the spending of Lilly largesse. The rooms below Ralph's offices became a gallery for contemporary art (63 on town map). Salomon Wolfe House, the gift of Phyllis and Bob Menke, was moved from south of town to the corner of Granary and N. Brewery Street in 1975 (62 on town map). That brick Harmonist house was carefully restored and prepared to receive an expertly crafted diorama of the town as it existed in 1826. Ralph engaged Lester Associates in Armonk, New York, which made dioramas

Visitors to New Harmony continue to learn about our
history from Ralph's posters inside the Mews.
Photograph by Janet Lorence, 2013.

for World's Fairs, to create ours. This concept of Ralph's imagination
continues to attract visitors of every age, who kneel in a darkened room
around a static merry-go-round with concealed lights that illuminate a
miniature village. Against a background of carefully researched and re-
created Harmonist music, modern visitors listen to excerpts from the
diaries of early Scots and Welsh visitors, narrated in the accents of their
respective countries.

As these impressive additions enriched the cultural and economic life
of the community, plans moved forward for the renovation of antiquated Murphy Auditorium. Since Evans Woollen, the architect I had
chosen to build the Entry House and both dormitories of the New Harmony Inn, was frequently in town from his Indianapolis office, Ralph
wisely selected him to bring old Murphy Auditorium from the nineteenth century into the twentieth. Woollen's quasi-monastic design for
the New Harmony Inn and Conference Center earned him a commission
for buildings at the Abbey of St. Meinrad. My daughter Annie brought
her considerable natural talent for decorating to the Conference Center,

creating an environment of simplicity and quality (65 on town map).⁴ *Sky Dance,* a red-painted steel sculpture designed by Larry Reising and fabricated by Tom and Elmer Helfrich, enlivens the front lawn of the New Harmony Inn.⁵

Ralph Schwarz acted with the speed of light, contrary to the slow pace I had traveled since 1941: it had taken nearly twenty years for the Robert Lee Blaffer Trust to assemble lots from different owners to provide adequate land for the Roofless Church as well as three years to plan and build it, and I had waited ten torturous years before a rebuilding of its walls could begin. My husband's pace had been even slower than mine: forty years passed before he began work on the Rapp-Maclure-Owen House and formed the Owen/Maclure Foundation, and forty-eight years before he placed the Granary in the nonprofit Rapp Granary-Owen Foundation for its restoration and operation.

If I was astounded by Ralph's ability to blitz through obstacles while retaining his supply lines with the Lilly board, his next maneuver left me breathless. We had agreed that a visitor orientation center and the training of guides were crucial to the interpretation of New Harmony's history. We further agreed not to replicate a Harmonist structure and to look for a "coming" architect who would speak the architectural language of the present. I did not believe, however, that funds for such an ambitious building would be available alongside the generous grants destined for other projects and, for the most part, already spent. But Ralph had exceeded his own record for speed and active imagination.

To my surprise and delight, Ralph informed me that the architect he had selected was Richard Meier, whom he described to the Lilly board as "an aspiring, talented man whose aesthetic, philosophy, and experience matched the need for a Propylaea where light, form, and function would create a dynamic approach to New Harmony's historic sites."⁶ Richard Meier would be arriving in the spring of 1974 to survey the site we had considered most suitable for a long-awaited visitors' orientation center, to be called the Atheneum. Ralph informed me that the word *atheneum,* apart from its historical context, translates as "a place of learning," which defines my mission for New Harmony.

Facing. Sky Dance.
Photograph by Darryl D. Jones, 2009.

Richard Meier, architect, The Atheneum, 1975–1979.

Photograph by Darryl D. Jones, 2009.

Closing my eyes, I can still envision a lean and lithe Richard Meier standing on that slight rise of land, recently sown with grass to cover the scarred surface of the town's erstwhile dump, his arms spread wide like the wings of a giant bird, his body inclined toward a curve of the Wabash below the knoll. Meier's eagerness and readiness for flight into uncharted space was contagious. Ralph and I were now fully convinced that Meier could design a building that would reflect not past but present time, while

nonetheless invoking, in modern dress, the memory of the paddle wheelers that had once plied the Wabash to bring passengers to New Harmony. Meier actually began his conceptual design July 15, 1975. We did not hesitate to bring our begging bowls to the Lilly Endowment. Once again, Ralph's powers of persuasion, not mine, won the board's consent to underwrite our ambitious project. None of us, however, foresaw that New Harmony's Atheneum would receive, among its many awards, the 2008 American Institute of Architects Twenty-Five Year Award for architectural design of continuing significance.[7]

Richard Meier's Atheneum, built of glass and white enamel on steel, was yet another windfall from heaven's unlimited storehouse. But let not its stellar and Oscar status obscure the human blessings that have poured forth from the same storehouse and continue to pour. The families and individuals who have restored houses since 1960 continue to improve the quality of community life. Peggy Rapp's enthusiasm for her own garden at Granary and Brewery Streets overflowed into the founding of a garden club, which grew to more than sixty members in its first year. Kent Parker has wisely observed, "You don't choose New Harmony; New Harmony chooses you." The list of individuals who have received nourishment from our Hoosier soil and who have, in turn, replenished it is a long one, and my gratitude is boundless.

The recent rediscovery—in the drawer of the Orkney chair in Mother Superior House—of a March 20, 1977, letter that Rev. Mother Ruth had sent surprised and humbled me. In closing, I bow my head to receive her blessing:

My very dear Jane,

The very kindly, thoughtful and generous hospitality on my visit to your "New Harmony" is greatly appreciated and will never be forgotten. From the time of my arrival until I left the Mother Superior's House on Thursday so many significant experiences took place that each contributed to and informed the last.

It seems to me that the central experience of my memorable visit was your dinner party with Kenneth present with his house-party following. It seems to me that everyone was at the top of his form that evening and that it was an experience to be treasured always.

The visits to your important and significant buildings were revealing and gave me an opportunity to capture some of your vision of what New Harmony is and is becoming. That is a legacy, Jane, for generations yet to come and work in the Spirit and harmony of your blest vision. I am so thankful for it all.

Every experience I had and which was shared with you, with Kenneth, with the dear Glovers [Rev. Mort and Genie of St. Stephen's] and with all your interested, interesting and friendly folk, I shall treasure always.

I pray and trust that you will have the joy in this life of realizing a task accomplished, a vision fulfilled. I thank my God that all is well and that you have the sense of freedom and joy that is yours because you are an obvious co-worker with the Holy Spirit of God.

God bless you, dearest Jane. I thank you most sincerely for every detailed plan and event of my visit and I hope with great earnestness that your inner "freedom" will always continue.

Lovingly and devotedly yours,
RUTH, CHS
Mother General[8]

Editor's Note

❖ IN THE SUMMER OF 2010, Jane Blaffer Owen hoped to begin three chapters to insert within the narrative before "Carol's Garden," which she always intended as the last chapter. She often indicated in our discussions that the primary focus of her memoir would be the years from her arrival in New Harmony in 1941 through the 1970s because the history of those years as seen through her perspective was limited. Thus, she felt comfortable delaying work on the following three chapters, since each had already been documented in some way.

"Rapp-Owen Granary" would emphasize the "community effort of its restoration." Grants from the National Park Service and the Lilly Endowment were supplemented by contributions from more than three hundred donors who also cared passionately about the Granary's restoration. David L. Rice, emeritus president of the University of Southern Indiana, guided the restoration as volunteer project coordinator, working with Ralph Glaser and Jeff Koester, as well as many skilled artisans. The aspect of community extended to include representatives from Iptingen, Germany, and New Lanark, Scotland, at its dedication in October 1999. The documentary *Old Stones in New Harmony: The Rebirth of the Rapp Granary,* produced by Parri O. Black at WNIN, a public television station in Evansville, Indiana, tells its story.

"The MacLeod Barn Abbey" would feature the importance of one of her spiritual mentors, Sir George MacLeod. She wrote: "My favorite place in New Harmony is the Barn Abbey because of its simplicity and intimacy, especially during Benedictine retreats. It didn't need an architect; our barn builders were natural architects. They knew proportion and soundness of structure" (66 and 67 on town map). She would also recount the commissioning of Tobi Kahn's *Shalev.* When first encountering the Orthodox Jewish artist's work, she described his talent as "a gift from God." She connected with his deep spirituality, which she recognized in the miniature sacred spaces called shrines that he had been creating since the late 1970s, and she commissioned him to create his first full-scale work *Shalev,* or *Angel of Compassion,* which she described as a place "to shelter and to heal us." Since the Rev. Terrence "Terry" Dempsey, founding director

The restoration of the Granary by the Rapp Granary-Owen Foundation began in
January 1997. In the distance, the Lab is obscured by the Granary's massive scale.

Photograph by Darryl D. Jones, 2009.

Barn Abbey with a view of Tobi Kahn's *Shalev*
near a floodplain of the Wabash River.

Photograph by Darryl D. Jones, 2013.

Shalev, by Tobi Kahn. Granite exterior, 150 × 98 × 44 inches;
bronze interior, 60 × 20 × 14 inches. © 1993 Tobi Kahn.

Photograph by Janet Lorence. Courtesy of Tobi Kahn.

Jane Blaffer Owen walking the Cathedral Labyrinth in 2008.
Chanoine François Legaux of Chartres Cathedral in France came
to New Harmony to bless the labyrinth in 1997.
Photograph by Christy Karll McWhorter. Blaffer-Owen family photograph.

of the interfaith Museum of Contemporary Religious Art at St. Louis
University, had introduced them, he was invited to dedicate *Shalev*. Knowing that Tobi Kahn is a *kohen*—the name Kahn is a variant on Cohen, often indicating descendants of the first priest, Aaron, from the tribe of Levi—Fr. Terry
chose the priestly blessing and prayer recited by *kohanim:* "May the LORD bless
you and guard you. May the LORD make His face shed light upon you and be gracious unto you. May the LORD lift up His face unto you and give you peace."

"Cathedral Labyrinth and Sacred Garden" would detail the labyrinth's
inspiration in the floor of Chartres Cathedral; its precision measuring by Kenneth "Kent" A. Schuette, clinical professor, landscape architecture, at Purdue
University, with Rob W. Sovinski, professor, landscape architecture, at Purdue University, and Robert Ferre, Labyrinth Enterprises; and its placement in
New Harmony under Kent's guidance. She would include details about Simon
Verity's *Orpheus Fountain* (68 and 69 on town map). Verity credits her with

The Cathedral Labyrinth and Sacred Garden, with
Orpheus Fountain by Simon Verity.
Photograph by Janet Lorence, 2013.

suggesting a lyre fountain so as to help tame the wild beast within those who walk the labyrinth and to wash their feet. She delighted in the many interesting visitors she met barefooted on the labyrinth's cool polished carnelian granite surface.

In early June 2010, however, her intense focus was on adding, to the otherwise complete epilogue, the names of those who had enriched New Harmony, and she was eager to include everyone. Her litany of thankfulness and appreciation remains unfinished—perhaps as could be expected, given her objective of an all-encompassing homage. Therefore, consider anyone omitted in print to be enfolded still within her generous heart.

N. M. M.

Afterword

LIFE WAS TO CELEBRATE

Anne Dale Owen

❖ AS ONE MIGHT WELL IMAGINE, mother was not a conventional mom. We children were treated as grown-ups, if not equals: free spirits, left to decide how far from the ground we chose to fly. We were allowed to run in the rain without wrappers, pad about barefoot, and, following her lead, skinny-dip. Discipline came from Daddy. For minor offenses, he would mostly shake his head at "Jane's hooligans." We were expected, however, to be present at every celebration, of which there were many.

I believe that through entertaining, Mother allowed herself to best express her joy. She was naturally shy, so celebrating others took the spotlight off her, and she did it all with her innate sense of style, grace, and humor. Mother celebrated everything you could think of and some we couldn't imagine.

She heralded in each spring with her Easter party in Houston. She could reconcile her love of entertaining and glorifying God in one fell swoop. Planning would begin with a guest list of twenty, "just family and a few friends." The caterer was called, menus chosen, tables and chairs ordered. She busied herself writing personal notes to all invitees. Once the invitations were sent, we realized the guest list had tripled. Mother would always insist that she simply could not have left out so-and-so. Brushing details aside, she would calmly return to her flower arranging, which she loved doing every year, and setting out the family linen for the tables. The troops rallied and lurched into high gear, once again contacting caterers and heaving another hundred colored eggs into the bushes. It was on one such Easter that half the guests munched on the chicken nuggets usually reserved for the children. Mother could never be persuaded to stop sending out those little handwritten invitations.

Aside from the typical Easter, Christmas, May Day, and Halloween, there was the annual English-Speaking Union garden party. Mother always had an affinity for everything British: the history, the Queen, and Her Majesty's consul general in Houston. As one of the founding members of the Houston English-Speaking Union, Mother felt it her duty to the Queen to entertain hundreds of

Anglophiles with the current consul general presiding.[1] She once noted that the Queen never carried a purse. Of course not. The Queen, always surrounded by a battalion of loyal protectors, probably has a Guard of the Purse! Never questioning the logic, Mother became stuck on the idea. Happily free of purse, she proceeded around Houston for weeks, until she had to buy something or was stopped for driving erratically, with no visible sign of a license. If you had ever had the chance to meet my mother, you'd be prepared for her signature, extra-large brimmed hats, each designed by Mr. John to match her every outfit, including one for gardening.[2] Stylish, yes, but while driving they acted like blinders, obliterating her peripheral vision. It was a miracle that she somehow survived Houston traffic with only the occasional fender-bender. While being hatted and without a purse was a bad idea in Houston, she blithely continued this practice in New Harmony, where everyone knew her and gave her a wide berth when she was out in her golf cart.

Another annual event or grand excuse for a party was to put the property on show for the River Oaks Garden Club of Houston Azalea Trail. Hundreds of strangers would pile through the house and tromp through the garden for several weekends. It seemed longer to me. Mother, however, was in her element; she greeted many and gave a select few a personal tour through the property. A self-taught gardener, she took every opportunity to put spade to earth. Begrudgingly, she permitted others the larger jobs. While she planted and prepared her garden beautifully, she conveniently forgot the subsequent mess; inevitably, grass had to be replanted, and floors resealed and buffed. Mother, ever ebullient, never tired of her garden or reading the hundreds of handwritten notes of praise.

I can't remember the lucky beneficiary for whom Mother had planned a performance of *A Midsummer Night's Dream* in our garden, but I do recall running around impaling the soft earth with hundreds of lanterns so the actors could see to perform on a moonless night. I then quickly retreated to Daddy's bedroom upstairs to watch the spectacle. The actors changed into their costumes in the Log Cabin, nestled at the very end of the property in a forest of pines, some hundred yards from central staging—the great lawn. The pine-needle paths, one leading north and the other heading east, were not lit; I had run out of lanterns long before. Thinking all roads lead to Rome, actors exited the cabin, confident and resplendent in costume; some landed on the lawn and the others at the goose pens. From my window perch in the main house I could hear the geese objecting to the intrusion. Those actors who had gone astray, while valiant, were abysmally lost and never showed up for their cues. The fact that some of the actors delivered their lines to no one did not disturb Mother, and she spoke of it proudly for years.

Not all her events were so populated. Mother reserved for her most special female guests, an informal lunch, holding court at her garden table shaded by the black haw tree. One time as I walked down the lawn on my way to join her, I stopped in my tracks; a voice clear and strong was emanating from the table, enveloping every living thing in the garden and enjoining every bird to become her chorus. I soon realized that I was in the presence of Adele Addison, who had decided to sing grace, "Let Us Break Bread Together." Another such lunch produced Beverly Sills, but we were not treated to her song, for she was saving her voice for *Die Zauberflöte* to be sung that night at the Houston Grand Opera. Ms. Sills was accessible and friendly. She spoke of her children: her daughter was born deaf—unable to hear her mother's greatest gift—and her son developmentally-challenged. What a beautiful strong woman. On another occasion, I had declined a luncheon but promised I would pass by for a brief hello. Upon entering the dining room, I immediately recognized First Lady Rosalynn Carter, deep in discussion, and there across the table was a fuller-bodied woman with fine features and the most beautiful iridescent skin. Mother introduced me to Olivia de Havilland. I quickly raced back to the cabin and returned with my copy of *Gone with the Wind*—unfortunately, an old yellowed paperback, but she graciously signed it.[3]

Mother always reserved cocktails and evenings for her male honorees. When Senator Eugene McCarthy ran for president, Mother organized a function. Black limousines, brimming with Secret Service, were having a hard time navigating the narrow stone bridge leading to our house. I was directing traffic when she breathlessly approached me. "We have forgotten to hang the doves of peace," she said, and pointed to the great lawn. It was obvious she used the royal "we" because I knew nothing of it. I left my post as traffic cop, grabbed a ladder, and proceeded to festoon every tree with paper doves. By the time I arrived at the party, hot and disheveled, there was such a crowd around the senator that I can't remember if I ever had a chance to meet him. As for Mother, she was calmly greeting everyone and treating them to her witticisms. As with most dreamers, Mother left the details to others.

I met Dr. Paul Tillich at one of her more intimate dinners; I was almost eleven and obviously curious because I knew how much his works mattered to Mother. He was dignified but seemed somewhat aloof, so I did not feel his magic. But I was no visionary.

My very favorite dinner partner was Lord Mountbatten. He was tall and stately and so approachable. He remains one of the loveliest men I have ever met: kind, intelligent, charming. I had missed my flight to New York in order to help Mother prepare for his visit; upon learning of this, he graciously offered me

Garden party at 300 Pinewold Lane, Houston.
Blaffer-Owen family photograph.

a ride up on someone's plane the following day. He queried me the entire flight about the speech he was going to give that night. I'm sure he only pretended to take my suggestions seriously.

There were many more receptions, lunches, dinners, and dedications. Mother's love of life and everything in it attracted a constant stream of fascinating and accomplished artists, actors, architects, and royalty as well as those who just loved her. It was all the same to Mother; if she enjoyed your company, you would be included. Her odd mixes of people, if not always interesting, were mostly entertaining and at worst a giggle, for we did not know from which planet these people had disembarked. All were enamored with her energy, intelligence, and slightly bawdy jokes, which she blamed on her brother, John.

I would be remiss if I forgot to mention one of Mother's greatest joys—dancing. She would find every opportunity to grace us with her repertoire. Having taken a few classes in New York with Martha Graham in the 1960s, she considered herself ready for prime time. She would share her talents at the slightest provocation: her version of the tarantella consisted of twirling around, somewhat in place, with her hands swaying in the air; the Kooty Hop (derivation unknown) consisted of jumping from one foot to the other, knees mid-high, with an impish grin, as if to say, "I know I'm ridiculous, but I am enjoying myself." Most frequently, it was her ballroom displays that everyone relished. She'd grab some unsuspecting guest; he would gallantly lead her to the dance floor, soon to realize that he was dancing alone, for she'd broken his hold and begun to gleefully perform in her long flowing Mr. John gown. She would twirl, lift legs to the side, and continue her version of the Martha Graham method; very shortly her guests would fill the dance floor, her partner relieved of his duties. Oh, by the way, she performed this at her ninetieth-birthday party (after two knee replacements). She was irrepressible.

I have spent a great deal of time recounting my fond memories of Mother in Houston. That said, it was in New Harmony where she refilled her bucket with her passion and love. There her accomplishments are extraordinary.

Mother's greatest single achievement to me was her collaboration with Philip Johnson. They together created a true masterpiece. Philip, not bound by an architectural degree, and Mother, with her innate sense of balance and form, divined the Roofless Church. Their imaginations were unconstrained when they envisioned this very unconventional place of worship. Its undulating shingled silhouette imitates the wheat fields below and appears to float heavenward, its only constraint four enormous smooth limestone stanchions to which it is tethered. For now it must stay earthbound like the rest of us. While Mother never said anything to me, I believe she and Philip were true intellectual and creative soul mates.

The first time I met Philip I was around six or seven. Mother and I were staying at her sister Titi's apartment in New York. While Mother was upstairs preparing herself for the evening out, I was sent downstairs to greet her guest. Even as a child, I noticed his tall slim frame and informal elegance. It was as if a sculptor had chiseled off a touch too much because to me he seemed too thin. I fetched him some water. His knees looked a little bony; nonetheless, I decided to sit on his lap, so I could be closer to his level. He put out his funny-smelling cigarette and our conversation commenced. I more than likely told some story about my animals. He had just acquired some swans. Philip was not grandfatherly, but he definitely had gentleness with a touch of shyness or sadness. Mother arrived soon, and my greeting duties were over. In retrospect, it must have been a great shock for him to have some child sit on his lap.

A year or two later, Philip, particularly proud of the restaurant he had just designed in the Seagram Building, was anxious for Mother to see it.[4] So there we were, the day before opening, lunching at the brand spanking new Four Seasons Restaurant. In spite of the bustle involved in readying the restaurant for the following day, we were immediately swished in and seated at a plush banquette. We were surrounded by glass; the other two walls were dark red or pomegranate with the tallest ceilings I had ever seen. I ordered steak and french fries. When our meals were served, I asked for ketchup. The waiter blanched and returned empty-handed. Philip whispered something to him. Shortly thereafter, ketchup appeared. He had sent the waiter out to some deli to procure my needed condiment.

Another time Philip invited Mother to his home in New Canaan, Connecticut, a very special invitation for her; once again I was in tow. We arrived in the morning, and there before us was his Glass House, set away from the drive on a gentle rise. It was glistening in the sun like a prism. We were struck by its simplicity and sheer beauty. His home was perfect for a bachelor, a one-story rectangular building surrounded by glass. There were only two opaque partitions: one between the kitchen and living room and the other separating his dressing room and bedroom. Living and dining were combined in the largest room. I was surprised that there were no curtains; perhaps there were in his bedroom. We had the full view of the grounds, including his large pond, recently occupied by his geese and swans. As Mother and he were in deep conversation, I wandered around the property, which was lush with grass, minimally but appropriately landscaped. There was a guesthouse some three hundred yards away, so he was afforded some privacy; inside there was a simple foyer and off the hall one bedroom. Upon entering the bedroom, I noticed there was a bed almost in the center of the room with an arched or domed ceiling lit by pin lights in its center. I don't remember any other adornment except for the first time I noted one entire wall was closed—curtained with fabric. Here, there was a rosy glow and the first feel of femininity on the property. Mother, tired from the trip, took a nap in this warm and serene room. I continued my wandering and found a pool, perfectly round. By then, Mother had joined me, and we concluded it was really for looks alone. You could only tread water in the center for fear of scraping yourself on the dark blue masonry. We were served a late lunch, cold soup and something else, but food was secondary; if there had been a butler or cook, they were invisible. The sun was setting, and the light emanating from the house was magical. Mother and I bid our adieux to Philip and his oeuvre. We felt like Alice exiting Wonderland as we departed this sanctuary surrounded by forest.

The last time I saw Philip was many years later at François de Menil's birthday party at Studio 54. He was sitting alone in the theater seats above the dance floor, waiting for the Pointer Sisters to perform. I didn't know if he would recognize me after all these years. I took the seat next to him and reintroduced myself. During our conversation, I asked him what, if anything, he wanted to do next. Without hesitation, he answered, "The Empire State Building," obviously with a touch of Philip. Not many years later, I was not surprised to see his version: a tower of glass with the appropriate indentations. The Transco Tower (now Williams Tower) stands in a park, the tallest building in Uptown, which can be seen some twenty miles away by air or automobile, a beacon to anyone who is lost. I use it daily to chart my course around Houston.

I most identified with Mother when she was gardening—simple, unadorned, and solitary. She would leave her entertaining and visionary hats on a hook to resume her earthbound state. I can still see her, in her denim frock and wide-brimmed hat, kneeling, hands deep in the earth, watering can at her side, planting bulbs for spring, including her favorite shady ladies. Patiently she'd deadhead spent flowers. Once on patrol, Mother's mission would be to remove anything that disrupted beauty or balance, scouring the grounds for errant sticks or fallen limbs, dragging them, no matter how heavy, to the shed for removal. If you were a weed, you'd better watch out. Eau de Earth would follow her all day long. Her greatest pleasure was sharing her bounty. I would see Mother coming up the lawn with a large basket of flowers: magnolias, tuberoses, ginger lilies, anything in season. She would rummage around my house for vases, cut or crush the stems, add water and a splash of gin for tulips. The fragrance filled my house for days.

New Harmony presented a bigger challenge. Unlike Houston, she could not just walk up the lawn, so her golf cart was summoned, and with baskets brimming, she'd set out on her quest to deliver flowers far and wide; an unwitting stranger might be the recipient of a stem.

I am constantly reminded of her every time something she planted fruits or blooms. I was one of the luckiest recipients of her adventures in Houston, New Harmony, and everywhere. I was Girl Friday, and she Robinson Crusoe. Mother gave me permission to be myself; she let me pick and choose from life's basket. I will always be grateful for that gift and could never have imagined a world without her. Being with her was truly an education, one that I could have received nowhere else. Mother was a magnet beckoning all the stars into her orbit; once captured, they were too transfixed by her beauty, wit, and charm to depart.

Afterword

Jane Dale Owen
1942–2014

❖ FROM A VERY YOUNG AGE, I knew my mother was a special person. She usually wore a broad-brimmed straw hat and carried a straw *panier*. Our downstairs coat closet at 3 Shadow Lawn was a treasure trove of headgear (including conical Asian hats), shawls and scarves of many fabrics and colors—soft, woven shawls, very cozy looking, silk scarves of bright colors, purple and green woven with silver threads—and a multitude of baskets from different countries. Baskets for all occasions: picnic baskets, flower baskets, and baskets to hold the many things she carried every day. I loved to explore the contents of this closet; it was like a visit to foreign lands.

Mother talked a lot to many people. She never encountered a stranger; it seemed to me as a child that she knew everyone. Later I realized her gregarious nature welcomed whomever she met.

I was always treated as an adult. She would ask me to entertain her guests, which included passing small glasses of sherry, while she finished dressing upstairs. Often we attended grown-up movies together; *Gone with the Wind* was my favorite, so romantic, so powerful. I was entranced. But Mother's interpretation focused on the horrors of war. As she talked, I wondered if we could possibly have seen the same film. As I matured, I began to understand and appreciate her perspective.

Mother really did approach life in a different way. I soon learned that she saw the best in everyone, qualities I somehow hadn't noticed. Often she was rewarded for her trust, but if not, she comforted herself with a favorite adage: "God rewards us for our faith, not our accuracies." I heard this often. God loved her. She was blessed and protected. Surely an angel sat on each shoulder, for she never came to any harm—not even when reading a book propped on the steering wheel while driving the Houston highways.

New Harmony was the love of her life and her mission. But her family also came first. I have a deep and lasting love for my unique and beautiful mother.

Biography

❖ JANE BLAFFER OWEN, CBE (1915–2010), graduated in 1930 from the Kinkaid School in Houston, Texas, and in 1933 from the Ethel Walker School in Simsbury, Connecticut. She selected Bryn Mawr College (1933–35) specifically to study under Georgiana Goddard King and Rhys Carpenter. An interest in finding peaceful solutions to world problems led her to the Washington School of Diplomacy (1938–39) during the buildup to World War II. In the 1950s, she attended some of Paul Tillich's classes at Union Theological Seminary.

Jane Blaffer Owen was a recipient of the Commander of the Most Excellent Order of the British Empire (CBE). She was the third recipient of the State of Indiana's highest honor, the Sachem Award, presented by Governor Mitch Daniels in 2007, for her lifelong dedication to enhancing the landmark historic community of New Harmony. The National Trust for Historic Preservation recognized her preservation and revitalization accomplishments in New Harmony with its highest honor, the Louise DuPont Crowninshield Award, in 2008.

She has received accolades and honorary degrees from many universities, including: Purdue University, Doctor of Letters, 2008; Ball State University, HHD, 1977; Northwood University's Distinguished Women Award, 1974; University of Southern Indiana, Doctor of Humane Letters, 1971; Kenyon College; and Butler University.

Michael S. Maurer included her in his book *19 Stars of Indiana: Exceptional Hoosier Women* as "Jane Blaffer Owen: The Buckwheat Bride" (Bloomington: Indiana University Press, 2009).

After a lecture and panel discussion honoring the significant roles that Robert Dale Owen and David Dale Owen played in establishing the Smithsonian Institution, held in the Castle on March 10, 2009, U.S. Senator Richard Lugar of Indiana also recognized the contributions of Jane Blaffer Owen and her late husband, Kenneth Dale Owen, in New Harmony, Indiana.

Jane Blaffer married Kenneth Dale Owen, a great-great grandson of Robert Owen, on July 12, 1941. Although based in Houston, the couple devoted themselves to New Harmony, Indiana.

KENNETH DALE OWEN (1903–2002) graduated from Cornell University
in 1926 and began his career as a field geologist for the Humble Oil Company in
Houston, Texas, before founding two companies, Gulfshore Oil Company and
Trans-Tex Production Company. He received an honorary Doctor of Science
degree from the University of Southern Indiana in 1987.

Kenneth D. Owen became a highly respected Standardbred horse breeder,
winning the coveted Hambletonian in 1967. He was commissioned a Kentucky
Colonel, the highest title of honor bestowed by the Commonwealth of Kentucky, and also named a Tennessee Ambassador of Goodwill by Gov. Don Sund-
quist. He was a founding member of the New Lanark Association, Ltd.,
in Scotland.

In his hometown of New Harmony, he established Indian Mound Farm, which
became renowned for its purebred Hereford cattle breeding operation. He also
worked to reclaim and restore historic properties belonging to his ancestors,
including the David Dale Owen Laboratory (his childhood residence) and the
Rapp-Maclure-Owen mansion.

Kenneth Dale Owen and Dr. David Rice, President Emeritus, University of
Southern Indiana, were together recipients of the Outstanding Preservation
Award of Indiana from the State Department of Natural Resources for their
roles in the restoration of the Rapp Granary–David Dale Owen Laboratory as
well as the AIA Indiana Honor Award for Preservation, 2000.

For his outstanding contribution to preservation, he was awarded Indiana's
highest civilian distinction, Sagamore of the Wabash, by Gov. Frank O'Bannon.

Kenneth Dale Owen and Jane Blaffer Owen were married for sixty-one years.
Both were also the recipients of awards in Houston where they actively partici-
pated in the community; their daughter Anne Dale Owen highlights some of
her mother's activities in Houston in the afterword "Life Was to Celebrate."

Notes

Most notes are by the author; brackets indicate information contributed by the Editor.

Foreword: John Philip Newell

1. [The memorial service celebrating her life and legacy was held in New Harmony at the Roofless Church on the evening of July 25, 2010.]

2. [Jane Owen reveals the origin of her name, *Descent of the Holy Spirit,* for the sculpture *Notre Dame de Liesse (Our Lady of Joy)* in chapter 7, "May Day Fête."]

Foreword: J. Pittman McGehee

1. [The burial office was held on July 10, 2010, at St. Martin's Episcopal Church.]

Preface

1. Founders included Marvin Halverson, James Luther Adams, Alfred H. Barr Jr., Truman B. Douglass, and Stanley Hopper. For more on the history of ARC, consult Betty H. Meyer's *The ARC Story: A Narrative Account of the Society for the Arts, Religion, and Contemporary Culture* (New York: CrossCurrents Press, 2003).

2. When Pope John XXIII convened the Second Vatican Council, Franck was the only artist to document all four sessions.

3. [Clara Maria Berndes-van der Drift "Claske" Franck died in 2013.]

4. The welcoming center was later rechristened with the gender-inclusive *Seafarers'* instead of the original *Seamen's.*

Historical Note

1. [Charles-Alexandre Lesueur's drawings show the boat's banner in French; others show it as the *Philanthropist.*]

2. [Donald E. Pitzer, "The Original Boatload of Knowledge Down the Ohio River: William Maclure's and Robert Owen's Transfer of Science and Education to the Midwest, 1825–1826," *Ohio Journal of Science* 89, no. 5 (1989): 128–42.]

3. [Connie Weinzapfel, Darrel E. Bigham, and Susan R. Branigin, *New Harmony, Indiana,* Images of America Series (Chicago: Arcadia Publishing, 2000).]

4. [Jane Blaffer Owen, interviewed by Connie Weinzapfel, May 2008, New Harmony, Indiana, collection of University of Southern Indiana/Historic New Harmony.]

1. Twin Vows

1. Walter Brookfield Hendrickson wrote a comprehensive biography entitled *David Dale Owen: Pioneer Geologist of the Middle West,* which was published in 1943, only a few years after my initial visit. My geologist husband's grandfather Richard Owen, David Dale's youngest brother, was also a prominent geologist.

2. Julie Dash, *Daughters of the Dust: The Making of an African American Woman's Film* (New York: New Press, 1992), 94–95 (screenplay 20–21).

3. He arrived in New Harmony on "The Boatload of Knowledge."

4. In *Centering Prayer and Inner Awakening* (New York: Cowley Publications, 2004), 86, Cynthia Bourgeault draws a parallel between St. Paul's great hymn and these lines of Rumi, which are from *Mathnawi*, VI: 1967–70, quoted from Kabir Edmund Helminski, *Living Presence: A Sufi Way to Mindfulness & the Essential Self* (New York: Tarcher/Putnam, 1992), 142.

5. There were concerns that the New Harmony Memorial Commission wanted to condemn "the property" and declare eminent domain. But this historic building was primarily a longtime Owen *home*.

6. Richard Wilson's story of the Wabash quotes La Salle's letter to Louis XIV in which he describes the great river to the north, which the Indians called "Ouabache."

7. A group of women, who had been studying the works of the Swiss psychiatrist Carl Gustav Jung under Ruth Thacker Fry, founded the C. G. Jung Educational Center of Houston, Texas, in 1958. Jung graciously consented to the use of his name for the center.

2. Indian Mound

1. The river was in the process of change during Harmonist times. A man called Pennypacker ran a gristmill at the Old Dam and hand-ploughed a ditch upon the site for the water to flow into the Wabash. The ditch widened and deepened until it separated that part of our mainland, which is now called Cut-Off Island.

2. Bromfield's Malabar Farm became an Ohio state park and National Historic Landmark. He is remembered as a Pulitzer Prize-winning author and conservationist.

3. I recently discovered a relevant passage concerning Tillich's *Theology of Culture* (Oxford: Oxford University Press, 1959) in Vincent J. Donovan's *Christianity Rediscovered* (New York: Orbus Books, 2003), 34, that provided me with a fresh insight into Abraham: "Paul Tillich points out that only if God is exclusively God, unconditioned and unlimited by anything other than himself, is there a true monotheism, and only then is the power over space and time broken. . . . Abraham's call was the turning point. It was the beginning of the end for polytheism. God must be separated from his nation to become the High God."

4. Walter Nigg, "Saint Bernard and the Cistercians," in *Warriors of God: The Great Religious Orders and Their Founders,* trans. Mary Ilford (New York: Knopf, 1959), 195.

5. Thomas R. Kelly, "Holy Obedience," pamphlet (Philadelphia: Philadelphia Yearly Meeting, 1939; republished electronically Quaker Heron Press, 2004), 11.

3. The Sixth Generation

1. It was my suggestion to honor Canada's Sanctuaire Sainte-Anne-de-Beaupré, associated with healing and the good Ste. Anne.

4. Harmonist House

1. On a commemorative poster in the entrance hall of the Laboratory, taken from "The Principles and Practices of the Rational Religion," tenth principle.

2. Sherry Underwood, who later became director of the Robert Lee Blaffer Trust Swimming Program, took lessons with Flossie as a child in 1964 and became an instructor herself during the summers of her high school and college years.

5. Harmonist Church and School

1. The booklet *One Plant, Many Branches…One Seed—The Adventure of the Adorers of the Blood of Jesus* was available in eight languages.

2. I explain how the mystery surrounding this translation was eventually solved in chapter 18, "Cornerstone Dedication."

3. Thomas Merton, *The Way of Chuang Tzu* (New York: New Directions, 1967), 147.

6. Acquiring the Granary and Mansion

1. Kosti Ruohomaa provided the photographs for "Life Visits New Harmony" in the September 17, 1945, issue of *Life* magazine.

2. Mindful of opportunities when they came, he did purchase the property to the west of the Lab. [Posey County deed record, grantor, Carrie S. Miller et al., to grantee, Kenneth Dale Owen, book 59, page 156, August 23, 1946; revised deed, book 60, page 586, August 21, 1948.]

3. When Miss Laura's brother John Corbin died in 1937, his siblings, who were the heirs of the estate, had considered the possibility of making the Corbin home and Granary available to the state. Miss Laura, however, had resisted. She considered the Granary and the Rapp-Maclure mansion, which her family had acquired from Kenneth's grandfather Horace Pestalozzi Owen, to be important historic properties and Corbin family treasures. [Richard Heckman owned Richard's Cafe.]

4. An explanation for why Miss Laura may have taken offense was discovered when my editor Nancy researched the details and reported them to me: "Everett Sanders, Law Offices of Sanders, Gravelle, Whitlock & Howrey in Washington, D.C., where Miss Laura's sister Helen Corbin Heinl lived, wrote a letter dated March 17, 1938, to Mr. Ross F. Lockridge, Chairman of the New Harmony Memorial Commission I, indicating that his firm was representing and advising the Corbin heirs as to the settlement of the estate of John Corbin, specifically, the historic properties. Lockridge, in a reply dated March 25, 1938, wanted to ensure that the Corbin heirs would not seek a high price for their property, but in doing so he spoke frankly and accurately, emphasizing that the Rapp-Maclure mansion 'is the least significant of all of the buildings from the standpoint of historic interest for genuine memorial purposes. The site which it occupies is of course of vital importance but this building is not in itself in any sense a memorial to either George Rapp or William Maclure since neither of them ever saw it. It is really a handsome memorial to Captain John Corbin and his heirs.'" [Elliott Family Papers—Helen Elliott—Organizations, fs, box XX, folder 95, 94–102, "Helen Elliott—New Harmony Memorial Commission I," Working Men's Institute Archives, New Harmony, Indiana (hereafter Elliott, folder number, WMI Archives). Courtesy of Working Men's Institute. Only four years later, in May 1942, the New Harmony Memorial Commission (Lockridge, Chairman; Balz, President) issued a pamphlet, *The New Harmony Memorial Movement: A Brief Review of Its Origin, Aims, and Progress,* which presents a dramatically different assessment of the Rapp-Maclure Place (Corbin home): "The impressive character of this stately building and spacious surroundings will be maintained in harmony with its historic significance. In the days of Father Rapp, it was a place of welcome and hospitality to distinguished guests. It served in that character also during the Community of Equality when William Maclure was its genial and generous master. It has had substantially that character ever since the days of Rapp and Maclure" (43). The mansion later came to be considered the heart of the memorial. Many archives and libraries have copies of the pamphlet, one of which has become accessible online at archive.org. Interestingly, the description makes no reference

to the fact that following a devastating fire the house was rebuilt and occupied by Maclure's brother Alexander and subsequent generations of the Owen family. Note that the New Harmony Memorial Commission was created by a joint resolution of the Legislature of 1937 (chapter 326, page 1401) and later by an act of the legislature of 1939.]

5. A member of the New Harmony Memorial Commission was said to have been making frequent visits to Miss Laura. Again, recent research confirmed what had seemed idle gossip at the time. [According to her report as president, dated September 12, 1947, Mrs. Frederick G. Balz confirmed that she had contacted Mrs. Laura Monical on each of her five trips to New Harmony with offers from the commission of thirty thousand dollars for immediate possession of the Rapp-Maclure mansion, grounds including the Thomas Say tomb, and the Harmonist Granary. She reported that each time Mrs. Monical decided "to not sell at that time." The commission also speculated about the possibility of acquiring the property through condemnation proceedings. Elliott, 96, WMI Archives. Courtesy of Working Men's Institute.]

6. [New Harmony Memorial Commission meeting minutes from June 24, 1948, indicate that negotiations were progressing with the Corbin heirs before Laura Corbin Monical's death and that the family requested a meeting following the funeral. Elliott, 96, WMI Archives. Courtesy of Working Men's Institute.]

7. [Posey County deed records, grantor, Amy A. Sandefur, to grantee, Kenneth Dale Owen, "for and in consideration of one hundred dollars," book 60, 392–93, July 14, 1948. A common practice to keep private the actual amount of real estate transactions during this time period was to simply record the minimum, one hundred dollars.]

8. A year later in a letter dated October 19, 1949, to the Memorial Commission president Mrs. Balz, Kenneth's thoughtful, measured handwriting communicates his motivation: "to preserve several structures, with which he has close family associations since the early eighteen hundreds."

9. [The Corbin heirs had sent a telegram, received on July 22, 1948, to the New Harmony Memorial Commission with the intent of "removing their property from further consideration and sale to the state," which was reported in the August 18, 1948, meeting minutes. Elliott, 96, WMI Archives. Courtesy of Working Men's Institute. The Posey County deed book records show the original transactions, for the Granary and the house and grounds, between grantor, Corbin Heinl et al./Corbin Ford, and grantee, Kenneth Dale Owen: (1) warranty deed 3342, book 60, pages 426–27, July 28, 1948 and (2) warranty deed 4415, book 61, pages 4–5, September 29, 1948. Both deed records state: "For and in consideration of one hundred dollars." Following a survey for Kenneth D. Owen, October 15, 1948, another warranty deed (5549) was "made for the purpose of correcting and clarifying the description of two deeds between the same parties in which three separate parcels made up the tract of land herein conveyed." The record also states, "for and in consideration of one hundred dollars." Dated September 14, 1949, deed book 62, 315. Again, a common practice to keep private the actual amount of real estate transactions during this time period was to simply record the minimum, one hundred dollars.]

7. May Day Fête

1. Rudyard Kipling, "Independence," Rectorial Address, St. Andrews, October 1923, in *A Book of Words* (London: Macmillan, 1928), 229–47.

2. W. B. Yeats, "Two Songs from a Play," in *The Collected Poems of W. B. Yeats* (New York: Macmillan, 1970), 210.

3. *Madonna and Child* by Umlauf was purchased and donated to the Museum of Fine Arts, Houston after the fête.

4. Rosamund J. Frost, "Lipchitz Makes a Sculpture," *Art News* XLII (April 1950): 36–39, 63–64.

5. William Shakespeare, *Antony and Cleopatra*, 5.2.79.

6. Greeting from the Book of Common Prayer.

7. [Thursday, January 19, 1950. Annual Report, 1949–50, Archives, Museum of Fine Arts, Houston.]

8. Upon reflection almost sixty years later, my spontaneous letter [April 12, 1950, from 3 Shadow Lawn, Houston, Texas] to Monsieur Lipchitz did not adequately communicate my thoughts, with its references to the children's performance, May wine, and baked bread, and to what I considered the misappropriation of May 1 by Russia: "In fact I don't know who Communism is seeking to crown or what it is hoping to impose—a pagan Ceres or Eastre at least one could use to sculptural advantage—unless it is amorphous matter. That physical matter, whether one is Leonardo or not, each one feels personally slave, and that 'heavier than air thing' with which you have managed to soar. So now you will understand, I hope, why you are so vulnerable to my request for one of your figures in our garden May 1st. . . . So, any joyful triumph that you have achieved over matter will be gratefully received." [Note: The Lipchitz family—Hanno D. Mott, Lolya R. Lipchitz, and Frank L. Mott—donated his correspondence in 2010 to the Archives of American Art, Smithsonian Institution: Jacques Lipchitz papers and Bruce Bassett papers concerning Jacques Lipchitz, circa 1910–2001, bulk 1941–2001 (hereafter Lipchitz, Correspondence, box, folder, item, AAA, SI). Originals of Jane Blaffer Owen's correspondence are collected there: Correspondence: Owen, Jane Blaffer, circa 1950–69, box 3, folders 35–37. When possible, originals, drafts, or duplicates will be cited from the Lipchitz papers. Original letter dated April 12, 1950 in Lipchitz, Owen, box 3, folder 35, 3–4, AAA, SI. Originals of some Lipchitz letters are in the Artists Archive, Green Gothic, Red Geranium Enterprises, New Harmony, Indiana.]

9. I no longer have the original photograph. An image was published a few months later in the September-October 1950 issue of *L'Art Sacré* dedicated to the church at Assy. Its articles and images were later collected by my friend Dominique de Menil in the book by M.-A. Couturier, *Art Sacré* (Houston: Menil Foundation, 1983), 55, and in the subsequent English version, M.-A. Couturier, *Sacred Art* (Austin: University of Texas Press, 1989), 55. The image used here is from an early study cast in bronze, rather than being in unstable plasticine. [Almost a year later John de Menil, in his capacity as chairman of the board of the Contemporary Arts Association of Houston, Inc., wrote to Lipchitz on March 9, 1951: "I have seen Mrs. Owen two or three times recently and she is growing more and more enthusiastic about the madonna. I am trying to convince her to give to our museum the reduced scale model—the one of which I saw a bronze casting when I visited your studio." Thus the study was cast in bronze quite early. Lipchitz, Contemporary Arts Association of Houston, Inc., box 1, folder 39, 1, AAA, SI.]

10. [Original letter in Lipchitz, Owen, box 3, folder 37, 17–19, AAA, SI.]

11. [Draft letter in Lipchitz, Owen, box 3, folder 37, 20–22, AAA, SI.] Courtesy of the Lipchitz family.

12. [May 12 letter to Jacques Lipchitz from 3 Shadow Lawn, Houston: "Our little Anne is doing beautifully and should be able to join her family in a week." Original letter in Lipchitz, Owen, box 3, folder 35, 6, AAA, SI.]

13. [May 12 letter from 3 Shadow Lawn, Houston, Texas. The precise source of the reference within the works of George Sand remains unknown to the author, as she probably read the passage during summers in France as an adolescent or in college. Original letter in Lipchitz, Owen, box 3, folder 35, 5–6, AAA, SI.]

14. Originals of some Lipchitz letters are in the Artists Archive, Green Gothic, Red Geranium Enterprises, New Harmony, Indiana. [Draft letter in Lipchitz, Owen, box 3, folder 35, 7 and 9, AAA, SI.] Courtesy of the Lipchitz family.

15. Also translated as: "Jacob Lipchitz, Jew, faithful to the faith of his ancestors, has made this Virgin for the goodwill of all mankind that the spirit might prevail."

16. [On JBO monogram stationery; at the conclusion dated May 24, 3 Shadow Lawn. Original letter in Lipchitz, Owen, box 3, folder 35, 10, AAA, SI.]

17. [On stationery from Ste. Anne's Farms, Grafton, Ontario, Canada, dated Saturday: "Dear Maître Lipchitz, I will be at the Pierre Hotel Friday and most of Saturday, 15th and 16th, and most earnestly hope nothing prevents our meeting at your studio shortly after three Friday afternoon. Call me that morning, or leave word, should that prove inconvenient for you. Yours in good faith, Jane Blaffer Owen." The 15th and 16th fell on a Friday and Saturday in September of 1950. Original letter in Lipchitz, Owen, box 3, folder 37, 69, AAA, SI.]

8. Lipchitz

1. Lest the reader become confused about the three castings, *Notre Dame de Liesse* is the title of the commission for the Catholic church in Assy, France. From our early correspondence, Lipchitz approved of my name *Descent of the Holy Spirit* for the New Harmony issue. The Iona Community adopted the slightly abbreviated *Descent of the Spirit* for the casting placed at Iona, Scotland. The sculpture has various informal names, which include Our Lady, the Virgin, the Madonna, and Lipchitz's *la Madone*. She temporarily acquired a few others along her unique journey. [Historical documents, such as correspondence, programs, and publications, use quotation marks for "Descent of the Holy Spirit" at New Harmony and "Descent of the Spirit" at Iona. Both communities, however, have known of the Lipchitz sculpture by these titles for more than fifty years. Owen subordinated her spontaneous name for the work to its title *Notre Dame de Liesse* through the use of quotation marks. For publication of her memoir, the titles conform to *The Chicago Manual of Style*, 16th edition, and are italicized.]

2. "The Assy Church: Famous Modern Artists Decorate Chapel in Alps," *Life*, June 19, 1950, 72–76; Marie-Alain Couturier, "Assy 1–2," in *L'Art Sacré*, September-October 1950, 17–18.

3. [The arrangements were made somewhat more formal in a letter on Number 5 New Harmony stationery, which includes "mon premier 'installment'" and encloses "a contrat privé ... pour 'La Descent du Saint Esprit'" in the amount of $15,000 for castings for Assy and New Harmony. After their meeting, Jane Owen begins corresponding to Jacques Lipchitz primarily in French. Lipchitz accepts the agreement (of September 27, 1950) in a penciled reply, thanking her for the check for $5,000, which will include casting both in bronze as well as providing blueprints for the altar. Original letter in Jacques Lipchitz papers, Owen, box 3, folder 35, 26–29, AAA, SI. Draft letter, Owen, box 3, folder 35, 31–33, AAA, SI.] Courtesy of the Lipchitz family.

4. [Original telegram of October 9, 1950, from New Harmony in Lipchitz, Owen, box 3, folder 35, 34, AAA, SI.]

5. Juan Larrea, *Guernica: Pablo Picasso* (New York: Arno Press, 1969), 61–62. A Spanish translation by Dr. Alexander H. Krappe was published by Curt Valentin in 1947.

6. After breaking with Larrea and professing Communism, Picasso responded to a question about the painting's symbolism, saying to an audience at the Museum of Modern Art, "This chicken is a chicken," for he understood that the artist creates, while others interpret and find meaning. Allen Leepa, "Guernica," in *The Challenge of Modern Art* (New York: Beechhurst Press, 1949), 235.

7. Larrea prepared me for what I would later hear from Paul Tillich in his lecture "Religion and the Visual Arts" at Connecticut College in November 1955. "Guernica was a small town . . . which was completely destroyed by a combined air attack of the Italians and Germans. It was the first exercise of what is called 'saturation' bombing, that is, bombing in such a way that nothing is left. Picasso has painted this immense horror—the pieces of reality, men and animals and inorganic pieces of houses tumbling together—in a way in which the 'piece' character of our reality, the character of being torn into pieces, is perhaps more visible than in any other of the modern pictures. During one of my lectures, I was asked, 'What would you think is the best present-day protestant religious picture?' I answered almost without hesitation, 'Guernica.' I named this picture, because it shows the human situation without any cover. It shows what very soon followed in most European countries in terms of the second World War, and it shows what is now in the souls of many Americans as disruptiveness, existential doubt, emptiness and meaninglessness. And if Protestantism means that first of all we have not to cover anything but to see the human situation in its depths of estrangement and despair, then this is one of the most powerful Protestant pictures." From his original typed notes, which he handed to me after the lecture. Courtesy of the Paul Tillich Estate, Dr. Mutie Tillich Farris, executor.

9. Enter Paul Tillich

1. [Lipchitz first began the enlargement of *Notre Dame de Liesse* in early 1951, after returning from New Harmony, at his Twenty-third Street studio, where he worked almost exclusively on the Virgin that year; after the April 12, 1953, reception at his new Hastings-on-Hudson studio, Lipchitz again devoted himself to the Virgin for over a year, according to two previously published sources—Jacques Lipchitz with H. H. Arnason, *My Life in Sculpture* (London: Thames and Hudson, 1972), 176, 187–90, 193, 231, and Irene Patai, *Encounters: The Life of Jacques Lipchitz* (New York: Funk & Wagnalls, 1961), 377, 387.]

2. In a 1954 Art Institute of Chicago exhibition catalogue, *Masterpieces of Religious Art,* Tillich wrote in "Authentic Religious Art": "If religious be defined as man's *ultimate concern for Ultimate Reality,* all art which reflects, however partially and distortedly, this ultimate concern is at least implicitly religious, even if it makes no use whatever of a recognizable religious subject-matter."

3. I have read so many of his works that the book in hand that day could have been *The Courage to Be* (New Haven: Yale University Press, 1952) or *The Religious Situation*, trans. H. Richard Niebuhr (New York: Henry Holt, 1932).

10. Polio Epidemic

1. [David M. Oshinsky, *Polio: An American Story* (New York: Oxford University Press, 2005), 161: "The year 1952 was the worst polio year on record, with more than 57,000 cases nationwide." Heather Green Wooten, *The Polio Years in Texas: Battling a Terrifying Unknown* (College Station: Texas A&M University Press, 2009), 69: "The brunt of polio epidemics in Texas was reserved for Houston and surrounding Harris County."]

2. [On stationery from 300 Pinewold, Houston 17, Texas, "jeudi soir," Jane Blaffer
Owen writes hastily to Lipchitz (about a proposed frieze she commissioned for him to
create for the exterior of the Blaffer Wing, designed by the architect Kenneth Franzheim
for the Museum of Fine Arts, Houston) with details about why she could not consult with
him: "À ce moment que Jane est devenue plus sérieusement malade. Carol et Anne
n'avaient qu'une légère attaque, mais Jane, subitement, a perdu le service de ses jambes."
("At that same moment Jane became more seriously ill. Carol and Anne only had a light
attack, but Jane suddenly lost the use of her legs." Translation by Monique Singley.)
Original letter in Jacques Lipchitz papers, Owen, box 3, folder 35, 95–98, AAA, SI. In a
reply to Franzheim on July 9, 1952, Jacques Lipchitz writes: "I think now is not the right
moment to bother Mrs. Owen with these details. We should wait until her worry for her
children's health is eased." Original letter in Lipchitz, Franzheim, Kenneth 1952, box 2,
folder 14, 10, AAA, SI. Courtesy of the Jacques Lipchitz family. According to architectural
historian Stephen Fox, Museum of Fine Arts, Houston board minutes indicate that
Lipchitz presented his proposal in August 1952. Ninny recounts family events in the
summer of 1952, Mary Lou Robson, "A Tragedy in the Household," in *Wings of the Morning:
Memoirs of Joyce Isabella Mann* (New Harmony: Mary Lou Robson, 1967), 125.]

3. [Harris County deed 975766, grantor, R. H. Goodrich and wife, Esther F. Goodrich,
to grantee, Kenneth D. Owen and wife, Jane Blaffer Owen, book 2409, pages 286–88,
February 29, 1952. JBO monogram stationery dated "le 20 mars" to Lipchitz reads in part:
"Une second raison est notre changement de maison. Ou à en de la chance, parce que c'est
une simple maison et une très belle propriété avec des beaux jardins que ne manquent que
de la sculpture" ("A second reason is that we moved to a different home. We are so
fortunate because it is a simple house and an absolutely beautiful property, with beautiful
gardens where only one thing is missing, sculpture." Translation by Monique Singley.)
Original letter in Lipchitz, Owen, box 3, folder 35, 83–84, AAA, SI.]

11. Sir George MacLeod

1. I have included the copy Susan Wunder, a retired dairy farmer and freelance
technical writer/editor in Bloomington, Indiana, gave me. The poem originally appeared at
the Poets Against the War website.

If You Think

If you think there's such a beast
as a war horse, walk up to my
Belgian and look straight in
his eyes.

You'll see no greed for glory,
no glint of malice, no
lust for blood. Just a warm,
ancient patience, infinitely

wiser than every excuse for war.

There is no such thing as a
war horse—only horses spurred
to war by soldiers under
distant orders.

Those giving them should look
my plow horse in the eye—then
explain to him the need for bombs,
missiles, tanks, or his own good

strength, misapplied.

Your talk would rise like vapor
into thin air before his calm demeanor.

He would walk away as if to find a
cool place in the woods without flies.
And if you follow him, you would not start
your war.
Courtesy of Susan Wunder.

2. [Jane Blaffer Owen to Jacques Lipchitz on stationery from 300 Pinewold, Houston 19, Texas, July 15, 1953: "Non—Notre Madone ne sera pas à Washington. Je viens de recevoir une letter de Francis Sayre." ("No—our Madonna will not be in Washington. I just received a letter from Francis Sayre." Translation by Ed.) Original letter to Lipchitz in Lipchitz papers, Owen, box 3, folder 35, 99–100, AAA, SI.]

3. Originally from Manchester, England, Gladys Falshaw became fluent in French and Sanskrit; she earned her doctorate from the Université de Paris for her 1923 work on comparative literature, "Leconte de Lisle et l'Inde," but chose to spend her next twenty years as a church worker among the untouchables in India. The Episcopal bishop of Texas accepted Dr. Falshaw's request to begin a series of lectures to raise awareness and funds for famine relief in her beloved India. She spoke at Rice University on February 10, 1950. Dr. Gladys Falshaw was a counselor, retreat leader, and authority on Christian healing. [Jane Blaffer Owen to Jacques Lipchitz on stationery from Number 5, June 28, tells about Dr. Falshaw, who is visiting her in New Harmony. Original letter in Lipchitz, Owen, box 3, folder 35, 13–14, AAA, SI.]

4. In the 1930s, when Dr. George MacLeod was a Church of Scotland minister in the slums of Glasgow, he realized that the churches had enormous difficulties in communicating with ordinary working and unemployed people. He resolved to make an experiment to rebuild the ruined Iona Abbey using the skills of unemployed masons and carpenters; the trainee ministers would be their laborers. And the clergy would also be trained to work in the slums of Scotland. Thus was born the Iona Community. What began as a training scheme for Presbyterian ministers developed into an ecumenical community for men and women, ordained and lay. Members, the vast majority of whom live not on Iona but across the world, commit themselves to a discipline of prayer, economic sharing, planning of time, meeting together, and working for justice and peace.

5. Five-year-old Annie would stay at Ste. Anne with Joyce Mann and my mother during our travels abroad.

12. Iona

1. On our way back to Oban, we took a large ferryboat, the *King George*. We had as a deck companion the charming and urbane Rev. Dr. Charles Warr, dean of the Thistle of St. Giles, Edinburgh's most venerable cathedral. He delighted Janie and Carol with an impious Scottish grace: "Some have meat and cannot eat. Some can eat but have no meat. But we have meat and we can eat. And for this, Lord, we thank Thee." Eventually the large

ferries replaced the Puffers, and today only a few of these "little engines that could" remain, perhaps in dry dock, if anywhere.

2. "The place of the wild goose in Celtic spirituality is partly ancient and partly modern. In many of the old prayers, there is an association between geese and resurrection because they return to the Celtic world in the spring. They are signs of new life. In the modern period, however, it was our dear George MacLeod who used this colorful inspiration to create an association between the goose and the Holy Spirit. It is a good strong native symbol for the Spirit. By the time George died, it was sometimes being referred to as an ancient symbol for the Holy Spirit in the Celtic world. When it was proposed to George that this was not an ancient symbol, his response was, 'Oh, well, it should have been.' Certainly by now it has been firmly established as a symbol of the Spirit, at least within the Iona community." From John Phillip Newell's letter to me, June 12, 2003, in answer to my question about the connection between the wild goose and the Holy Dove.

3. Ron Ferguson, ed., *Daily Readings with George MacLeod: Founder of the Iona Community* (Glasgow: Wild Goose Publications, 1991), 84.

4. "Thus shall we have communion with thee, and, in thee, with our beloved ones. Thus shall we come to know within ourselves that there is no death and that only a veil divides, thin as gossamer." From George F. MacLeod, "A Veil Thin as Gossamer," in *The Whole Earth Shall Cry Glory: Iona Prayer* (Glasgow: Wild Goose Publications, 1985), 92.

5. [According to its history, late in the medieval period, the abbey church dedicated to Mary also became the seat of the Bishop of the Isles (Sodor) and, as such, was known as St. Mary's Cathedral; that medieval name faded long ago. After the restoration, the red granite church structure was simply called the Abbey Church.]

6. George MacLeod's vision to rebuild the domestic buildings symbolized the need for us to rebuild the spirituality of our day-to-day lives.

7. These lines were first sent in a letter to me from George MacLeod on April 25, 1959. Years later, they became a challenge and finally a tribute to the workers who translated into reality one of the most complex set of plans ever to leave the drafting board. These workers, like the Harmonist builders before them, realized that the highest craftsmanship arises only when the worker brings a deep reverence to the task and that ownership rests in this and not in possession.

8. [The statue's title on Iona appeared as *Descent of the Spirit* in several early publications, including a pamphlet entitled *An Interpretation* to explain the theological significance of the work of art, followed by *Ecclesiastical Thoughts* (to dispel any notion of idolatry or association with Roman theology), and George F. MacLeod's "The Descent of the Spirit," *The Coracle: The Journal of the Iona Community* 34 (1959): 1–4, reprinted from *The Scotsman.* Lipchitz's statue on Iona would never have been accepted as *Notre Dame de Liesse,* a title suitable for a Catholic church in Assy, France.]

9. For readers unfamiliar with cloisters and to underscore the rightness of MacLeod's vision, I shall quote from Ewan Mathers's book *The Cloisters of Iona Abbey* (Glasgow: Wild Goose Publications, 2004), 9–10: "Cloisters form an environment in which to be and in which to think. I believe that their original purpose was both physical and spiritual. Firstly, they provide a practical covered pathway linking the various parts of a monastic building; secondly they provide space for meditation, contemplation, and silence. This arrangement reflects the twofold nature of life in a monastery of daily work and worship: a theme explored today by the Iona Community, who now occupy the Abbey buildings on Iona. The need for places of quiet reflection is no less now than when these cloisters were first built."

10. The casting that Lipchitz and I had agreed would also occupy a spiritual site like the two other castings, for Assy and New Harmony.

11. From an essay George MacLeod gave to me, dated Pentecost 1962.

12. I am pleased to report that the Scots lack of ease with Catholicism has now abated somewhat, and there is considerable discussion about the possibility of restoring the nunnery. In 1997, the house of prayer Cnoc a' Chalmain (Hill of the Dove) was dedicated to establish a permanent Roman Catholic presence on Iona for the first time in four hundred years and to foster ecumenism on the island through work and prayer.

13. Assy

1. According to the article "The Assy Church: Famous Modern Artists Decorate Chapel in Alps," *Life,* June 19, 1950, 72: "In paying for the church, Devémy and Couturier have received contributions from all over France, as well as a small donation from the Pope himself."

2. Couturier often distributed a particular quotation, which he used in his outreach for unity, from Cardinal Mercier's *The Testament:* "In order to be united, it is necessary to love another; in order to love another it is necessary to know one another; in order to know one another we must go to meet one another."

3. [Jane Blaffer Owen letter to Jacques Lipchitz on stationery from a restaurant on the route down the mountain reveals the visit to Assy with immediacy:
Restaurant du Père Bise, Maurice Bise, Prop., Talloires, Lac d'Annecy, le 5 août:

Je viens de passer une aprèsmidi remarquable avec l'Abbaye Devémy. Ayant rendu hommage à *Notre Dame de Liesse,* nous avons lu ensemble votre lettre. Que venait d'arriver. Comme vous avez rendu heureux ce brave et digne homme! Pour lui la plus grande sensibilité de votre oeuvre se trouve dans les mains. En parlant de la grande puissance de la statue, et de sa demeure temporaire dans le Baptistère, il a remarqué qu'il y avait une possibilité qu'elle serait dehors. J'ai dit que je pense que ça vous plairait, et j'espère n'avoir pas parlé injudic[ieuse]ment. Elle rend tout autour d'elle si petit.

Monsieur l'Abbaye a tant d'admiration pour vous. Il fut si touché de vos lettres capitaux quand il s'agissait de la Madonne. Il a voulu que je vous décris haut ou court, votre physionomie, etc. Il était aussi amoureux de votre écriture. Que je fus heureuse d'être témoigne à sa grande joie!

L'église fourmillait de pèlerins. Les uns et les autres réagissait d'elle comme s'ils participaient à une *événement* non une sculpture.

En quittant l'Abbaye il à dit "nous sommes liés par un bel lien."

(I just had the most wonderful afternoon with Abbot Devémy. After presenting my respects to *Notre Dame de Liesse,* we read your letter together, which had just arrived. You made this good and worthy man so happy! For him, the greatest sensitivity of your work shows in the hands. While talking about the great power of the sculpture and her temporary home in the baptistery, he mentioned the possibility of its being kept outside. I told him that I thought you would like that idea, and I hope that I did not speak out of turn. She makes everything around her appear so small.

The abbot has so much admiration for you. He was so touched by your capital letters, especially when referring to the Madonna. He wanted me to describe you thoroughly, your physique, etc. He was enamored with your writing. How happy I was to be a witness to his great joy!

The church was buzzing with pilgrims. One and all were reacting to her as if they were participating in an <u>event</u>, not [viewing] a sculpture.

In leaving the abbot he said, "We are united [or bound] by a beautiful link." Translation by Andrea Heggen.) Original letter in Jacques Lipchitz papers, Owen, box 3, folder 37, 27–28, AAA, SI.]

4. In her book *Mysticism* (New York: E. P. Dutton, 1930), 136, Evelyn Underhill quotes from the sermons of the German philosopher Johannes Eckhart in Franz Pfeiffer, *Meister Eckhart*, trans. C. de B. Evans (London: Watkins, 1924).

14. Kilbinger House

1. [Posey County deed records: grantor, Fred Lichtenberger, administrator of the estate of Mary Kilbinger, to grantee, Jane Blaffer Owen, book 66, page 298, recorded January 25, 1952.]

2. Helen Duprey Bullock came to New Harmony in December 1953 and returned at my request in the spring of 1954. She authored "National Trust Report and Recommendation for New Harmony, Indiana," June 1954.

3. Helen Duprey Bullock, *My Head and My Heart* (New York: G. P. Putnam's Sons, 1942), vi.

4. [A letter from John Nicholson, dated August 9, 1954, to the author indicates that work on Kilbinger House is "progressing nicely." Also, Helen Duprey Bullock notes its progress in her "National Trust Report and Recommendation for New Harmony, Indiana," June 1954, 9.]

5. Visitors to New Harmony can view the Maximilian-Bodmer Exhibit in the Lichtenberger Building as part of the tour that begins at the Atheneum Visitors Center (28 on town map).

6. [A letter from the author written to Dr. Herman B Wells, then president of Indiana University, dated May 17, 1955, provides insights into the professional approach to this Harmonist home: "Personally, I plan to concentrate my funds and my wits—such as they are!—on a bang up, historically correct and artistically beautiful restoration of the Jacob Ruff [Reiff?]-Kilbinger House. [W]hen the Commission turns over its holdings to the Conservation Department I hope, as my friend and interpreter, that you will strongly urge the new Trustees to explore old records housed at Economy, Pennsylvania. . . . In this connection, I should like to make available the help of Lawrence Thurman. As you recall, he has charge at Economy of the original Harmony Society records. In our advancing work on the Ruff [Reiff?]-Kilbinger house, when seemingly insoluble problems arise Mr. Thurman flies down to place his invaluable advice and experience at our disposal; I would love to offer to the Conservation Department the services of a man eminently qualified and really dedicated, to advise us both when the need occurs. For instance, when he arrives at my expense in June to consult on the Ruff [Reiff?]-Kilbinger house, I would like nothing more than to share his time with the Conservation Department." According to Sarah Buffington, Curator, Old Economy Village, both surnames, Ruff and Reiff, are listed in Eileen Aiken English's *Demographic Directory of the Harmony Society*.]

7. Hannah Tillich contributed books and personal items to the collection.

8. Inside the drawer of the Orkney chair, I have placed a copy of a book by the Reverend Mother Ruth, CHS, *In Wisdom Thou Hast Made Them* (New York: Adams, Bannister, Cox, 1986).

9. New Harmony's oldest work of art is a stone carving of Our Lady and the Christ Child from Isle Ste. Louis, France, the work of an unknown fifteenth-century sculptor; this

wayside *Shrine of Our Lady, Queen of Peace* near the Roofless Church was dedicated to Thomas Merton by a trustee of the Merton Trust (71 on town map).

15. Poet's House and Beyond

1. Walter Starkie, CMG, CBE, LittD, recounts his fascinating life in the books *Scholars and Gypsies: An Autobiography* (Berkeley: University of California Press, 1963) and *Raggle-Taggle: Adventures with a Fiddle in Hungary and Roumania* (New York: E. P. Dutton, 1933).

2. In 1827, William Owen, another son of Robert Owen, had established theater in New Harmony. During the mid- to late 1800s, New Harmony was home to the Goldens, a famous theatrical troupe and family who performed throughout the United States.

3. Lesley Frost arrived, shortly after Gustav Davidson of the American Poetry Society, to prepare for a visit by Robert Frost that did not materialize because of her father's untimely death in early 1963.

4. I have placed a copy of John Hubbard's *From the Poet's House: A Portrait of New Harmony, Twelve Facsimile Etchings,* published by the RLB Trust, on the fireside coffee table in the Entry House of the New Harmony Inn for the enjoyment of our guests. Hubbard's line drawing *Fish above the Lab* appears on the title page of both that book and mine.

5. A term taken from Owen's two 1825 addresses, concerning his new system in society, delivered in the Hall of the Representatives of the United States Congress in Washington, D.C., en route to New Harmony.

17. Enter Philip Johnson

1. [Johnson's public lecture for Tuesday, November 20, at 8:30 PM was announced in the article "N.Y. Architect to Speak at St. Thomas," *Houston Chronicle,* November 18, 1956.]

2. [The AFA convention was held April 3–6, 1957. Records of the Office of the Director (RG02:02:01). Lee H. B. Malone correspondence and miscellaneous subject files 1949–60, box 1, folder 23. AFA program booklet, ibid., folder 17. Archives, Museum of Fine Arts, Houston.]

3. [The Shamrock Hilton Hotel had joined in the citywide western theme for the Houston Fat Stock Show and Rodeo, held February 20–March 3, 1957.]

4. [T. S. Eliot, *Collected Poems, 1909–1962,* "Four Quartets: Little Gidding" (New York: Harcourt, Brace & World, 1970), 209. The two last lines here he quoted from Dame Julian of Norwich.]

5. April 19–20, 1957.

6. [The brochure designed by Jane Blaffer Owen in 1960 recounts a similar version. An original was enclosed in a letter to Lipchitz dated December 6, 1962, in Jacques Lipchitz papers, Owen, box 3, folder 36, 113–20, AAA, SI. A letter written from Marion, Massachusetts, to Jacques Lipchitz, on August 14, 1957, however, provides the following details: "J'étais contente que vous étiez déjà en vacance[s] la fin de juillet, ça vous en aviez besoin, j'en suis sûre, mais, tout de même, j'aurais voulu partager avec vous l'énorme plaisir de ma visite au bureau de Philip. Le nouveau modèl[e] vous plaira beaucoup. Les arcs du toit sont plus élevés, ce qui donne l'impression qu'un grand souffle a rempli un parachute. Donc, notre Madonne descend doucement à terre. Trois heures avec le modèl[e] et les élévations (en étapes successifs) sont passées comme trois minutes. Tout cela j'aurais voulu goûter avec

vous, surtout au moment de placer votre statue, car Elle est formée en minuscule pour mieux comprendre ses désirs. On pense qu'Elle sera contente de se trouver exposée complètement à ceux approchent la chapelle, afin que le triangle semble soutenir la voûte du toit, mais que le Saint-Esprit soit couvert. Une fois entré on découvre la colombe. Naturellement, on attend votre opinion pour placer votre œuvre; on espère simplement qu'on marche sur le bon chemin. Avez vous jamais l'impression, bien cher Maître, qu'on est dans le service de la Madonne, comme si Elle était notre patronne?" ("I was glad that you were already on vacation at the end of July, because I am sure you needed it, but I would have liked to share with you the great pleasure of my visit to Philip's office. You will be very pleased with the new model. The arches of the roof are higher, which gives the impression of a mighty breath of wind filling a parachute. Our Gentle Lady descends slowly to earth. Three hours with the model and the elevations (in successive stages) went by like three minutes. I would have liked to taste all this with you, particularly the moment of setting into place your statue, for a model, in miniature, has been made of her in order to better understand her desires. We think she will be happy to be completely exposed to those approaching the chapel, so that the triangle seems to hold up the vault of the roof, but the Holy Spirit is covered. Once you have entered her space, you discover the dove. Naturally, we await your opinion on where to place your piece. We merely hope that we are on the right path. Have you ever thought, my dear Master, that we are in the service of the Madonna, as if she were our patroness?" Translation by Dr. Leslie Roberts.) Original letter in Lipchitz, Owen, box 3, folder 36, 20–25, AAA, SI.]

7. [On Ste. Anne's Farm stationery, August 24, she wrote: "I feel that I must send you my condolences on the sad loss of two months of your time and effort. I am capable of imagining your sense of horror upon entering your studio that day, but I also know that you are formed of much sterner clay than your plasticine. You should likewise be grateful now, more than ever before, to the strong metaphysical wings you have acquired during a lifetime of disciplined work and aerial longings. I can think of no one better equipped to soar above disappointment than yourself." Original letter in Lipchitz, Owen, box 3, folder 3, 58–59, AAA, SI.]

8. [A consoling note was sent the next day, postmarked Janurary 7, 1952: "Mon cher et brave ami, je me suis si humble devant les grands événements que viennent de s'accomplir, que je ne peux pas essayer de vous écrire, ou. D'une chose, cependant, nous sommes toutes les trois certaines. C'est non l'ouvrage du diable, mais de Dieu, et petit à petit le noir s'éclaircira. Tout se montrera dans une nouvelle et plus belle lumière. Vous avez fait des grands sacrifices toute votre vie et vous verrez que même de venir a ce moment. S'il vous plaît accepter avec ma profonde sympathie le petite chèque se enclos [ci inclus] envers un nouveau studio, preferablement pres de chez vous, à Hastings. J'ai téléphoné seulement Dominique de Menil et ma mère, qui furent aussi sans paroles. Pas un a été fait en vain. Dieu est impliqué dans tous ce chaos présent et un jour on saura sûrement pourquoi. Avec tout mon coeur."

("My dear and brave friend, I am so humbled by the tragic events that just took place that I cannot even try to write to you. However, there is one thing the three of us are sure about: this is not the work of the devil but the work of God. Slowly but surely the darkness will dissipate. Everything will appear in a new and more beautiful light. You have made great sacrifices throughout your life, and you will see that even in the time to come. Please accept this small check with my deep sympathy to help you with a new studio, if possible near your home in Hastings. I only called Dominique de Menil and my mother. Both were speechless. None of this happened in vain. God is involved in this current chaos, and one day we will probably understand why. With all my heart.") Translation by Monique Singley, who explains that the closing, a literal translation of an apt English phrase, "With all my heart," to express condolence at the great loss of Lipchitz's life work, is not a common way to end a letter in France, adding that the French equivalent in this context would be similar to "You are in my thoughts and prayers." Original notecard in Lipchitz, Owen, box 3, folder 35, 79–80, AAA, SI.]

9. [Mid-July 1955 for Église Notre-Dame de Toute Grâce du Plateau d'Assy; early summer 1956 for New Harmony (arriving with minor damage during transport and returned to the foundry for repair); and, as was previously mentioned, mid-December 1957 bound for Scotland (arriving in Iona a year later).]

10. [From a letter dated April 23: "Le Chanoine West de la cathédrale de St. John the Divine à New York, désire vivement m'accompagner à Hastings, mais ne pas quitter la Cathedral dimanche. Est-ce-que le lundi après midi, le 3 mai, vers cinq heures, vous sera convenable?" ("Canon West of the Cathedral of St. John the Divine in New York wishes very much to accompany me, but cannot leave the cathedral on Sunday. Would Monday afternoon, May 3, around five o'clock, be convenient for you?" Translation by Ed. Note: May 3 occurred on Monday in 1954.) Original letter in Lipchitz, Owen, box 3, folder 35, 104–105, AAA, SI.]

18. Cornerstone Dedication

1. T. S. Eliot, "Four Quartets: Little Gidding," in *Collected Poems 1909–1962* (New York: Harcourt, Brace & World, 1970), 209.

2. [Helen Duprey Bullock, Robert Lee Blaffer Trust, letter to author, Februrary 3, 1959: "I could not reach Father Goodrich, but Anna did. He will happily come to New Harmony for our May Day. . . . I telephoned Jack Clinger of Byrd Mill. He too, will come with us. We can all use Lloyd's car from D.C. to New Harmony." Roofless Church, box 7, folder "Jane Owen," Robert Lee Blaffer Trust Archive, Robert Lee Blaffer Foundation, New Harmony, Indiana. Jack Clinger was also the official miller for Colonial Williamsburg.]

3. [William Blake, "Jerusalem," in *Selected Poetry and Prose of William Blake,* ed. Northrop Frye (New York: Modern Library, 1953), 244.]

4. [John August(e) Blaffer served in 5th Company, Battalion Washington Artillery, Louisiana Artillery, CSA, according to Andrew B. Booth, *Records of Louisiana Confederate Soldiers.*]

19. May Day Dedication of the Roofless Church and Barrett-Gate House

1. The Harmony Way Bridge is now on the Register of National Historic Places.

20. Tillich Visits Houston

1. According to William R. Crout, "Tillich accepted appointment as University Professor, the most prestigious of academic positions, at Harvard on April 12, 1954 (taking a year's leave of absence to give the Fall 1954 second series of his Gifford lectures in St. Andrew's Scotland and agreeing to return to Union Theological Seminary as 'Visiting Professor' for the Spring 1955 term) and completed his seven-year Harvard tenure with retirement on June 30, 1962."

2. Tillich's evening lectures, which were open to the general public, included "The Historical Dimension of Reality," April 4; "The Dynamics of Human History," April 5; and "Historical Time and the 'End' of History," April 6. [Program saved from attendance and

filed in folder 1, "Tillich—Articles by," Tillich Archive, Robert Lee Blaffer Foundation, New Harmony, Indiana.]

3. This version from a stone in Tillich Park differs slightly from Tillich's sermon, "By What Authority," published in *The New Being* (New York: Charles Scribner's Sons, 1955), 85: "He who lives without authority is trying to be like God, who is by Himself alone. In so doing, he brings down destruction, be it a person, a nation, or a period of history like our own."

4. A written confirmation came to me from Professor Niels C. Nielsen Jr., of the Rice Department of Philosophy, dated March 9, 1961: "I have written to his [Tillich's] Secretary that he will have tea with us on Thursday and trust that our plans will work out satisfactorily." The tea occurred on Thursday, April 6, 1961. Letter in folder "Tillich Park," Tillich Archive, Robert Lee Blaffer Foundation, New Harmony, Indiana.

21. MacLeod's Dedication of the Lipchitz Gate

1. There is a photograph of the bronze model for the gate of the Roofless Church in both Jacques Lipchitz with H. H. Arnason, *My Life in Sculpture* (London: Thames and Hudson, 1972), 173, and H. H. Arnason, *Jacques Lipchitz: Sketches in Bronze* (New York: Frederick A. Praeger Publishers, 1969), 189.

2. Ron Miller, *The Gospel of Thomas: A Guidebook for Spiritual Practice* (Woodstock, VT: Skylight Paths Publishing, 2004), 58–59.

3. Ron Ferguson, ed., "The Life of Life: Sermon on Prayer, July 1955," in *Daily Readings with George MacLeod: Founder of the Iona Community* (Glasgow: Wild Goose Publications, 2001), 22.

4. Kenneth's hope came to fruition when Janie's son, Erik, chose to restore the center-gable Gothic Revival cottage and expand it with an ample and historically sensitive addition to accommodate a family. The building is now called Miller-Arneberg House.

5. Suzanne Glémet was my French governess, who taught all who knew her the meaning of life through service to mankind and God.

6. Such as an exhibit in the Owen Community House of religious paintings by William Congdon; a talk in Murphy Auditorium by MacLeod, "Youth and the Future," from his experience with the Iona youth; a concert including works of Haydn, Beethoven, Orrego-Salas, and Prokofiev by the Berkshire Quartet in the Roofless Church; and a press conference featuring George MacLeod, Philip Johnson, and Jacques Lipchitz.

7. Adele Addison also sang "Lord Jesus Christ" (fragment from *Prayers of Kierkegaard*) by Samuel Barber. She had recorded "Let Us Break Bread Together," arranged by William Lawrence, with the Jubilee Singers on her 1959 album *Little David Play on Your Harp*.

22. Estranged and Reunited

1. The Committee for Intellectual Interchange had committees in New York and Japan. Professor Yasaka Takagi served as chairman of the committee in Japan. From Paul Tillich's "Informal Report on Lecture Trip to Japan," Summer 1960.

2. From "Professor Paul Tillich Visits New Harmony, Indiana, for the Dedication of the Ground of Paul Tillich Park and the 'Cave of the New Being,' Pentecost, June 2, 1963," Robert Lee Blaffer Trust, Program Services.

3. Philip Johnson had asked Robert Zion, of Zion and Breen Associates, to redesign and expand the Abby Aldrich Rockefeller Sculpture Garden at the Museum of Modern Art in the early 1960s. Not long after Zion completed Tillich Park, he published *Trees for*

Architecture and Landscape and had numerous award-winning designs during his long career as a renowned landscape architect.

4. Some have expressed surprise that Hannah and I "got along" so well. When we first met she seemed unapproachable, but once she recognized the purity of my intention to honor her husband, we became dear friends for the rest of her life. She died in 1988.

5. From Paul Tillich's "Nature Mourns for a Lost God," in his collection of sermons, *The Shaking of the Foundations* (New York: Charles Scribner's Sons, 1948), 83. At a ceremony on June 23, 1965, Secretary of the Interior Stewart Udall recognized as a National Historic Landmark the New Harmony Historic District. Secretary Udall, in his presentation speech, quoted from Tillich's sermon "Nature Mourns for a Lost God."

6. A February 1966 letter from Hannah to the author provided specific reasons for her decision: "And you will be pleased by the fact that Paulus said in Santa Barbara to a friend of ours . . . when we talked about your 'park' 'there I want to be buried.' . . . He refused to buy a lot at the East Hampton cemetery. . . . I did it, because I had reserved it, hoping to get his permission and then the cemetery people gave me a deadline . . . I had to buy or not to buy." [The quotation marks around "there I want to be buried" are handwritten and all ellipses appear in the original letter, which is preserved in the Paul Tillich Archive, Robert Lee Blaffer Foundation, New Harmony. Courtesy of the Hannah Tillich Estate, Dr. Mutie Tillich Farris, Executor.]

7. Whitfield "Pat" Marshall's letter is dated December 23, 1965.

23. The Undying Dead

1. Ritsert Rinsma, *Alexandre Lesueur, tome 1, Un Explorateur et Artiste Français au Pays de Thomas Jefferson* [Explorer and Artist in the Land of Thomas Jefferson] (Le Havre: Éditions du Havre de Grâce, 2007).

2. *Alex l'Explorateur, tome 1, La Malédiction du Serpent* [The Curse of the Serpent] (Le Havre: Éditions du Havre de Grâce, 2007). The graphic novels are created in collaboration with artist Yves Boistelle and archivist Hervé Chabannes. Ritsert Rinsma lectured in New Harmony at Thrall's Opera House on October 30, 2008. He is finishing his doctorate at the University of Le Havre and teaches history and English in Le Havre and Bolbec.

24. Paul Tillich Park

1. An invoice for the transport of the stones was duly submitted March 15, 1966, by Ralph Esarey, who was also a geologist at Indiana University and at one time the state geologist, like Kenneth's ancestors.

2. They would return to New Harmony in the early 1970s for the Ten Commandments tablets that surround Waddams Chapel.

3. Ralph Beyer, letter to author, March 9, 1966.

4. Paul Tillich, *Theology of Culture*, ed. Robert C. Kimball (Oxford: Oxford University Press, 1959), 42.

5. A year later in 1967, the portrait bust would be placed in his park and unveiled by James Rosati in an intimate gathering (42 on town map). Two close friends of Tillich led that ceremony: Klaus Ritter dedicated the portrait bust, and Alfonso Ossario was a memorial speaker. While it is a recognizable portrait of the philosopher-theologian, it is more than a likeness. The firm jaw and sadness in the eyes give the face a Lincolnesque quality; the expression of a man who has lived through world wars is like that of a man who has lived through a civil war. All wars are fratricides.

6. Our Fragrant Farms (fragrantfarms.com; see area map) uses sustainable horticultural practices to grow peonies, other flowers, and grapes for wine on lands once tilled and harvested by the Harmonists. The peonies are ready in May to be sold and shipped anywhere.

7. From "Professor Paul Tillich Visits New Harmony, Indiana, for the Dedication of the Ground of Paul Tillich Park and the 'Cave of the New Being,' Pentecost, June 2, 1963. I. 'Estranged and Reunited: The New Being,' Professor Tillich's Address in the Roofless Church. II. The Act of Dedication of the Ground of Tillich Park and the 'Cave of the New Being.' III. Professor Tillich's Response to a Community Reception, Sunday Afternoon." Robert Lee Blaffer Trust, Program Services.

25. Paul Tillich Commemorative Service

1. A two-page, mimeographed statement from the Robert Lee Blaffer Trust, which I wrote in early January 1966, was included with the letters.

2. Tillich was invited to speak at MoMA on two occasions. The first was a lecture, "Art and Ultimate Reality," delivered on February 17, 1959; the second was an invitation to dedicate the new galleries and sculpture garden on May 24, 1965, but because Tillich became ill, his address was read by Wilhelm Pauck, his friend and former colleague at Union Theological Seminary. Information provided by William Crout.

3. Caren Goldman and William Dols, *Finding Jesus, Discovering Self: Passages to Healing and Wholeness* (Harrisburg, PA: Moorehouse, 2006), 59, quote these lines from Stanley Kunitz's "The Mound Builders," *The Collected Poems* (New York: W. W. Norton, 2002).

4. The hymns were: "A Mighty Fortress Is Our God," "Come Creator, Spirit Come," and "Hail Thee Festival Day."

5. Rollo May selected this passage from a letter Tillich had written to comfort a friend on the death of a mutual friend.

26. Open Windows

1. Paul Tillich's *The Religious Situation* was first published in German in 1926 and in English in 1932.

2. The Red Geranium opened to the public on July 16, 1963, serving lunch and dinner to 135 guests that day. The popularity and reputation of "The Red" continued to grow.

3. Esther de Waal, *A Seven Day Journey with Thomas Merton* (Ann Arbor, MI: Servant Publications, 1992).

27. Tumbling Walls

1. Probably adapted from Carl Sandburg's *The People, Yes*, published in 1936: "Sometime they'll give a war and nobody will come."

2. [State of Indiana, County of Vanderburgh, in the Vanderburgh Superior Court, Ralph Schwartz [sic, Schwarz], as Trustee of the Robert Lee Blaffer Trust, versus Philip Johnson and Philip Johnson Associates, Defendants, Cross-Claimants, Cross-Defenders, 1975 Term, No. 71-CIV-2933.]

3. Such as one by Bob Weil, "Roofless Church an Eyesore? Shrine's Walls Starting to Look Like Jericho's," the *Evansville Press*, Friday, July 9, 1971, replete with photographs by Don Goodaker.

4. After my mother's death (May 11, 1975), I had visited Janie on Mother's Day. Leaving services at St. Mary's Episcopal Church with my grandchildren Ingrid and Erik, we walked

past the Modern's sculpture court wall, and I saw efflorescence, which reaffirmed to me that having sought a legal remedy for the walls of the Roofless Church was just.

28. Glass House

1. She had dressed me for my wedding as a Russian empress in a gown she designed with wimple and veil like a nun, understanding that marriage is a sacrament.

2. Paul Tillich, "The Lost Dimension of Religion," *Saturday Evening Post,* June 14, 1958, 28–30, material in brackets mine.

3. [Susan Bielstein read the memoir in connection with *Forms of Spirituality: Modern Architecture, Landscape, and Preservation in New Harmony,* which Jane Blaffer Owen considered as a "companion book" to her own. A portion of Ms. Bielstein's comments relates to this and the preceding chapter and accurately assesses the tone and intention of Owen's narrative style: "I had only one serious conversation with Mrs. Owen about writing this book. The two of you were well along with it, and she was concerned about communicating situations that, while important to the history of New Harmony, were not entirely flattering to all parties concerned, such as the difficulty with Philip Johnson over the walls of the Roofless Church and how that unfolded. I was pleased to see in 'Tumbling Walls' that she handled that event matter-of-factly, simply, without blame, but indicating what the loss of friendship meant to her. Then, the most brilliant part of the situation is that in the following chapter she tells the story of visiting Johnson's Glass House during much better times—causing the narrative to resolve on an up note." Susan Bielstein, Executive Editor for Art, Architecture, Film, and Classical Studies, University of Chicago Press, email to Nancy Mangum McCaslin, May 30, 2011.]

29. Orchard House

1. This was confirmed when he later published *Mark Hampton on Decorating* (New York: Random House, 1989), a collection of his columns in *House & Garden,* and *Legendary Decorators of the Twentieth Century* (New York: Doubleday, 1992), edited by Jacqueline Onassis. His widow Duane Hampton's forthcoming book *Mark Hampton: An American Decorator* (New York: Rizzoli, 2010) celebrates his life and career. I dedicated a small garden at Orchard House to his memory.

2. C. S. Lewis, *Miracles* (London: Collings/Fontana, 1947), 247.

3. Mark decorated Blair House with Mario Buatta and Lucky Roosevelt.

30. Rapp-Maclure-Owen House Restoration

1. At the time, Kenneth had engaged Earl Reed, head of historic preservation of buildings with the American Institute of Architects, to research the history of the house.

31. Art and Carol's Garden

1. Even though Tillich left Germany for the sake of his family, he did not forsake involvement. I was most interested to learn recently that he made top-secret radio broadcasts for Voice of America during the war. Ronald H. Stone and Matthew Lon Weaver, ed., *Against the Third Reich: Paul Tillich's Wartime Radio Broadcasts into Nazi Germany* (Louisville, KY: Westminster John Knox Press, 1998).

2. Herold Witherspoon had met Paul Tillich walking along a beach in East Hampton in the summer of 1964.

3. The doors were dedicated at the convocation of the Society for the Arts, Religion, and Contemporary Culture meeting on the evening of May 17, 1968. The architect for the refectory dining room was Evans Woollen.

4. Doug Adams, *Transcendence with the Human Body in Art: George Segal, Stephen De Staebler, Jasper Johns, and Cristo* (New York: Crossroad, 1991). Doug Adams, "Becoming One Body: Stephen De Staebler's Family of Winged Figures," *Image: A Journal of the Arts & Religion* 3, no. 37 (Winter 2002): 29–36.

5. Edward Gilbert also designed a benefit ball when he came with me to Houston and a birdcage for my garden at Pinewold.

6. After George died and Annie decided to return to Ontario, I relocated in about 1966 from my No. V house on Steammill to their former residence. Located on Granary, directly across the street from the Rapp-Maclure-Owen House and the Laboratory and adjacent to Poet's House, it is also close to the center of activity on North Street. I named the house in grateful memory of them and their numerous contributions to our community.

7. Carl Gustav Jung, *The Archetypes and the Collective Unconscious,* trans. R. F. C. Hull (New Haven: Yale University Press, 1981), 384.

8. David Rodgers said he had begun to carve in limestone because it is "a gorgeous material." An educated carver with a graduate degree in fine arts, he neither looked to re-create past forms nor to imitate the Hoosier landscape. He searched instead "down into the depths of our flesh—bones, wombs, birth canals—and into the hidden structures of nature." From Scott R. Sanders, "Three Carvers," in *Stone Country* (Bloomington: Indiana University Press, 1985), 104.

9. Robert Lax, "Morning" in *The Circus of the Sun* (New York: Journeyman Books, 1960).

10. Carroll Harris Simms, letter to author, July 30, 1983. Carroll was the first African American to be accepted at and to graduate from Cranbrook Academy of Art. He then began the sculpture program at Texas Southern University in Houston, joining the faculty in 1950.

Epilogue

1. Wardelmann and Son Garage was followed by Ed Garrett Garage, owned by Everett and Nora (Wardelmann) Garrett, when its exterior was painted white.

2. Numerous events and lectures have been held here. On May 21, 1977, Professor Richard W. Leopold recounted his eight-week visit to New Harmony in 1935 to research the subject of his doctoral dissertation, which had been recommended by Arthur M. Schlesinger and was published in 1940 as *Robert Dale Owen: A Biography* by Harvard University Press.

3. A brochure for the New Harmony Inn during this time reads: "The Red Geranium Bookstore offers the reading public various aspects of New Harmony's past and future through both the written word and photographs. The visitor will find books on subjects pertinent to our history. A fine selection of children's books seeks to honor the memory of Robert Owen, who cared deeply about the well being and education of young people. The visitor who looks up from the book shelves shall discover a pictorial account of people and places in the town's history. He shall catch a glimpse not only of the educators and builders who made New Harmony a place of enlightenment in nature's wilderness, but of those in recent history who have helped keep a light burning in the wilderness that men can make." Written by Jane Blaffer Owen, designed and printed by Creative Press, Inc., circa 1970s.

4. The interior features original designs crafted by Posey County artist Kenny Fisher as well as the skill of designer Herbert Wells of Houston.

5. Larry consulted with me about the red color for his sculpture, which I advised should mirror nature. He wrote to me later that day, Monday, December 31, 1984, "Shortly after our conversation I took the color samples over to the greenhouse and discovered there a red begonia with the deeper underside of the petals close in coloration to that of the selection. The sculpture will certainly be a bright spot on the lawn—dancing away both day and night." He continued, "The Helfrichs are executing very professional and sensitive work" regarding the fabrication. Tom Helfrich created the chandelier in the Granary, Mark Hampton's Gate at the Orchard House, and the metal entrance doors to the Cathedral Labyrinth and Sacred Garden.

6. Ralph Schwarz, letters to author, February 24, 2010, and March 4, 2010.

7. Earlier awards included the Progressive Architecture Award in 1979 and the AIA Honor Award in 1982.

8. Courtesy of the Community of the Holy Spirit, New York.

Afterword: Anne Dale Owen

1. For her many endeavors, she was awarded Commander of the Most Excellent Order of the British Empire (CBE) by Queen Elizabeth II.

2. Mr. John of New York was hatter to the stars, including Audrey Hepburn and Vivien Leigh.

3. A hunting lodge built in 1931 and converted to the family guest house. It became my residence after I graduated from high school.

4. Philip had completed the Seagram Building in 1956 and the Four Seasons in 1959.

Town Map Legend

31. Sycamore
32. Poet's House Lawn with Elm
33. Roofless Church
34. Lipchitz, *Descent of the Holy Spirit* (*Notre Dame de Liesse*)
35. Farmland view from balcony of Roofless Church
36. Barrett-Gate House
37. 1860 Miller/Arneberg House (on area map)
38. Lipchitz, *The Suzanne Glémet Memorial Gate*
39. Paul Tillich Park
40. Thomas Say tomb
41. Fauntleroy House
42. James Rosati, *Head of Tillich*
43. The Red Geranium Restaurant
44. St. Stephen's Episcopal Church
45. The New Harmony Inn (see 3 above)
46. Entry House
47. Waddams Chapel
48. Orchard House
49. Tillich Dining Room
50. Stephen De Staebler, *Angel of the Annunciation*
51. Stephen De Staebler, *Pietà*
52. Stephen De Staebler, *Chapel of the Little Portion* (*Saint Francis Chapel*)
53. 1840 Garden House
54. Owen Community House, the Artists' Guild
55. Carol's Garden
56. David Rodger, *Fountain of Life*
57. Carroll Harris Simms, mother-daughter bench
58. Thrall Opera House and Golden Troupe Exhibit
59. Antique Showrooms at the Mews
60. New Harmony Inn Swimming Pool
61. J. Breith Building
62. Salomon Wolfe House
63. New Harmony Gallery of Contemporary Art
64. New Harmony Conference Center
65. Historic New Harmony
66. The MacLeod Barn Abbey
67. Tobi Kahn, *Shalev*
68. Cathedral Labyrinth and Sacred Garden
69. Simon Verity, *Orpheus Fountain*
70. Sarah Campbell Blaffer Studio
71. *Shrine of Our Lady, Queen of Peace*, wayside shrine, dedicated to Thomas Merton

Jane Blaffer Owen stands in the doorway of her home on
Pinewold in Houston. April 18, 2015 marks the centennial
of Jane Blaffer Owen's birth in Houston, Texas.

Photograph by Christina Girard, 2009.

Facing. Jane Blaffer Owen gathers peonies at Fragrant Farms
in New Harmony to distribute to friends and visitors.

Photograph by Randa Christy.
Courtesy of Fragrant Farms (fragrantfarms.com).

My greatest hope for New Harmony
is that this place be one
of healing and reconciliation.

—*Jane Blaffer Owen*

Proceeds from the sale of my memoir will benefit the foundation named in honor
of my father, the Robert Lee Blaffer Foundation, P.O. Box 399, New Harmony,
Indiana 47631. Should you wish to support personally our ongoing mission in
New Harmony, donations are gratefully accepted and put to good use.

Index

345

EDITOR · *Linda Oblack*
EDITORIAL ASSISTANT · *Sarah Jacobi*
PRODUCTION DIRECTOR · *Bernadette Zoss*
INTERIOR AND JACKET DESIGN · *Pamela Rude*
PROJECT MANAGER · *Westchester Publishing Services*
PROJECT EDITOR · *Darja Malcolm-Clarke*